The Secret Lives of Tentmakers

American Society of Missiology Monograph Series

Chair of Series Editorial Committee, James R. Krabill

The ASM Monograph Series provides a forum for publishing quality dissertations and studies in the field of missiology. Collaborating with Pickwick Publications—a division of Wipf and Stock Publishers of Eugene, Oregon—the American Society of Missiology selects high quality dissertations and other monographic studies that offer research materials in mission studies for scholars, mission and church leaders, and the academic community at large. The ASM seeks scholarly work for publication in the series that throws light on issues confronting Christian world mission in its cultural, social, historical, biblical, and theological dimensions.

Missiology is an academic field that brings together scholars whose professional training ranges from doctoral-level preparation in areas such as Scripture, history and sociology of religions, anthropology, theology, international relations, interreligious interchange, mission history, inculturation, and church law. The American Society of Missiology, which sponsors this series, is an ecumenical body drawing members from Independent and Ecumenical Protestant, Catholic, Orthodox, and other traditions. Members of the ASM are united by their commitment to reflect on and do scholarly work relating to both mission history and the present-day mission of the church. The ASM Monograph Series aims to publish works of exceptional merit on specialized topics, with particular attention given to work by younger scholars, the dissemination and publication of which is difficult under the economic pressures of standard publishing models.

Persons seeking information about the ASM or the guidelines for having their dissertations considered for publication in the ASM Monograph Series should consult the Society's website—www.asmweb.org.

Members of the ASM Monograph Committee who approved this book are:

Recently Published in the ASM Monograph Series

George Shakwelele, *Explaining the Practice of Elevating an Ancestor for Veneration*

Peter T. Lee, *Hybridizing Mission: Intercultural Social Dynamics among Christian Workers on Multicultural Teams in North Africa*

The Secret Lives of Tentmakers

Navigating Missionary Identity in Restricted Access Nations

A. G. Smith

American Society of Missiology Monograph Series 78

PICKWICK *Publications* · Eugene, Oregon

THE SECRET LIVES OF TENTMAKERS
Navigating Missionary Identity in Restricted Access Nations

American Society of Missiology Monograph Series 78

Pickwick Publications
An Imprint of Wipf and Stock Publishers
199 W. 8th Ave., Suite 3
Eugene, OR 97401

www.wipfandstock.com

PAPERBACK ISBN: 979-8-3852-5720-1
HARDCOVER ISBN: 979-8-3852-5721-8
EBOOK ISBN: 979-8-3852-5722-5

Cataloguing-in-Publication data:

Names: Smith, A. G., author.

Title: The secret lives of tentmakers : navigating missionary identity in restricted access nations / A. G. Smith.

Description: Eugene, OR: Pickwick Publications, 2026. | American Society of Missiology Monograph Series 78. | Includes bibliographical references and index.

Identifiers: ISBN 979-8-3852-5720-1 (paperback). | ISBN 979-8-3852-5721-8 (hardcover). | ISBN 979-8-3852-5722-5 (ebook).

Subjects: LCSH: Missions—Arabian Peninsula. | Christianity and other religions—Asian. | Intercultural communication—Religious aspects—Christianity.

Classification: BV2082 S65 2026 (print). | BV2082 (ebook).

VERSION NUMBER 04/17/26

For those who sacrifice simplicity, easy answers, and their very selves
so that the name of Jesus might be known
among those who have never heard.

Contents

Acknowledgments

I AM SO GRATEFUL to the many people surrounding me in prayer and encouragement who made the following pages a reality. Thank you to the individuals, families, and churches who have faithfully supported our family in ministry of all kinds—even the ministry of qualitative research.

I am deeply grateful to the missionaries whose stories are contained in these pages. Thank you for generously sharing your joys, your pain, and your very selves with me for this research. I do not take your trust and your generosity lightly. I pray I have honored your complex experiences in these words, though I know I cannot capture it all. You have impacted me deeply.

Many thanks to my doctoral supervisor, Dr. Trevor Castor. You spent many hours reading drafts, making comments, asking questions, and pointing out my inconsistencies and muddled thinking. I am grateful for how you have shaped this dissertation, and me as a researcher.

Thank you to the family God gave me through marriage and where I have found so much support and encouragement. I love you all!

Thank you to my incredible children, who provided their original soundtrack for my studying, endured my terrifying "thinking face," and who celebrated "Dr. Mom" the hardest. I have thrown away the "Nope, go ask your dad" sign hanging on my door for good!

I am grateful to my husband, whose experiences, struggles, and identity crisis as a tentmaker inspired this research. You sacrificed so much so that I could research and write this work. It was no small thing to shift the normal routines of our well-established family system, but you took up a significant burden of the homeschooling and housework with joy, while shouldering weighty tasks of your own. Thank you for cheering me on the loudest, supporting me the most, and valuing what I do so deeply.

Finally, I am grateful to the one triune God, who alone is worthy of the worship of all nations in every tongue.

Abbreviations

AP	Arabian Peninsula
Apps	Applications
BAM	Business as mission
BMB	Believer from a Muslim background
CIA	Central Intelligence Agency
CP	Church planting
CPM	Church-planting movements
CSI	Concealable stigmatized identities
DBS	Discovery Bible studies
DMM	Disciple-making movements
GCC	Co-Operation Council for the Arab States of the Gulf
GPA	Growing Participator Approach
GRI	Government restrictions index
HMA	Home ministry assignment
IRB	Institutional review board
KSA	Kingdom of Saudi Arabia
MBA	Master of business administration
MENA	Middle East and North Africa
MMM	Marketplace mission movement
OED	*Oxford English Dictionary*
RAN	Restricted access nation

Abbreviations

SLS	Short, legitimate statement
T4T	Training for Trainers
TCK	Third-culture kid
TESOL	Teaching English to speakers of other languages
UAE	United Arab Emirates
UPG	Unreached people group
VPN	Virtual private network

1

Contemporary Missions in Restricted Access Nations

INTRODUCTION—SECURITY, IDENTITY, AND MISSION

My husband and I are American members of an evangelical missionary organization that emphasizes church planting among UPGs. We lived on the Arabian Peninsula, first as Arabic students on tourist visas, then on my husband's investor visa. My husband owned two small for-profit businesses, providing legitimate services to the local community. These businesses also provided residence visas for two additional missionary families as employees. After three years of running these small businesses, my husband made enough capital to cover his business expenses and pay a local employee part-time wages. The rest of the profit supplemented a Global South missionary family's support-raised salary, as they came from a country with high inflation rates that impacted their support. Our own family never drew any financial benefit from the businesses, remaining on full-time support through donations to our mission organization. Within our mission organization, we functioned as team leaders for new missionaries while they learned Arabic, training them for life and ministry in the Arabian Gulf. We also engaged in local relationships with other missionary colleagues across several organizations for evangelism and discipleship, with the goal of establishing a locally led Arab church.

Our work as missionaries in a country where it was illegal to be a missionary sometimes resulted in an experience of living a double life. Among our social circles in the US, our organization, our teammates, and colleagues on the field, we were known as missionaries. We raised and lived on full financial support from ministry partners, and received extensive training in international church planting. However, among non-missionary expatriates, local Arabs, and even believers from a Muslim background (BMBs), we were known as Christian business owners. We actively concealed our missionary identity in many social situations to protect our visas, believers from a Muslim background (BMBs), and the missionaries we associated with. We framed travel for church-planting training or ministry furloughs as "family vacations" to our local friends—which was partly true, as we often took those opportunities to take a holiday. We carefully cultivated our online presence by monitoring churches' websites for our names or photos, deleting our friends' online "outing" of us as missionaries on social media, and even blocking some friends from contacting us when they consistently failed to keep security protocols. We often avoided friendships with non-missionary expatriates, who couldn't comprehend why we would bother learning Arabic or even live in this country without a job that made a tremendous salary, as they did. If they asked too many questions, our story would fall apart, and our missionary intentions would become obvious.

My closest Muslim friends knew of me as a stay-at-home mom to my young children, a category they well understood. However, they did not know about other significant parts of my life: that I was working on my master's degree in theology, that I was publishing research, or that I worked significant hours to train and lead a team. These were dear friends I loved, and I often felt they knew such a small part of who I was. My husband felt like a fraud as he presented a businessman identity, as he had no training in business and was figuring it out as he went. In many of our relationships, we faced challenging questions that we tried to answer with truth, but not the whole truth. We had secret identities that many people could not know, an entire life that had to be hidden from beloved friends. All our words were carefully weighed with an internal cost-benefit analysis of disclosure to protect our family, other missionaries, and especially BMBs. These and other practices proved stressful to my husband and me in many ways, as they competed with our core identity of honest, godly Christians. Over time, we grew increasingly uncomfortable with having a hidden identity and misleading others about who we were.

Police and government agents frequently interrogate missionaries and BMBs in this country, and persecution for leaving Islam is high. My family's sudden exit from the country resulted from a security incident when a ministry project we did unexpectedly went viral on social media. My husband was imprisoned on a false charge of "forced conversion." Our hidden missionary identities and intentions were exposed. I fled the country in the night with our young children to avoid arrest. Only then did my younger children discover that their parents were missionaries, which was profoundly disorienting for them. The charges against my husband were dropped months later, and my husband was released from the country with a lifetime ban.

We have spent the years since that time processing our identity presentation, concealing practices, and issues of security for tentmakers in restricted access nations (RANs).[1] Was it right? Should we have done things differently? How do you maintain integrity and protect others in a context of high security? The construction, management, and navigation of identity is a complex issue for missionaries in RANs today, and the research that follows arises from my experiences as a member of the missionary community in the Arabian Peninsula.

THE UNREACHED PEOPLE GROUP PARADIGM

The Lausanne Conferences of the 1970s and 1980s focused on people group thinking—the concept that specific ethnolinguistic groups, rather than nation-states as a whole, should be the locus of missionary strategy. People group thinking was spearheaded by Ralph Winter through his 1974 address at the Lausanne Congress, as well as through papers he published on the topic. In "The Highest Priority: Cross-Cultural Evangelism," Winter addressed the triumphalist myth that the gospel had already penetrated the whole world simply because Christians or churches existed within each nation-state. In the same paper, Winter also responded to the 1973 World Council of Churches' proposed moratorium on traditional missions.[2] This moratorium on sending both missionaries and church funds from the West was intended to allow local Christians in those countries to finish the task of evangelism.[3] However, Winter argued that despite the existence of a national church within a particular country, the gospel may not transcend social, linguistic, and cultural boundaries of groups within that country.

1. Synonyms include "closed," "creative access," or "limited access" countries or nations. For simplicity, this study uses only the term "restricted access nations."

2. Winter, "Highest Priority," 213.

3. Reese, "John Gatu," 245.

In addition, the historical animosities between different people groups sometimes prevented the gospel from spreading from one people group to another within the same national borders.[4] Winter's work on hidden people groups sought a paradigm change in missiology from a focus on planting churches in a nation, to planting churches among particular ethnolinguistic groups.

Winter introduced the E scale: E-1 is evangelism within one's own culture and language; E-2 is evangelism to a nearby culture and language; E-3 is evangelism to a different culture and language. E-3 requires a wide variety of additional cross-cultural communication skills.[5] Within this framework, Winter argued that the task of cross-cultural evangelism was still of deep concern so that all sociolinguistic groups in each nation might hear the gospel.[6] He concluded, "We are thus forced to believe that until every tribe and tongue has a strong, powerfully evangelizing church in it, and thus, an E-1 witness within it, E-2 and E-3 efforts coming from outside are still essential and highly urgent."[7] Thus, Evangelicals began conceptualizing Christian foreign missions in terms of reaching unreached people groups (UPGs), rather than simply establishing a number of healthy churches within a particular nation-state. A UPG is defined as a social unit with shared language and cultural norms, with little to no ability to evangelize the people group without cross-cultural assistance from outsiders.[8] This UPG paradigm is significant for the nations of the Arabian Peninsula, where international expatriate churches often legally exist to provide spiritual services for expatriates. However, these churches often function in languages and cultural norms quite different from the people groups indigenous to the Arabian Peninsula, and must overcome significant barriers to effectively communicate the gospel.

However, many of the world's UPGs live in countries where proselytization, or sometimes even religious conversion, is illegal. Religious conversions of locals in some contexts may result in persecution, imprisonment, deportation, or even death. In the wake of modern decolonization, secularization, or legislation limiting religious freedom, many nations either

4. Winter, "Highest Priority," 213–15.

5. Winter, "Highest Priority," 213.

6. Winter, "Highest Priority," 214–15.

7. Winter, "Highest Priority," 216.

8. Parks et al., "Hidden and Forgotten People."

reduced or eliminated missionary visas.[9] The professional missionary identity was no longer a viable platform for evangelical ministry in these countries, and an alternate identity became increasingly necessary.

The Rise of Tentmaking and Business as Mission

Missionaries desiring access to the UPGs in RANs must gain residency visas through other means, often through a vocation. This impacts the presentation of their identity: they often present a missionary identity in their passport countries, but primarily identify with their vocation in their host countries to maintain legal residency. In addition, they often conceal their missionary identity while in their host country. Identity management is thus a significant issue for evangelical tentmaking missionaries in RANs. Following the Lausanne Conferences, a broad spectrum of "tentmaking" practices emerged as "creative access platforms." These strategies enabled missionaries to obtain residence visas and present a non-missionary identity to government authorities.[10]

For the task of world evangelization, the Lausanne Covenant acknowledges the realities of governmental persecution against Christians and religious propagation as a scheme of Satan, which seeks to thwart the advances of the gospel.[11] Thus, the Lausanne Congress affirms the authority of Scripture over, and sometimes against, governmental legislations when they oppose God's clear commands for the gospel's propagation. In 2010, the Third Lausanne Congress' *Cape Town Commitment* encouraged mission organizations to integrate tentmaking Christians into global mission strategies, noting that "Christians in many skills, trades, businesses, and professions can often go to places where traditional church planters and evangelists may not."[12]

Long before this Lausanne Congress, at the turn of the twentieth century, Roland Allen had strongly advocated the concept of tentmaking, taken from Paul's model of missions alongside Priscilla and Aquila (Acts 18:1–3).[13] Allen argued for self-sustaining models of mission rather than missionary board financing, the primary model of missionary sending at the time. Allen presented the tentmaking model not only for reasons of

9. Stefan, *Business in Islam*, 273.

10. Barnett, "Creative Access Platforms," 89–90.

11. Stott, *Lausanne Covenant*, 74–80.

12. Third Lausanne Congress, *Cape Town Commitment*, 59–60.

13. Allen, *Missionary Methods*.

economic pragmatism, but primarily for the missiological strategy and adherence to biblical precedent.[14] Allen argued for a voluntary clergy force that spread the gospel, rather than predominantly theologically educated missionaries paid by denominational and agency structures. He contended that these lay missionaries would more closely share the life experiences of those they sought to reach, enabling higher effectiveness:

> Among our own people also the church sorely needs clergy in close touch with the ordinary life of the laity, living the life of ordinary men, sharing their difficulties and understanding of their trials by close personal experience. Stipendiary clergy cut off by training and life from that common experience are constantly struggling to get close to the laity by wearing lay clothing, sharing in lay amusements, and organizing lay clubs; but they never quite succeed. To get close to men, it is necessary really to share their experience, and to share their experience is to share it by being in it, not merely to come as near to it as possible without being in it. The church needs clerics who really share the life of their people.[15]

In order to have such a laity force in mission, these voluntary clergy needed self-supporting vocations that enabled them to live ordinary lives without being paid by the church or any missionary society. Allen called them "non-professional missionaries," and his writings demonstrate a strong opinion that they most closely follow Paul's missionary strategies.[16]

The concept of tentmaking became popular in missiological literature in the 1970s and 1980s with the writings of J. Christy Wilson, Ruth Siemens, and Don Hamilton.[17] Like Allen, they advocated for a flattening of the sacred-secular dichotomy between paid missionary clergy and self-supported evangelistic Christians. In addition, they considered tentmaking the solution to the increasing number of RANs closed to professional missionaries.[18] Some mission organizations utilized tentmaking platforms as modes of entry only, setting up shell companies that provided visas. This strategy kept missionaries' time free for evangelism and discipleship, though it was

14. Allen, *Missionary Methods*, 49–50.

15. Paton, *Roland Allen*, 150.

16. Rutt, *Roland Allen*, 142–43.

17. Wilson, *Today's Tentmakers*; Siemens, "Vital Role of Tentmaking"; Hamilton, *Tentmakers Speak*.

18. Siemens, "Vital Role of Tentmaking," 121; Lewis, *Working Your Way*, 15; Yamamori, *God's New Envoys*.

not without controversy, discussed below.[19] However, many missionaries increasingly considered tentmaking as a way to integrate work and ministry more holistically, rather than simply a means of access to a RAN.

Like Roland Allen, tentmaking authors also argued for the credibility that tentmaking gave to missionaries. Their vocation created an everyday platform for the display of Christian character, lending credibility to the message they shared.[20] In addition, tentmaking missionaries provided a tangible model of a Christian layperson's work ethic and witness for new believers to imitate.[21] However, some missiologists remained skeptical of tentmaking. They noted the difficulty in splitting time between work and ministry goals. They also questioned whether a model separate from denominations or missionary boards would lead to renegade, independent missionaries with no accountability.[22] Ruth Siemens reacted to this skepticism regarding tentmakers at that time, saying, "Tentmakers are often made out to be second class [to traditional, supported missionaries]." She also grieved, "The mission community is not even sure whether to accept tentmakers as valid workers."[23]

Following the growing discussions about tentmaking in mission, the concept of business as mission (BAM) emerged in the late 1990s, and slowly gained traction in the early 2000s.[24] BAM advocates argued for a more holistic approach to mission that included not just evangelism, but also broader societal improvements such as poverty alleviation and economic development.[25] In addition, BAM theologians argued for the sacred work of business as it brought glory to God through Christian principles applied to business.[26] They emphasized the value of nonreligious vocation, against the dichotomy of the sacred-secular divide.[27] Some BAM advocates began to voice concerns over the dishonest tentmaking practices of "undercover missionaries,"

19. Barnett, "Creative Access Platforms," 89.

20. Siemens, "Vital Role of Tentmaking," 123; Lewis, *Working Your Way*, 35; Barnett, "Creative Access Platforms," 94–95.

21. Lewis, *Working Your Way*, 19; Siemens, "Vital Role of Tentmaking," 124.

22. Albright et al., *Scholars Needed*, 5.

23. Siemens, "Vital Role of Tentmaking," 128.

24. Albright et al., *Scholars Needed*, 7.

25. Myers, *Walking with the Poor*; Kirk, *What Is Mission?*

26. Novak, *Business as a Calling*.

27. Baer, *Business as Mission*, 140; Rundle and Steffen, *Great Commission Companies*, 16–17.

who set up shell companies in order to gain access to RANs or who worked minimal hours for a business in order to have more time for ministry.[28] BAM advocates called for greater integrity, and argued for the transformational power of business in a community as a witness to the gospel.

There is wide variation in BAM practices and goals.[29] Many BAM advocates argue for Christian businesses that fulfill various kingdom or Great Commission purposes. These may include creating jobs in impoverished areas with low employment, raising the standard of living in a society, reaching unreached people groups with the gospel, and demonstrating Christian character and values through operational excellence.[30] BAM practitioners are frequently encouraged to aim for a "triple bottom line," which includes profitability and sustainability, social impact, and spiritual impact.[31] In 2024, BAM Global published a report calling for a quadruple bottom line for BAM businesses: financial, social, spiritual, and environmental.[32] Steve Rundle and Tom Steffen describe "Great Commission companies" that go beyond developmental enterprises in their BAM model. Rundle and Steffen also strongly emphasize the task of evangelizing UPGs, citing globalization as a new reality presenting tremendous opportunities for missions. Great Commission companies "bring good news in word and deed to the neediest parts of the world. The good news about globalization is that the barriers that once prevented people from hearing this message are falling and the missions baton is being handed to a new breed of messenger."[33] Many believe BAM and kingdom-oriented vocational workers are the future of mission, sometimes in place of traditional, supported missionaries.

Some consensus exists regarding the individual definitions and boundaries of tentmaking, bi-vocational ministry, BAM, and Christian expatriates taking employment overseas; however, in the literature and in real life, their roles and motivations often blend into one another. BAM practitioners are sometimes called tentmakers,[34] but elsewhere, tentmak-

28. Rundle and Steffen, *Great Commission Companies*, 26–27, 184; Roemmele, "Cloak-and-Dagger Tentmakers"; G. Taylor, "Don't Call Me a Tentmaker."

29. This can be demonstrated in the plethora of alternate names, which all carry slightly difference nuances: Great Commission companies, kingdom businesses, Business for Transformation (B4T), or kingdom entrepreneurs, among others.

30. Baer, *Business as Mission*, 9–10, 119–20; Johnson, *Business as Mission*, 35.

31. Johnson, *Business as Mission*, 270–77.

32. Plummer, *BAM and Mission Agencies*, 2.

33. Rundle and Steffen, *Great Commission Companies*, 29.

34. Lai, *Tentmaking.*

ing is distinguished as those who take up employment rather than those who start a business.[35] C. Neal Johnson describes BAM and tentmaking as separate but related endeavors that both fall under another category called marketplace mission movement (MMM).[36] Christian expatriates who take employment in a foreign country with no missionary training are sometimes called tentmakers.[37] In fact, J. Christy Wilson includes Marco Polo and Christopher Columbus in his historical overview of tentmakers since they were Christian laymen who traveled the world.[38] C. Neal Johnson notes the wide variety of uses of the term "tentmaker," as well as the replacement words utilized in an attempt to more accurately define such a person. Some of these alternative terms include lay missionaries, self-supporting witnesses, bi-vocational missionaries, kingdom professionals, holistic entrepreneurs, and "bussionaries"—a combination of "business" and "missionary."[39] In 2004, the Lausanne Working Group 30 on BAM gathered sixty-eight BAM experts in order to form a working definition of BAM. They could not achieve consensus on how to define BAM.[40] However, a growing consensus and conceptual convergence has occurred in the past twenty years.[41] The complex landscape of mission and vocation can lead to confusion regarding nomenclature, goals, and measures of effectiveness. The definitions used for this study are discussed below under the heading "Defining of Terms."

Missionary Identity and Security in a Modern Age

In addition to the changes in vocational and visa status for missionaries, technology and globalization complicate both security and identity for missionaries today. Patrick Lai and Rick Love outline the communication

35. Johnson, *Business as Mission*, 147; Tunehag et al., "Business as Mission," 13.

36. Johnson, *Business as Mission*, 112. Johnson notes that MMM itself is still poorly defined due to its recent emergence.

37. Lewis, *Working Your Way*, 1.

38. Wilson, *Today's Tentmakers*, 11, 27.

39. Johnson, *Business as Mission*, 115–99.

40. Kruger, *Tentmaking*, 133.

41. Plummer, "Business as Mission?" Plummer describes the current definition used by BAM Global, which includes four common denominators of BAM endeavors: "Profitable and sustainable businesses; intentional about Kingdom of God purpose and impact on people and nations; focused on holistic transformation and the multiple bottom lines of economic, social, environmental and spiritual outcomes; concerned about the world's poorest and least evangelized peoples" (para. 4).

complexities that modern Christians face in mission due to technology, noting that nothing can any longer be assumed to be private or "in-house."[42] Globalization has blurred the once-distinct lines between the missionary's home identity and host country identity, sometimes creating trouble if these identities are not congruent.[43] Emails, texts, and other digital communications are always at risk of hacking or decryption, potentially exposing missionaries to security breaches. In response to the threats posed by terrorism, widespread video and audio surveillance are standard in many countries. In addition, information gathering for law enforcement and national services may not be restricted by privacy laws.[44] Younger missionaries may have grown up as "digital natives" in the internet age, posting widely and freely on social media sites, blogs, and websites, leaving a digital footprint that is difficult to erase. Missionaries today simultaneously straddle multiple worlds and identities through technology in ways that previous generations never did. The missionary identity is becoming more difficult to conceal and protect, leaving missionaries increasingly vulnerable to expulsion from their country of service. The missional landscape—with both opportunities and challenges—has changed significantly in recent decades.

RATIONALE AND NEED

Evangelism, discipleship, and church planting among locals in RANs can be interpreted as proselytization. As a result, the missionary agenda and identity must be managed so that tentmakers can continue living in RANs. The vocational identity may be presented on the field, while the missionary identity is hidden. But in the home country, the missionary identity may be prominently presented. This can create the feeling of living a double life or having a dual identity. Living such a life may negatively impact the tentmaker—as it did for me.

Tentmaking and business as mission (BAM) are accepted and even standard practices among most church-planting organizations today. However, missionaries who use their vocations as a platform for entry and long-term legal residence in RANs may face ethical and theological issues surrounding concealment, duplicity, and identity. Missionaries interpret, experience, and cope with these issues in different ways. This study seeks to elucidate the effects of this identity management on missionaries'

42. Lai and Love, "Integrated Identity," 337.

43. Nehrbass, "Managing Missionary Identity," 193–94.

44. Greenberg and Hier, *Surveillance*, 15–18.

self-concept today. The goal is to understand missionaries' experiences and practices of managing and concealing their missionary identities, how they cope with challenges that arise, and how they narrate their own identity through these experiences.

One of the broader benefits of the study is that mission organizations, churches, and missionaries may better understand the unique challenges that missionaries in RANs face in managing their identity. This study will have implications for pre-field training, member care practices, and debriefing of missionaries as they leave the field. From a pre-field perspective, this study could benefit future missionaries as they consider issues of identity and concealment in preparation for entering their country of service. The study's outcomes could impact seminary and missionary training curricula to serve the current ethical, theological, and practical needs of missionaries living in RANs. From a member care perspective, a greater understanding of the modern challenges to identity that missionaries face is an important first step to managing the ill effects that such challenges may bring. In her book *Honourably Wounded: Stress Among Christian Workers*, Marjorie Foyle describes the many sources of stress among cross-cultural missionaries, including culture shock, interpersonal conflict, raising children on the field, and reentry into the home country, among others. Surprisingly absent from her research, first published in 1987, is a discussion on security issues relating to tentmaking in RANs. Research on missionaries serving in RANs is needed to assess whether such a lifestyle increases stress, emotional and psychological distress, or unhealthy coping mechanisms. The hope for this study is to impact missionary practices for greater wholeness, longevity on the field, and more effective witness in RANs.

RESEARCH QUESTION AND SUBQUESTIONS

The primary question of this study is, How does presenting a missionary identity back home and a non-missionary identity overseas impact one's self-concept? Four subquestions support this primary research question:

1. How do tentmakers present their identities across various social fields?[45]
2. What concealing practices do tentmakers use to manage their missionary identities in RANs and online?

45. For the purposes of this study, if I do not refer to both "tentmaking" and "BAM" together, I will use the term "tentmaker" in a broad sense to include BAM.

3. How do tentmakers perceive the experiences of navigating identity in a RAN?
4. What strategies do tentmakers use to reconcile illegal, hidden, or deceptive activities with their moral identity?

SCOPE AND LIMITATIONS

An interdisciplinary approach in intercultural studies allows for a holistic and more comprehensive perspective on complex issues. This study represents an intersection between missiology, culture, and the social sciences. Because identity and morality are embedded within complex social and cultural systems, I have limited this study to American missionaries who serve with evangelical mission organizations with an emphasis on church planting among UPGs. American evangelical missionaries may have shared cultural values and understandings of direct communication, individual rights and responsibilities, privacy, truth telling, and openness.[46] These cultural values and assumptions form the basis of their perceptions of reality, identity, and morality. Further, individualism is a cultural pattern in the United States that profoundly impacts interpretations of experiences surrounding self-concept.[47] Limiting the study to American missionaries allows for a deeper exploration of identity construction and management among people with shared cultural values. While many Christians living and working overseas identify in some way as missionaries or tentmakers, this study limits participants to those who are members of evangelical church-planting organizations. Affiliation with a church-planting organization likely requires some level of concealment and identity management for security, even if missionaries do not conceal their Christian identity.

Different locations may yield differing practices contextualized to the realities that missionaries face there. This study focuses on the specific context of the Co-Operation Council for the Arab States of the Gulf (GCC) countries on the Arabian Peninsula. The GCC is comprised of Bahrain, Kingdom of Saudi Arabia (KSA), Kuwait, Oman, Qatar, and the United Arab Emirates (UAE). Yemen, while located on the Arabian Peninsula, is excluded from this study as it differs significantly from the GCC states in significant issues such as wealth, national stability, power structures, technology and surveillance, and terrorism threats. Further information on

46. Adeney, *Strange Virtues*, 43.

47. Triandis, *Individualism and Collectivism*, 12, 33.

the GCC is found below under the heading "Setting." The results may not necessarily be extrapolated to other missionaries or the RANs they serve. However, this study may provide insight for further research in other RANs.

DEFINITIONS

Restricted access nation (RAN): Nation-states that do not provide missionary visas for entry or residence and maintain legislation against religious proselytization.[48] In these countries, missionaries intending to verbally proclaim the gospel, encourage conversion from one religion to another, distribute or teach Christian literature, or gather national believers into a church likely need to hide these activities from the government and locals. If they do not conceal these activities, they risk prosecution or deportation.

Missionary: Missionaries in this study are defined as Christians living cross-culturally who intend to proclaim the gospel, disciple locals in the faith, and promote Christian beliefs among UPGs. Missionaries in this study are affiliated with an evangelical church-planting mission organization and thus have received training toward these goals.

Evangelical: Following the Bebbington quadrilateral, Evangelicalism is marked by the priorities of:

1. *Conversionism*—The belief that people must be "born again" for salvation
2. *Activism*—The lived expression of faith in action
3. *Biblicism*—A high regard for the Bible as authoritative
4. *Crucicentrism*—A belief in the central role of Christ's sacrificial death on the cross.[49]

This definition of Evangelicalism will be assumed throughout the study, rather than any political alignments or other definitions of Evangelicalism that have come into colloquial usage in recent years.

Church planting (CP): Intentionally gathering Christian believers into a fellowship and organizational structure. No particular ecclesial structure

48. Although they do not provide missionary visas, some RANs do at times provide work visas for clergy in expatriate churches registered with the government. These churches are often highly regulated by the government and must provide member lists, install cameras on the premises, and gain approval for gathering tithes or other financial resources. See Office of International Religious Freedom, *2021 Report*, United Arab Emirates.

49. Bebbington, *Evangelicalism in Modern Britain*, 2–3.

is assumed in this study, as the participants are broadly evangelical rather than from a specific denomination. Church planters participate in activities such as evangelism, gathering local believers for worship and discipleship, and training local leadership for ecclesial responsibilities.

Business as mission (BAM): Using BAM Global's definition, business as mission is "the seamless integration of excellent business with intentional mission. It is doing business for God's glory, the gospel, and the common good."[50] On the Arabian Peninsula, only people with certain nationalities can start and own businesses, and in some GCC countries, they must also have a national partner who is a co-owner. Those who start and own businesses are called tentmakers in this study, as explained below.

Tentmaking/tentmakers: Derived from the apostle Paul's vocation as a tentmaker alongside his work as a missionary, modern tentmakers have a part-time or full-time vocation alongside their missionary role. In this study, tentmakers are missionaries affiliated with mission organizations who hold residence visas through their vocation, whether they take employment within a company, start their own business, or work in a business started by other missionaries. They may be either fully financially supported through their employment, fully supported through missionary support structures, or partially supported by both. Tentmakers often rely on their profession for their public identity in their country of service, to supply or supplement their income, and perhaps as a platform for ministry activities.

Self-concept: The cognitive understanding that a person possesses about themselves, including their social, emotional, physical, religious, and intellectual attributes. Self-concept includes evaluations and descriptions of the self, often in comparison to others.[51]

Identity: Closely related but distinct from self-concept, identity contains both internal and external elements pertaining to who or what a person is. Identity is a complex set of meanings that includes a person's characteristics, memberships in and allegiances to social groups, roles they play in society, and the meanings applied to all of these categories.[52] Rather than fixed and singular, as the word "identity" can imply, identities are often fluid and multiple, developing across a person's life as they inhabit various social spheres

50. Plummer, "Business as Mission?," para. 1.

51. Byrne, "Validating Measurement of Self-Concept," 901.

52. Burke and Stets, *Identity Theory*, 1.

and roles. At the same time, there are abiding and stable elements of the self that endure.[53] The concept of identity is discussed further in chapter 3.

RESEARCH METHODOLOGY

This study uses qualitative methodology to explore missionary identity presentation and management arising from security concerns in RANs. I have chosen ethnographic methods for this study, including semi-structured interviews, fieldwork involving participant observation, and informal conversations with tentmaking missionaries in GCC countries. Researchers often use ethnography to explore a culture or a "community of practice" with shared understandings of belonging, beliefs, practices, and assumptions.[54] As security issues necessitated a high level of trust between the participants and the researcher, I recruited participants first through personal contacts in my multiagency missionary network, and then through snowball sampling. I located field leaders of various church-planting organizations and received permission from them to interview their field personnel. These field leaders then shared my recruitment materials with their field personnel.

The semi-structured interviews prioritized participants' narratives to analyze in depth how they construct and present their identities in their context. In addition to interviews, I conducted fieldwork in several different countries of the GCC, combined with five years of residence in the GCC. Thirty-eight tentmakers participated in this study. This study adheres to a high level of confidentiality to protect participants, while prioritizing the voices of participants. Further information on data collection, participants, security protocols, researcher positionality, and data analysis are discussed in chapter 4.

SETTING: THE GCC STATES

This study takes place in the GCC countries of the Arabian Peninsula: Bahrain, the Kingdom of Saudi Arabia (KSA), Kuwait, Oman, Qatar, and the United Arab Emirates (UAE). These countries formed the GCC in 1981 to strengthen regional ties as an economic and military union with a shared history.[55] The GCC countries all experienced a dramatic increase in wealth

53. Brubaker and Cooper, "Beyond 'Identity,'" 6–7.

54. Wolcott, *Ethnography*, 251.

55. Co-Operation Council, "Charter."

from the production and export of oil since the 1970s. The member states of the GCC are monarchies: two absolute monarchies (Saudi Arabia and Oman), three constitutional monarchies (Qatar, Kuwait, and Bahrain), and one federal monarchy (the UAE). The GCC states also host an unusually high number of expatriate guest workers, comprising significant percentages of the population. These high expatriate populations indicate the abundant opportunity for tentmakers to gain access to these RANs through employment. The demographics of the GCC nations are summarized in table 1 below.[56]

Table 1: GCC States Statistics and Demographics

	Bahrain	**Kuwait**	**Oman**	**Qatar**	**Saudi Arabia**	**UAE**
GDP—Total 2025 USD	$47.83 billion	$153.1 billion	$104.35 billion	$222.78 billion	$1.08 trillion	$548.6 billion
Population 2025	1,660,000	5,112,000	5,500,000	3,109,000	36,006,000	11,083,000
Percentage of Population Comprising Expatriates	53.4%[57]	70%[58]	43%[59]	88%[60]	44.4%[61]	90%[62]
Government Structure	Constitutional monarchy	Constitutional monarchy	Absolute monarchy (sultanate)	Constitutional monarchy	Absolute monarchy	Federal monarchy

Religious and Journalistic Freedom Restrictions in the GCC

All six GCC states are Arabic-speaking nations where Islam is designated as the official religion. In all six GCC countries, religious proselytization of Muslims is illegal, though the severity of punishment differs among each nation. In Bahrain, there are no official laws against blasphemy, proselytization, or apostasy from Islam in the penal code, which is unique among

56. GDP and population estimates from World Economic Outlook, Apr. 2025.
57. Government of Bahrain, "Facts & Figures."
58. Total Population by Country, Kuwait, 2025.
59. National Centre for Statistics and Information.
60. Total Population by Country, Qatar, 2025.
61. Global Media Insight, Saudi Arabia, 2025.
62. Total Population by Country, United Arab Emirates, 2025.

the GCC states. However, the Bahrain *2021 International Religious Freedom Report* states that in 2021, at least twenty-seven individuals had been investigated, and one prosecuted, for blasphemy and defamation of Islam, which may include proselytization.[63] This suggests that while the official penal code may not forbid proselytization or even blasphemy, those who engage in proselytizing may still face legal problems. In Kuwait, there is no official penalty for proselytization, but in practice, some non-Muslims have been prosecuted for "contempt of religion."[64] In Oman, it is illegal to proselytize in public, except where permission is granted to certain Islamic groups. However, promoting religions other than Islam carries a penalty of up to seven years imprisonment.[65] In Qatar, proselytization by non-Muslims is penalized by up to ten years imprisonment, as well as two years imprisonment and a fine of up to 10,000 riyals for possession of written materials used for missionary activity.[66] For Saudi Arabia, the GCC state with the least religious freedom, proselytization is illegal, as well as displaying symbols of any religion other than Islam. Official penalties for the proselytization of Muslims are unclear, but in practice, imprisonment, deportment, lashings, and death have all been utilized. Apostasy from Islam may be punishable by death. While practicing a religion other than Islam is technically illegal in KSA, Christian expatriates working in Saudi Arabia are sometimes permitted to hold private worship services on residential compounds.[67] For the UAE, the penalty for any proselytization is up to five years imprisonment.[68]

In 2009, the Pew Forum on Religion and Public Life released the *Global Restrictions on Religion* report, which measured the degrees of religious restriction experienced in various countries. They rated each nation on a government restrictions index (GRI), with zero being religiously free with no restrictions and ten being the highest level of restriction. All six nations of the GCC are classified as "Religiously Repressive Muslim Majority States."[69] In 2019, the Pew Research Center did a follow-up study measuring government religious restrictions. Over the decade, the GRI increased for five of the six GCC states. The only GCC state that loosened restrictions

63. Office of International Religious Freedom, *2021 Report*, Bahrain.
64. Office of International Religious Freedom, *2021 Report*, Kuwait.
65. Office of International Religious Freedom, *2021 Report*, Oman.
66. Office of International Religious Freedom, *2021 Report*, Qatar.
67. Office of International Religious Freedom, *2021 Report*, Saudi Arabia.
68. Office of International Religious Freedom, *2021 Report*, United Arab Emirates.
69. Philpott, *Religious Freedom in Islam*, 116.

was Saudi Arabia, the nation with the highest religious restrictions in the GCC.[70]

Authoritarian government structures also lead to extreme censorship of the press in the GCC, and professionals in the media must officially support state policies. Journalists in the GCC do not have legal protection against the government, and critics of the state may be censored, imprisoned, or deported.[71] While five of the six GCC states have legislation protecting freedom of speech in some way (Saudi Arabia is the exception), caveats are made within that legislation for "libel and slander, some campaign speech, calls for violence, indecency and obscenity, securities regulation, and rules surrounding advertising."[72] The functional result of these caveats is that freedom of speech in GCC media is heavily restricted. Reporters Without Borders released the results of both quantitative and qualitative studies on world press freedoms for 2023. This study considers journalist harassment and endangerment, government transparency, legislation surrounding media, and other factors. One hundred eighty countries were ranked from 1 (most free) to 180 (most restrictive).[73] All members of the GCC states ranked either "high" or "very high" for levels of government restriction on the freedoms of the press. The 2023 index rankings of press freedom and the GRIs of each GCC state from the 2009 and 2019 studies are listed below in table 2.

Table 2: GCC States Religious and Journalistic Restrictions						
	Bahrain	**Kuwait**	**Oman**	**Qatar**	**Saudi Arabia**	**UAE**
Global Restriction on Religion Index 2009 (0–10)	4.0	5.0	4.5	3.9	8.4	4.1

70. Majumdar and Villa, "Globally, Social Hostilities."

71. Al-Kindi, "Press Freedom and Corruption." Interestingly, Matt Duffy reports that one factor in media restriction is that all six GCC states have ties to Great Britain as former protectorates or colonies. Great Britain historically practiced extreme censorship in order to control colonial populations by guarding the stream of information given to them. British advisors helped set up legislation before leaving the gulf (Duffy, "Arab Media Regulations," 1–3).

72. Duffy, "Arab Media Regulations," 4.

73. Reporters Without Borders Index, 2023.

Table 2: GCC States Religious and Journalistic Restrictions						
	Bahrain	**Kuwait**	**Oman**	**Qatar**	**Saudi Arabia**	**UAE**
Global Restriction on Religion Index 2019 (0–10)	6.4 (+2.4)	6.2 (+1.2)	5.4 (+0.9)	5.4 (+1.5)	7.2 (-1.2)	5.8 (+1.7)
Reporters Without Borders Index 2023 (1–180)	171 very high restrictions	154 very high restrictions	155 very high restrictions	105 high restrictions	170 very high restrictions	145 high restrictions

Digital Authoritarianism

The great wealth of the GCC nations allowed for development of advanced technological resources for surveillance that lower-income nations often cannot achieve.[74] Combined with authoritarian government structures, this technological surveillance is used to control local populations—an area of growing concern. Marc Lynch reports that in the Arab Spring uprisings of 2011, the most popular social media applications (apps) were public facing, such as YouTube and Twitter. However, posting on these apps led to disappearances and imprisonments across the Middle East during the Arab Spring. Since 2011, users in the Middle East have increased usage of encrypted and private in-network applications, such as WhatsApp and Telegram, to prevent retribution. Lynch writes about these apps,

> Their encryption possibilities may also provide an unwarranted sense of safety to their users. In all cases, seemingly apolitical apps can quickly take on political roles for creative activists—which, in turn, increases the incentive of autocratic regimes to control and surveil them.[75]

Digital surveillance is a significant human rights concern for political activists in the GCC since the Arab Spring, as GCC governments seek to control information and political narratives.[76] Retinal scans, ubiquitous video surveillance, phone tapping, government-sponsored disinformation

74. Lynch, "Digital Activism," 5–6.
75. Lynch, "Digital Activism," 5.
76. Shaheed, "Binary Threat."

campaigns, internet monitoring and data mining, and email decryption are all of rising concern to activists against "digital authoritarianism."[77]

Researchers on digital authoritarianism in the Arabian Gulf have noted that these surveillance measures have advanced and accelerated due to the COVID-19 pandemic.[78] In 2020, the governments in the Middle East and North Africa (MENA) region enacted high numbers of internet shutdowns in order to slow communications and control narratives.[79] Downloading national COVID-19 tracking apps became a normal and sometimes mandatory practice in the GCC. Amnesty International rated Bahrain and Kuwait's national COVID-tracking apps as among the most dangerous in the world. They categorized them as "highly invasive surveillance tools" that "go far beyond what is justified in efforts to tackle COVID-19."[80] These apps were found to track real-time locations of users by frequently uploading GPS coordinates to a server in a central government database. Bahrain and Kuwait paired the app with a Bluetooth bracelet worn by the user to ensure that the user's location and phone location were identical. In addition, users registered for the apps with identification numbers linked to other private information. Bahrain published private information about users online, including COVID-19 health status, nationality, age, gender, and travel history. Amnesty International also listed Qatar's COVID-19 tracking app as concerning, as the government mandated its use and required registration with users' national ID numbers. The app experienced a security vulnerability, risking users' personal information. In the wake of the COVID-19 pandemic, digital security and privacy are of increasing concern for all who live in the GCC, not just missionaries.

These realities surrounding religious freedom restrictions, journalistic freedom restrictions, and digital surveillance create a unique setting for missionary tentmakers. Missionary visas may not be obtained in any of these six Islamic nations, as proselytizing is illegal.[81] However, the high numbers of expatriates residing in these countries as professionals demonstrate an opportunity for obtaining residence visas through work. The

77. Ziadah, "Surveillance, Race, Social Sorting," 606–7.

78. Lynch, "Digital Activism," 6; Shaheed, "Binary Threat," 8; Amnesty International, "Bahrain, Kuwait and Norway."

79. Shaheed, "Binary Threat," 10.

80. Amnesty International, "Bahrain, Kuwait and Norway," para. 4.

81. While there are no missionary or religious visas, there are some designated work visas available for clergy in registered churches in the GCC.

government restrictions index on religion of each country has increased since 2009, except in Saudi Arabia, showing that security concerns regarding evangelism, conversion, and discipleship are not decreasing despite the globalizing factor of high expatriate populations.[82] Should missionaries face interrogation, imprisonment, or deportment, the factors of low media freedom and high censorship may increase the opportunity for human rights abuses. However, missionaries among Muslims acknowledge that the risks may be highest for locals who convert from Islam.[83] Three GCC countries are featured on the 2025 Open Doors watch list, which annually ranks the top fifty countries of the world where Christians face extreme persecution. Saudi Arabia was ranked twelfth in the world for persecution of Christians, Qatar was ranked forty-first, and Oman was ranked thirty-second.[84] This unique combination of limited religious freedom, authoritarian government structures, high relative wealth, expatriate population, and technological advancement make the GCC states a unique setting for studying the impact of missionary identity management and concealment practices.

CHAPTER BREAKDOWN

This first chapter introduced the concept of missionary identity management in RANs, the rationale and need for the study, and the research questions that guide this study. It also described the scope and limitations of the study and defined key terms. Included was a brief summary of the methodology and a description of the current landscape of GCC nations related to religious freedom, surveillance, and other factors impacting tentmakers.

Chapter 2 is a review of the literature. This review focuses on four main topics relating to tentmaker identity management and presentation. First, the literature review explores research on missionary digital security and the management of identity online. Second, the review covers literature regarding the construction and presentation of both the missionary identity and the vocational identity, and the tensions experienced between the two. Third, the concepts and ethics of dual identity and the "undercover

82. Majumdar and Villa, "Globally, Social Hostilities."

83. Little, *Effective Discipling*, 58, 178. Little's research revealed that the most frequent obstacle in discipleship for BMBs was pressure arising from within the Muslim family. The second most frequent obstacle was local Muslim community hostility, rejection, or expulsion. The twelfth most frequent was living in a police state where Muslims were unable to officially change their religion. See also Brogden, "Identity, Security, and Community."

84. World Watch List, 2025.

missionary" are explored. Finally, emerging missiological works on integrated, rather than bifurcated, identities for global missionaries are presented. This literature review demonstrates the timeliness and need for further qualitative research on the experiences of identity presentation among tentmakers in RANs.

Chapter 3 explores identity from a social-scientific perspective. This includes research on how culture impacts the construction and perception of identity. Chapter 3 discusses Charles Taylor's work on the modern Western features of identity construction, and the link between identity and moral reasoning. This chapter also examines identity theory and how identities are constructed and maintained in social interactions. Of special significance are role identity, identity dissonance, and distress arising from a concealed stigmatized identity. This framework supports the present study and supplies a series of lenses for analyzing the data collected in this study.

Chapter 4 delineates the qualitative methodology for this study. It describes the ethnographic methods used for gathering data among tentmaking missionaries in GCC countries. This chapter describes the participants and researcher access, data collection methods, and security precautions used for data collection. Chapter 4 also outlines the data analysis protocols used to generate the findings, and discusses researcher positionality and reflexivity.

Chapters 5 and 6 present the findings from data gathered through interviews, observations, and field notes. American church-planting missionaries in the GCC describe in their own words their varied perspectives and practices of missionary identity presentation, management, and concealment. Both chapters begin with the story of a participant managing their identity in various ways. Chapter 5 describes the management of the missionary identity, organized by social interactions with various role partners across multiple social fields. The presentation and management of participants' identity fluctuated based on role partners and context, as each role partner had a specific set of expectations and interpretations of behavior for the tentmaker. Six role partners or social fields are described, as well as the management of missionary identity when multiple social fields collide into a blended context.

Chapter 6 continues the analysis of the research findings, focusing on the impact of identity management practices in RANs on tentmakers' self-concept. Chapter 6 reports patterns that emerged regarding identity dissonance among tentmakers. It also describes the theological, cultural, and ethical strategies that tentmakers use for coping with the experiences of duality and dissonance. Finally, chapter 6 describes factors contributing to experiences of identity consonance and integration among participants.

Chapter 7 concludes this study by placing the findings within the context of the literature. This chapter describes the implications of the study, recommendations for missionaries and mission organizations, as well as suggestions for future research.

CONCLUSION

As the church seeks the fulfillment of the Great Commission across all nations, special complexities arise in places where such activity is illegal. Missionaries must navigate between boldly proclaiming of the truth of the gospel and carefully managing security to avoid deportment or imprisonment, and to protect BMBs from unnecessary persecution. This tension of proclamation and concealment may present particular challenges for missionary self-concept.

This study does *not* seek to answer the debates about whether the future of missionary sending should be separated from missionary organizations and funding, whether clandestine activity is justified or not, or which model(s) constitute best practices for mission in a globalized world. Rather, this study seeks to describe the personal impact of a lifestyle where a person has a missionary identity in one location and a vocational identity in another in contexts of high security. This study will also describe the behaviors, processes, and strategies of missionaries who make daily decisions individually and collectively to navigate both proclamation and concealment. This study places a high value on the particular context of each missionary, including their overall personal narratives, values, core personal identities, and the communities in which they are embedded. All of these contribute to the complex ways missionaries manage their identities across their social fields.

2

Literature Review

THIS STUDY EXPLORES HOW presenting a missionary identity back home and a non-missionary identity in a restricted access nation (RAN) impacts one's self-concept. This literature review is divided into four main headings on various topics relating to missionary identity presentation, management, and concealment. The first section explores current research on how missionaries in RANs present and manage their identities online. It also explores concerns and stressors for missionaries amid increasing technological advances and surveillance. The second section surveys the current literature regarding the tensions of presenting missionary and vocational identities. The third section explores the concept of dual identity and the ethics of undercover missionaries with hidden agendas in RANs. Finally, the last section describes emerging concepts of an integrated and unified identity among tentmakers in RANs.

MISSIONARY IDENTITY PRESENTATION AND MANAGEMENT ONLINE

An important aspect of research for missionary identity in the twenty-first century is how the digital age impacts identity management and self-presentation. At the turn of the twenty-first century, several identity scholars began to write about how the internet and social media were changing how people constructed and presented their identities. Leigh Doster calls this self-presentation through social media "elective identity"—that is, people present curated aspects of their real or idealized identities as a method of identity management.[1] These elective identities are often achieved through signs and symbols, accentuating positive traits and downplaying negative ones in order to project an idealized self.[2] On social media, this might occur through posting particular photos, crafting captions or status updates, or tweeting quotes to present a particular self to the world. The presentation of a curated identity may be especially relevant to missionaries in RANs, as they may conceal or withhold their missionary identity.

Ron Cole-Turner argues that just as businesses and companies sought out brand identities in order to facilitate trust in the marketplace, individuals in the 1990s began marketing themselves as a brand.[3] Self-branding is a method of self-presentation whereby an individual markets their skills, accomplishments, and personality in order to secure social benefits. Cole-Turner argues that this branding and self-presentation online raises questions about the ontology of the self, as internet-mediated relationships now complicate the dynamics of social interactions. He writes, "At first glance, self-branding via hand-held social media access seems to offer unprecedented freedom to define and redefine the self." However, he argues that this freedom is balanced by the ever-changing market, which the personal brand must constantly adapt to: "Elective identity needs constant updating, not just because we change our minds about how to present ourselves but because we want to change our identities in response to feedback from others."[4] While much of this feedback may be from other humans, he notes that a significant amount of feedback may also be from bots, creating a false feedback loop. Thus, a branded identity must be in constant flux; self-reflection is not done to attain ideals but to adapt to performance feedback such as likes or views.

Cole-Turner also explains "context collapse," an issue exacerbated by social media usage and self-branding.[5] In everyday human interactions, people change their self-presentation slightly to adapt to the context.[6] Different levels of information are shared with different groups—strangers, spouses, children, and neighbors. Sharing certain details can lead to support in some contexts, but harm or negative evaluations in others. However,

1. Doster, "Teen Identity, Social Comparison," 54.
2. Doster, "Teen Identity, Social Comparison," 33.
3. Cole-Turner, "Commodification and Transfiguration," 3.
4. Cole-Turner, "Commodification and Transfiguration," 4.
5. Cole-Turner, "Commodification and Transfiguration," 5.
6. Goffman, *Presentation of Self*, 46–49.

on social media sites, these varied and distinct contexts collapse, and all parties receive the same information.[7] The college student's self-presentation as a vivacious and adventurous friend to her peers on social media may appear to future employers as undependable and unprofessional. The contexts have collapsed into one. This collapse of contexts may lead to "a lowest common denominator approach to self-presentation" that pleases the majority.[8] This context collapse is especially relevant to missionaries in RANs, who are known in their home contexts as missionaries and known in their country of service by their vocation. As these multiple and varied contexts flatten in a digital age, the collapse forces missionaries to either reduce their identity presentation to a one-dimensional character across all contexts, or carefully disclose information in one context that must be concealed in another.

In RANs, where evangelistic activities may be illegal, digital security and identity are paramount concerns. Thus, online missionary identity presentation and management activities are significant. Kenneth Nehrbass conducted qualitative and quantitative research on missionary usage of digital communication to manage the different aspects of identities among various social groups. Nehrbass argues that the "cultural shift from print to digital is impacting the missionary communication world."[9] In previous generations, missionaries were expected to communicate much less often via physical letters sent back to their supporters, perhaps once per year. The frequency of communication has shifted as missionaries are encouraged to send shorter updates more often. They are also encouraged to reach more people by using multiple digital platforms. In addition to frequent email newsletters, many missionaries have Facebook pages, blogs, Instagram, and other digital platforms that give their supporters real-time updates and insights into missionary life previously unavailable to them.

In addition to increasing the frequency and platforms for communication, missionaries in Nehrbass's study also shifted the audience to whom they communicated. In their social media posts, missionaries communicated to multiple audiences at once through these digital platforms and performed their various expected roles and identities—such as family member, "effective worker," or foreigner in an exotic land. Nehrbass found that missionaries used cultural scripts in their digital communications,

7. Cole-Turner, "Commodification and Transfiguration," 5.

8. Santer et al., "Narratives of the Self," 80.

9. Nehrbass, "Managing Missionary Identity," 185.

each with cultural symbols and meanings behind them depending on the expectations of their multiple social groups. These cultural scripts include (1) validating the work, (2) demonstrating the exotic, (3) chronicling the family, and (4) chronicling what God is teaching.[10] Nehrbass found that the divisions between home and host country were flattened as people from both "worlds" were brought together on social media platforms. Knowing they were communicating to multiple audiences at once caused missionaries to post with caution, as they had to consider how various social groups might interpret each post. Some missionaries sought to keep the home world and ministry world separate by setting up multiple social media sites.

These findings are significant for missionaries in RANs, whose security may depend on keeping home and ministry fields separate. In addition, missionaries in RANs may enact their missionary identity over digital media differently than missionaries living in non-RANs. Nehrbass's research did not include missionary identity management in RANs. However, he did note that missionaries in Asia and the Middle East were much less likely to publicly identify as missionaries on social media, but rather resorted to secure digital or face-to-face communication.[11] This present study builds on his work of missionary identity management, exploring how missionaries in RANs manage and present their identities online, especially in contexts of significant surveillance.

Jaron Evans (a pseudonym) is an American church planter and tentmaker on the Arabian Peninsula. In his article "To Be or Not to Be (Online)," he delineates his approach to digital security and the identity he presents online. His approach has changed over the course of his ministry and as technology has advanced. When he and his wife arrived in Saudi Arabia over a decade ago, social media was new and they approached it cautiously. They had a Facebook account only for connecting with family back home, not local Arab contacts. They locked all commenting or tagging, and did not post pictures. When they discovered that Saudis wanted to connect with them online, they created a separate Facebook account only for Arab contacts but immediately recognized that this looked suspicious; why would they not have any American friends on Facebook? Evans notes that his attempts to keep his home and field worlds separate suggested that he and his wife were "hiding something."[12] These realities, along with lo-

10. Nehrbass, "Managing Missionary Identity," 185.

11. Nehrbass, "Managing Missionary Identity," 194.

12. Evans, "To Be (Online)," 13.

cal BMB online practices, helped shape a new digital paradigm for Evans's practices.

Evans argues that missionaries should present an identity through an online presence that is more open and authentic to their Christian identity. He believes this helps missionaries connect with locals in RANs and also reduces security risks:

> It may sound counterintuitive, but an increased online presence may actually help make us safer from the risk of unwanted labels being attached to us. When we are intentional about it, we can be the ones who write the narrative of what our friends see when they search for us on the web. One common philosophy of security-risk management for missionaries involves defining and maintaining a consistent, truthful, and legitimate identity and purpose for being in the countries where we serve. While sometimes we may seek to remove information from the web that might lead to unwanted labels, we can also positively flood the net with the story we want to be read by our community.[13]

Evans's argument for missionaries purposefully narrating their online identity contrasts with the normative practice of deleting social media accounts and not interacting online. While many missionaries in RANs often delete evidence of their missionary identity online, especially after speaking in churches, Evans argues for going the extra step to intentionally project an identity online—in their own words and on their own terms. In this way, missionaries can have some control over how their identities are presented online. Evans controls his family's narrative through his Facebook page, his LinkedIn account, and a public Vimeo page using his real name. On these platforms, he projects his family identity, his Christian identity, his professional identity, and his traveling expatriate identity. In presenting and narrating these authentic aspects of his identity online, Evans believes he now looks less like he is hiding something and more like a normal adult participating in the online world.

Evans argues against missionaries having a *secular* identity online, but rather cultivating an openly Christian identity:

> In my experience in Saudi Arabia, I found that being transparent about these things online did not hinder our ministry but actually empowered us to shine Jesus more authentically to those in our community. When we post about the things we love, why shouldn't

13. Evans, "To Be (Online)," 14.

> Jesus be the center of it? The representation of who we are online is reflective of who we really are. I am not saying we need to get preachy on our Facebook profiles, but we can express our love for Jesus and others in real and authentic ways.[14]

However, when engaging in online evangelistic activities, Evans is much more careful to protect his identity. Advancing technology has allowed for new possibilities in evangelism and discipleship in RANs through online media. Sometimes, secret police or Muslims who are not truly seeking may also access these ministries to find out information about missionaries, BMBs, or underground churches located in RANs. Due to these security concerns, Evans protects his identity when initially contacting these individuals. He does this by setting up alias Facebook and Google accounts, using a second phone with an out-of-country number for texting, and using proxy servers and other digital security measures. Evans notes that both the opportunities and the challenges of digital communication have increased since the COVID-19 pandemic. In response, he argues that missionaries must be online more than ever rather than withdrawing from an online presence, as has been the more frequent practice in the GCC.[15] Evans's description of practices for managing and narrating his identity in the GCC is foundational for this study on methods of missionary identity management.

Few studies have been conducted on the impact of digital security or surveillance on missionaries. David Dunaetz studied the psychological impact of modern technological advances on missionaries. He defines *technostress* as "the psychological discomfort people feel when interacting with technology, such as the pressure to respond quickly to emails and text messages, to post regularly on social media, or to master and use a new app."[16] Perhaps surprisingly, technostress affects younger generations of missionaries more than older ones. Dunaetz argues that "in addition to being able to put stressful situations into perspective because of their maturity, they [older generations] tend to have more power in organizations, have more control over what technologies they choose to use, and are better able to judge how important it is to learn a technology."[17] Dunaetz does not

14. Evans, "To Be (Online)," 16.

15. Evans, "To Be (Online)," 19–20.

16. Dunaetz, "More Harm Than Good," abstract.

17. Dunaetz, "More Harm Than Good," 121.

report whether generational differences in how *often* missionaries engage with technology also impact their higher susceptibility to technostress.

Dunaetz explores six areas of technostress related to missionary activity. *Techno-overload* is the pressure to do more tasks in less time due to technological advancements.[18] *Techno-invasion* is the stress caused by technology enabling greater access to a person's life, making them available to others, and contributing to a disintegration of a work-life balance.[19] *Techno-complexity* involves the time required and the intimidation experienced in learning a new technology. *Techno-insecurity* arises when a person feels their job is threatened by technology that could replace them, or by younger people who may be capable of learning technology faster.[20] *Techno-uncertainty* produces stress due to the constant upgrades or changes in technology. Finally, *techno-comparison* is the stress arising from social comparisons made by viewing others' idealized lives on social media. Dunaetz notes that younger generations may be more susceptible to depression stemming from techno-comparison.[21]

Surprisingly, Dunaetz does not mention security issues across digital platforms as causes of technostress among missionaries. However, he does explore some consequences of technostress, including role overload and role conflict. In role overload, missionaries experience the pressure of an increasing number of tasks to complete, which may include language and culture acquisition, meeting local needs, responding to text messages and emails, and managing social media sites.[22] In role conflict, missionaries struggle with the competing expectations of supporters, local relationships, ministry programs, field leadership, and the missionary's own expectations. Dunaetz writes, "It may not be possible to accomplish all these things, a problem compounded by continual electronic communication with various stakeholders."[23] The research questions of this present study expand on Dunaetz's research into missionary technostress, as it will elucidate some of the modern challenges missionaries face in managing and protecting their identities online.

18. Dunaetz, "More Harm Than Good," 117.
19. Dunaetz, "More Harm Than Good," 117–18.
20. Dunaetz, "More Harm Than Good," 118.
21. Dunaetz, "More Harm Than Good," 119.
22. Dunaetz, "More Harm Than Good," 122.
23. Dunaetz, "More Harm Than Good," 123.

TENSIONS BETWEEN MISSIONARY AND VOCATIONAL IDENTITY

Tentmakers frequently express variation regarding their primary calling and motivations, sometimes creating tension between the missionary and vocational identities. These differences impact tentmaker practices both in ministry and in their vocation, particularly in RANs where the missionary identity may be concealed and the vocational identity publicly presented. This can create the feeling of having a dual identity: the home country identity of missionary, and the field identity of vocational worker. The motivations, callings, goals, time commitments, and prioritizations of each identity can sometimes be experienced as two competing identities. This experience of navigating two competing identities is often described as "schizophrenia" in tentmaking literature.

Dan Gibson divides tentmakers into two main categories: Pauline and Priscillan, after the Christian tentmakers in the book of Acts. In Gibson's paradigm, Pauline tentmakers prioritize teaching and preaching full-time when possible. They are primarily funded by churches and donor support, though they may supplement this income with another vocation. Pauline tentmakers are highly trained in evangelism and discipleship, and view these activities as of primary importance. Gibson identifies one potential obstacle for Pauline tentmakers: the sense of "ministry schizophrenia," in which the tentmaker feels like a missionary fraudulently disguising themselves as an engineer or teacher since their primary goal is evangelism or church planting.[24] Gibson notes that Paul, Priscilla, and Aquila did not have these issues of identity and integrity, as they did not need visas into "closed" countries as missionaries do today.[25] Priscillan tentmakers in Gibson's paradigm follow the model of Priscilla and Aquila. Gibson describes them as models of Christian skilled, self-supported vocational workers whose ministry flows from their role as tentmakers.[26] Priscillan tentmakers see themselves primarily through the lens of their vocation due to experience and training, but look for ministry opportunities through their full-time work. Self-image is a significant category for Gibson; Priscillan tentmakers may see themselves primarily in terms of their professional vocation, whereas Pauline tentmakers identify primarily as full-time ministers of the gospel.

24. Gibson, *Avoiding the Tentmaker Trap*, 25.
25. Gibson, *Avoiding the Tentmaker Trap*, 25–26.
26. Gibson, *Avoiding the Tentmaker Trap*, 22–23.

Gibson identifies several challenges for both Pauline and Priscillan tentmakers. Time management between vocational commitments and ministry commitments is a significant challenge for all tentmakers. He argues that the inability to balance the demands of both work and ministry frequently leads to burnout among tentmakers.[27] Another potential "trap" that Gibson lists is the expatriate community, which may place additional time demands on the tentmaker, detracting from the tentmaker's original goals with locals.[28] Learning the local language is often more difficult for Priscillan tentmakers, as their employers rarely give them sufficient time to devote to it. Pauline tentmakers often have ministries that demand a high language proficiency, such as teaching Scripture or making apologetic arguments in the host country's language.[29] Job satisfaction and success may also be measured differently by Pauline and Priscillan tentmakers. Priscillan tentmakers may prioritize vocational success over ministry success, potentially leading to low spiritual fruit. Pauline tentmakers may prioritize ministry goals, potentially leading to poor vocational outcomes and compromising their witness.[30] Gibson's advice to tentmakers particularly focuses on the tension between the missionary and vocational identities, assuming they are distinct identities.

Many BAM theorists consider this tension and distinction between the missionary and vocational identity problematic, a sign that the tentmaker has fallen prey to the sacred-secular divide between clergy and laity. In "Ministry, Profits, and the Schizophrenic Tentmaker," Steven Rundle points to this sacred-secular divide as a primary cause of missionary failure to impact a local community. He identifies missionary ambivalence about profit as a core concern, as many missionaries believe their supporting churches might drop needed financial support entirely if they knew the missionary was making money on the field. Missionaries also express discomfort over making a profit; they are much more comfortable with nonprofit or charitable endeavors, especially when combined with evangelistic intentions. Rundle argues for Christians to establish profitable, sustainable businesses as a key part of their evangelistic witness:

> This ambivalence about income-producing activities handicaps the tentmaking movement in several ways. It creates an erroneous

27. Gibson, *Avoiding the Tentmaker Trap*, 51–52.
28. Gibson, *Avoiding the Tentmaker Trap*, 56–57.
29. Gibson, *Avoiding the Tentmaker Trap*, 50.
30. Gibson, *Avoiding the Tentmaker Trap*, 27.

> distinction between sacred and secular activities, as if God is more interested in the soul than in the body. This apparent conflict creates a sense of guilt in the tentmaker, which strains the family and the entire ministry. It also leads to a struggling business, which adds more pressure on the tentmaker.[31]

Demolishing the sacred-secular divide is frequently upheld as the solution to the tension experienced between the missionary and vocational identities. However, there remains a dearth of qualitative research on identity construction and management among tentmakers in RANs. Such research can potentially confirm whether tentmakers hold to a sacred-secular divide, and draw out other potential causes of tension in identity experienced by tentmaking missionaries.

Patrick Lai provides a comprehensive handbook for those who want to serve as missionaries in RANs by gaining employment or starting businesses in those countries, based on his research of over 450 tentmaking missionaries. His treatment of dual identity—the missionary and vocational identities—for tentmakers in RANs is particularly relevant to this study. Lai also decries the division of sacred and secular vocation as an arbitrary and Western dichotomy that needs to be discarded. At the same time, he categorizes ministry and vocation in terms of "religious" and "secular" work and admits that the two sometimes conflict:[32]

> It is important to understand there is no dichotomy between work and ministry. Work and ministry are to be one. However, as an experienced tentmaker knows, there are times when I must defer going to the office so I can meet with Abdullah to study the Bible. I cannot be in two places at once. Sometimes I can do evangelism or discipleship at work, but often I cannot. In this sense, work and ministry do conflict. Thus, in real life there are times when we must choose between our vocational work and our ministry outreach.[33]

Thus, while Lai is consistent in arguing against missionaries dividing their lives into sacred and secular spheres, he also acknowledges the conflicts many tentmaking missionaries experience between their missionary identity and the expectations of their vocational role. The goals or tasks of vocation may sometimes be different or distinct from the goals and tasks of

31. Rundle, "Ministry, Profits," 299.
32. Lai, *Tentmaking*, 10, 14, 43, 46.
33. Lai, *Tentmaking*, 10–11.

mission, and when they conflict, a tentmaker may have to choose between one or the other.

Later, Lai argues that tentmaking provides "a secular identity" that presents opportunities for ministry that those with a public missionary identity may not have:

> We are not known as missionaries or religious professionals. We have a secular identity. A tentmaker, unlike a regular missionary, is free from the stigma of proselytizing. Having natural access to people creates unexpected opportunities to witness. As tentmakers, we do not wear the Christian label; we are one of the crowd.[34]

Lai argues that a secular identity gives a tentmaker more credibility, making locals more likely to seek the tentmaker out if they have religious questions than they might for a religious professional.[35] Tentmakers can build trust by demonstrating their character through their everyday actions and habits. Lai argues that tentmaking missionaries need to be comfortable with their role and identity—which is invested primarily in vocational identity as far as the government is concerned. He argues that when a tentmaker's work is legitimate and clearly understood as the source of income to those observing, it eases the pressure from the missionary and affirms the authenticity of their identity.[36] To demonstrate integrity, the answer to the question "What are you doing here?" should always be "To earn a living." Otherwise, more questions will arise.[37]

Ian Prescott describes the construction and management of missionary and vocational identities along a spectrum. His tentmaker scale from 1 to 5 describes ways that people experienced a sense of calling (to missions, to a vocation, or both), how they self-identify (missionary, professional), what their "sense of vocation" is, and how they relate to an agency (missionary, tentmaker, field friend, or supporter). He also describes special issues that each type may face as they manage and present their identities. Type 1 missionaries are traditional church-planting missionaries with an open

34. Lai, *Tentmaking*, 40.

35. Lai, *Tentmaking*, 41–43. For clarification, it appears that when Lai uses the term "secular identity," he is more accurately describing a "vocational identity." His terms can be confusing when paired with his arguments against a division between sacred and secular categories in a believer's life. Furthermore, though he says tentmakers "do not wear the Christian label," much of the book describes how tentmakers use their vocation as a natural platform for displaying their Christian identity, rather than a secular identity.

36. Lai, *Tentmaking*, 77.

37. Lai, *Tentmaking*, 77.

missionary identity. Types 2 and 3 are both bi-vocational tentmakers. For Type 2s, the missionary calling is the perceived primary calling, and their profession is how they gain access to the ministry field. Their vocation may change over time to flex to ministry needs. Prescott's Type 2 tentmaker corresponds to Gibson's Pauline tentmaker paradigm. For Type 3s, the professional career is primary. Type 3s view their vocation as a significant part of their calling to reach the unreached. Their field of service may change, but their vocation is unlikely to change across locations. Prescott's Type 3 corresponds to Gibson's Priscillan tentmaker paradigm. Type 4s are Christian expatriates working jobs outside their home country and are committed to living Christian lives wherever they are, but may not identify as missionaries. Type 5s are professionals who remain in their home country and may also support mission efforts. Prescott also identifies a Type 2.5, who feels an equal or dual calling as a missionary and a professional, and is not sure which should take preeminence should the two roles conflict.

Prescott identifies various issues among these types of tentmakers as they understand their role and identity in light of God's calling on their lives. One primary issue is confusion over how much time and effort should be devoted to "reaching people" and how much to devote to vocational excellence, which is a witness to Christian character and righteous living. A closely related issue to the management of time and priorities is the judgment experienced or perceived between tentmaking missionaries over their decisions regarding time in ministry and vocation. Prescott argues that Types 2 and 3 are especially prone to misunderstanding one another's callings and activities. Type 2s may think Type 3s are unfocused and not devoted enough to mission; Type 3s may believe Type 2s suffer from a lack of integrity and professionalism. Prescott addresses the unsatisfactory proposed solutions for this tension between tentmakers, which focus on a "holistic balance":

> Some writers try and tackle this by advocating a holistic balance between the two. While the concern for holism is valid, the solutions offered rarely satisfy. Holistic tends to be used to label the user's own preferred position, thus labelling all other positions as inadequately unholistic and not always recognizing that different balances are right for different people.[38]

Prescott instead advocates for an acceptance that all types of tentmakers are needed for mission, rather than one "correct" type. Prescott also describes

38. Prescott, "Identity and Platform," 17.

the "schizophrenia" experienced by tentmakers, the feeling of being pulled in two directions simultaneously between ministry and vocation goals. He postulates that this may be especially present for Type 2.5s, who feel equally called to both roles. Prescott affirms the need for integrity but acknowledges the complexities of identity for missionaries in RANs, including a sense of calling and how missionaries self-identify. How missionaries perceive their calling, vocation, and ministry roles impacts their self-concept as they present and navigate their identity in RANs, and this study builds on Prescott's tentmaker categories.

Like Ian Prescott, Steve Rundle and Min-Dong Paul Lee seek to categorize the complex experiences of identity among business-owning tentmakers. Rundle and Lee describe four categories of business-focused tentmakers using identity theory from the field of social psychology. The categories are based on the person's primary motivations, training, and practices. They describe four BAM identities: (1) evangelists, (2) faith-driven entrepreneurs, (3) BAMers, and (4) explorers. Evangelists have background experience primarily in ministry roles, and their primary objective is spiritual impact rather than entrepreneurial success. For evangelists, business is likely viewed as a means to an end—an entry platform for gaining access to RANs.[39] Faith-driven entrepreneurs primarily have training and experience in business, and identify a well-run business as a significant aspect of their Christian calling. Their goals primarily focus on business sustainability and profitability, though they also pursue spiritual outcomes.[40] BAMers have experience in both ministry and business, and hold both business and spiritual objectives in "a balanced and productive tension." As Prescott notes about BAM and tentmaking literature, this "holistic balance" of ministry and business is somewhat vague and perhaps reflects the authors' preferred position. Explorers have neither extensive ministerial nor business experience or training, but want to explore BAM as well as their calling to make Christ known among the nations.[41] Their identity formation is still vague and taking shape, and they may be more susceptible to both mission drift and not achieving sustainability in business.[42]

39. Rundle and Lee, "Motivations, Backgrounds, and Practices," 428.

40. Rundle and Lee, "Motivations, Backgrounds, and Practices," 427.

41. Rundle and Lee, "Motivations, Backgrounds, and Practices," 421.

42. Rundle and Lee, "Motivations, Backgrounds, and Practices," 429.

Rundle and Lee differentiate these categories by the degree to which a person feels high or low salience to either the missionary identity or the business identity.[43] Identity salience is reflected in prior training or background experience, organizational affiliation, source of income, goals, priorities, and the rationalizations behind business practices. These rationalizations often showed allegiance to for-profit business expectations and norms (high business identity salience) or nonprofit sector expectations and norms (high missionary identity salience).[44] Table 3 below is taken from their article, showing the four categories based on missionary or business identity salience.[45]

Table 3: Missionary and Business Identity Salience Among BAM Practitioners			
		Missionary Identity Salience	
		Low	High
Business Identity Salience	Low	Explorer	Evangelist
	High	Faith-driven entrepreneur	BAMer

This study builds on Rundle and Lee's study of tentmaker identity salience and other relevant categories from identity theory. This study seeks to answer further questions about tentmaker identity construction and management, particularly in the context of security concerns in RANs. In addition, this study expands to include not only those starting businesses, but also those who take up employment in various other professions. Identity salience also forms a significant aspect of a person's self-concept. Identity salience towards either a vocational or missionary identity (or both) may impact security practices and identity management, a question this study seeks to answer.

Adding a perspective on tentmaker identity presentation in a North American setting, Jared Siebert presents the findings of his qualitative study on self-concept among "multi-vocational" tentmakers—primarily pastors—in Canada. Siebert's research reports on the positive effects on the minister's self-concept that presenting a non-ministry identity can bring,

43. Identity salience and other aspects of identity theory are discussed in ch. 3.

44. Rundle and Lee, "Motivations, Backgrounds, and Practices," 425–26.

45. Rundle and Lee, "Motivations, Backgrounds, and Practices," 426.

as well as the challenges for tentmakers. For identity, Siebert found that pastors reported having a stronger self-concept by not presenting their primary identity as a pastor or professional minister to various social fields. This led to a sense of freedom in constructing identity around different roles, enabling pastors to make difficult decisions they might not otherwise be brave enough to make if their whole identity was fixed on the role of pastor.[46] These decisions included speaking about emotionally charged topics, confronting issues within a church, or having tough conversations with congregants. Participants also reported positively that their vocation allowed them to interact with people they usually wouldn't interact with daily, leading to more ministry opportunities. Siebert's conclusions about the potential benefits of presenting a vocational identity apart from a ministry identity are congruent with Patrick Lai's.

However, challenges for multi-vocational pastors in Canada centered around expectations and burdens of responsibility across multiple roles—work, church, denomination, family, and personal, especially regarding time availability.[47] Canadian tentmakers reported that they sometimes delayed telling people they were also pastors if they intuited that it might be salient to withhold that information until trust was built. People would often "shut down" once they discovered the tentmaker was also a pastor.[48] This may indicate a loss of trust towards the pastor for withholding a crucial part of their identity and may be relevant to a missionary's contacts discovering their missionary identity. There is a gap in the literature focusing on tentmakers, identity, and self-concept in RANs, which adds complex factors such as illegal missionary activity. Issues of identity salience are different from actively concealing a significant aspect of identity, as missionaries in RANs often do. In addition, it is essential to note the difference in ministry context. Identifying as a religious worker in secular Canada may have a different impact on relationships and disclosure than a religious worker identity in an Islamic setting. Therefore, tentmaking practices and dual identities may have a different impact on self-concept for tentmakers on RANs than in Canada, which this study explores.

46. Siebert, "Tending to the Tentmakers," 96.

47. Siebert, "Tending to the Tentmakers," 102.

48. Siebert, "Tending to the Tentmakers," 96.

DUAL IDENTITY AND THE UNDERCOVER MISSIONARY

While the previous section focused on the sometimes-competing roles of missionary and vocational work, this section focuses on the concealment of the missionary identity in RANs. This concealment causes tentmakers to present their identity one way in some social fields and another way elsewhere, which is the primary focus of this study. The concept of missionary "dual identity" is well established in missiological literature. A dual identity involves maintaining two distinct, though perhaps overlapping, identities across various geographic locations or social groups, involving some level of withholding or concealing information, or even deception, to maintain the identities. In the literature, these two identities are (1) the missionary identity in the passport country and (2) the vocational identity in the country of service. In RANs, many missionaries sometimes conceal their missionary identity, leading to concerns regarding deceit and subversion as "undercover missionaries." In the literature, many missiologists and practitioners use the terms "schizophrenic" and "living a double life" to describe the experience of navigating between these two identities.

In 2003, *Time* magazine published an article called "Missionaries Under Cover," written from the perspective of someone who does not share the evangelical worldview. In the wake of September 11 and with tense international relations boiling in the background, David Van Biema describes the world of evangelical missionaries living in the Middle East. He depicts missionaries as "aggressively" seeking the conversion of Muslims to Christianity:

> The new arrivals mean well: in addition to the Christian Gospel, which they consider their most precious gift, they have channeled millions of dollars in aid and put in countless hours of charitable work. But some fieldworkers for more liberal Christian organizations claim that some of the more aggressive evangelical tactics can put all religious charities at risk, as when the Taliban, angered by missionary activities two years ago, shut down every Christian aid group in Kabul. Muslim critics accuse missionaries of lying about their identities and their faith to achieve their goals. And as the tensions between Islam and the West continue to boil, some familiar with the Middle East have begun asking whether the missionaries, who love Muslims but despise Islam, are the sort of non-appointed goodwill ambassadors the U.S. really needs in a region dense with the rhetoric of holy war.[49]

49. Van Biema, "Missionaries Under Cover," 38.

The article is especially scathing towards overzealous evangelical short-termers, who Van Biema describes as arrogantly and openly defying anti-proselytization laws. They then leave before experiencing the consequences of their actions, which fall on those who live there. Van Biema contrasts evangelical zeal for conversion with the social projects of mainline Protestant and Catholic groups among the poor:

> Claims that Christian aid groups engage in charity as a "cover" for proselytizing do a disservice to the sometimes heroic humanitarian efforts by workers who believe that Christians should heed not just Jesus' message of salvation but also his example as a feeder and a healer. Yet there should be no question that while most evangelical missionaries love Muslims, they hope to replace Islam.[50]

Van Biema contrasts seeking conversion, as Evangelicals do, with humanitarian efforts; Van Biema considers conversionism highly problematic. He thus describes the lives of these undercover tentmakers, who enter countries closed off to missionaries, in a negative light:

> But the sometimes clandestine status can breed bad habits. Visa bans turn many Evangelicals, usually straightforward to a fault, into truth stretchers, if only at the customs desk. They use encrypted e-mail and code words or smuggle Bibles. "Some," says a Christian minister in Morocco, "seem to have been inspired by the book of James, verse 007."[51]

This *Time* article, which evaluated evangelical missionaries' lives and goals from a secular perspective, triggered some soul-searching among missiologists for how Christians should communicate in a digital and globalized world.[52] These outside perspectives are important in considering how tentmakers in RANs manage and present their identities to non-Evangelicals, as there are stigmas associated with evangelistic motivations and activities.

Missiologists and practitioners have frequently debated the ethics of maintaining a dual identity—especially the practices required to adequately conceal a missionary identity when it is illegal to seek conversions. In *The Changing Face of World Missions*, the authors write,

> Is it ethical? In other words, is it right, is it honest, is it fair to enter a country and work as a marketplace person when your real motive

50. Van Biema, "Missionaries Under Cover," 44.

51. Van Biema, "Missionaries Under Cover," 41.

52. Love, *Glocal*; Rundle and Steffen, *Great Commission Companies*, 26.

> for being there is to convert people to Jesus Christ? Isn't that being deceitful, dishonest, and untruthful? In many cases, this is the most critical question facing creative-access mission workers. If they cannot clearly answer the question, they will face the perils of self-questioning, identity crisis, and ethical doubt throughout their lives and work as mission workers.[53]

The authors argue that inner tension regarding this issue of deceitfulness is due to a Western division between religious life and everyday life—the sacred and the secular. They note that most religious workers throughout history and across many religions also worked in the marketplace. Western discomfort with this dual identity, they contend, is due to the false sacred-secular divide. They claim,

> For much of the rest of the world, faith and everyday life and work are not separate realms but equal parts of the whole of life. In comparison, Western church culture teaches us that clergy cannot and should not take the role of a teacher, farmer, or business person. They are paid solely by the church to do the work of the church.[54]

The authors conclude that missionaries holding marketplace vocations is not an ethical issue. Likewise, doing mission activity in a country where those activities are illegal is also not an ethical issue.[55] However, the authors do not explore the daily practices of concealing a missionary identity, in which some additional ethical issues may arise.

In the literature on tentmaking and BAM, the most frequent solution to resolving the inner moral tension arising from a dual identity, or from tentmaking itself, is more education on the secular-sacred divide and recognizing that all of the Christian's life is to honor God.[56] They argue that the "sacred" role of professional missionary or clergy and the "secular" role of full-time employment in business or other fields should not be such sharply divided categories. Rather, if tentmaking missionaries view all of life as sacred, including nonreligious vocation such as accounting or nursing, it can alleviate inner tension and dissolve the dual identity.

53. Pocock et al., *Changing Face of Missions*, 223.

54. Pocock et al., *Changing Face of Missions*, 224.

55. Pocock et al., *Changing Face of Missions*, 224.

56. See Johnson, *Business as Mission*, 156, 161–62; Lai, *Tentmaking*, 40–44, 411–13; Lai and Love, "Integrated Identity," 344, 347; Onongha, "Tentmaking in Twenty-First Century," 190–91; Bailey, "Business as Mission," 370; Roemmele, "Cloak-and-Dagger Tentmakers."

In *Great Commission Companies*, Steve Rundle and Tom Steffen describe a "spiritual-vocational hierarchy" pyramid. This hierarchy places businesses and trades at the bottom, "helping" vocations such as nursing and teaching above that, then pastors, and finally, foreign missionaries at the top.[57] They claim that many Christians believe the professions at the top of this pyramid are more God honoring than those at the bottom. Instead, they advocate for a theology that embraces all vocations as part of the mission of God. Their book then focuses on "Great Commission companies," which are businesses that bring transformation and the message of the gospel to underdeveloped countries with the least access to the message of Christ—places where "professional missionaries" are no longer welcome.[58]

In addition, Rundle and Steffen decry the "undercover missionary" model in RANs as deeply dishonest:

> One model that has little to commend it is the "missionary in disguise" approach. This is one that uses a business merely as a "cover" for people who quite frankly have little interest in business except for its usefulness as an entry strategy into countries that are off-limits to traditional missionaries. The aim is to do the least amount of work necessary to appear legitimate (at least in their own eyes; few others are fooled so easily). While there have been some successes, the results have been generally mixed, and many Christians now recognize that this "ends justifying the means" approach to ministry is dishonest and a poor witness.[59]

Rundle and Steffen compare these clandestine missionary activities with spies and terrorists, who also use businesses as a "cover" for their hidden agendas. Instead, they argue that owners of Great Commission companies are often quite evangelistic and known for their faithful witness, but they are rarely deported because of the value they bring to the communities they live in.[60]

Larry Poston considers three areas where missionaries may be faced with practices involving deception and subterfuge for the sake of the gospel: tentmaking, contextualization, and insider movements. He considers the practices of each of these missiological concepts from the biblical narrative, noting that the ethics of the biblical authors are not as "black and white" as Western Christians might want them to be:

57. Rundle and Steffen, *Great Commission Companies*, 16.

58. Rundle and Steffen, *Great Commission Companies*, 18.

59. Rundle and Steffen, *Great Commission Companies*, 26.

60. Rundle and Steffen, *Great Commission Companies*, 27.

> From the standpoint of ethics, if the host government of such a nation [RAN] was aware of the person's primary motivation for entering the country (i.e., to bring about religious conversions), would that government have given permission to enter? If the answer is "no" and the person is aware that the answer would have been "no," then the person has essentially used subterfuge to enter. This kind of situation may not be problematic so long as the visa or work permit application does not ask concerning one's motivations for entering the country, or does not specifically restrict one from "religious proselytization." But what if the paperwork includes such questions or prohibitions? Is a bit of "data dropout" justifiable in such cases? Or even an outright falsehood—"for the sake of the Gospel?" If we are withholding data in order to establish or maintain our freedom to act on behalf of Kingdom concerns, could such an approach be seen as essentially the same as that which Jesus adopted when he repeatedly told different groups *not* to reveal his true identity?[61]

By Poston's definition of subterfuge, even legitimate businesses such as Great Commission companies could be potentially accused of subterfuge if their primary motivations for entering the country involve conversions of the unreached.

Poston brings out several ethical tensions held in the biblical narrative to navigate these complex ethical questions. First, God condemns falsehood in Scripture but also rewards the Hebrew midwives and Rahab for their subterfuge (Exod 1:17; Josh 2:4–6). Further, God not only allowed but *commanded* a lying spirit to go to Ahab to deceive him (1 Kgs 22:20–23). Jesus commanded his disciples, those he healed, and demons to withhold information revealing his true identity (Matt 8:4; 12:16; 16:20; Mark 3:12). The apostles declared they must obey God rather than human authorities (Acts 5:29), yet Paul commanded obedience to governing authorities as God's agents (Rom 13:1–2). Poston concludes from these biblical tensions that God perhaps has flexible rather than rigid requirements for openness, honesty, and truthfulness. Poston also speculates that the consciences of different Christians might be "tuned to different allowance levels" of subterfuge and deception.[62] This study explores how missionaries may navigate these complex ethical issues of subterfuge, withholding, concealment, and

61. Poston, "Ethics of Missionary Dissimulation," 414–15.

62. Poston, "Ethics of Missionary Dissimulation," 415.

even deception for the sake of the gospel. It seeks to uncover the impact of the "varying allowance levels" on the tentmaker's self-concept.

James A. Tebbe also discusses personal integrity among "undercover missionaries" and the inner turmoil that can arise when missionaries have one identity in their home country and another in their country of service. He describes the stories of missionaries who have left their missionary organizations over these questions of conscience, unable to resolve the dissonance they experienced. Tebbe particularly identifies the differences in how missionaries portray their identity back home and how they present their identity in their country of service as an integrity issue. If there is a discrepancy between these two identities, Tebbe says the tentmaker is guilty of deception and subterfuge. Even so, Tebbe suggests that missionaries prepare careful answers ahead of time regarding their identity. As Lai suggested, Tebbe recommends missionaries answer questions with more questions, such as "What is a missionary? What do you mean by 'missionary'?" Tebbe reasons, "Missionaries need not tell everything about themselves, either. God does not lie, but He does keep secrets."[63] Tebbe does not discuss how this secret keeping is distinguished from presenting a different identity in the home and host countries. He promotes the former while standing against the latter.

Like Poston, Tebbe also notes the cultural differences in disclosure. Tebbe contends that compared to American or British missionaries, Eastern European Christians are more adept at navigating questions about identity because they have lived under oppressive regimes. Ultimately, however, Tebbe says that careful answers and asking clarifying questions will not resolve all integrity issues:

> The question of integrity arises, as we have seen, when missionaries feel they must misrepresent who they are and what they are really doing. There is value in learning how to respond to questions and to try to turn the tables on our questioners as Jesus did. But learning what to say, or changing the name of your mission, doesn't solve everything. We must be who we say we are.[64]

Tebbe rejects a simple acceptance of the great chasm between the identity a missionary presents in their home country and in their country of service. Tebbe identifies the daily practices of identity presentation as the source of identity dissonance leading to crisis and missionary attrition. This study

63. Tebbe, "Matter of Integrity," 49.
64. Tebbe, "Matter of Integrity," 51.

seeks to elucidate these daily practices and their impact to identify areas where missionaries in RANs most deeply experience tension and dissonance as they manage their identity.

In his article "Shrewd Yet Innocent," Robert Morris evaluates the ethics of the hidden and double agendas of tentmaking missionaries. He argues that hidden agendas are often necessary, such as when an engineer takes a job in a RAN in order to look for opportunities to share his faith. He argues that God may bless these hidden agendas. He cites 1 Sam 16, in which God commands Samuel to tell Saul he is presenting a sacrifice to God. In reality, Samuel is also anointing David as king. Morris presents this story as a biblical example of double and hidden agendas that God blessed and commanded. However, he argues against having a double agenda when one of those agendas is a lie, which corrodes integrity:

> Problems arise when one of our agendas is false or deceptive. For example, someone on a student visa who attends one university class per week and spends the rest of the time evangelizing in the villages is acting fraudulently. Someone on a student visa should be a student, and if evangelism is his calling, let him witness to the academic world that he has been given permission to enter. Then neither his hidden or overt agenda lacks integrity.[65]

Morris argues that tentmakers should do what their visas allow them to do as a matter of integrity, but this does not mean they are wrong for having a hidden agenda that the government has not approved.

In regards to truth telling and deception, Morris says that tentmakers should adopt an ethos that is less North American and more Eastern and even biblical. He says, "The cardinal rule for wise tentmakers is, 'Respond to what has been asked, no more.'"[66] He cites Jesus's example of enjoining others to secrecy about his identity, and his speaking in parables in order to withhold information about the kingdom from some of his listeners. In the same vein, he argues that tentmakers who regulate the flow of information through encryption, pseudonyms, and withholding information act in wisdom and shrewdness, not deception. By doing the job they committed to do, tentmakers can therefore maintain their integrity in RANs, even with hidden agendas.

Zachary Harris presents the most extreme evangelical stance on security and undercover missionaries on the spectrum. Harris argues against

65. Morris, "Shrewd Yet Innocent," 7.

66. Morris, "Shrewd Yet Innocent," 7.

taking any security precautions in RANs—including underground churches, using tentmaking as a platform, using pseudonyms, or encrypting email. He argues that these practices, designed to circumvent persecution or prevent deportment, imprisonment, or death, are unbiblical. Harris advocates instead for open-air proclamation in the manner of Paul and Jesus, even in contexts of hostility toward the gospel. Harris argues that there is no model of secrecy in the New Testament, and that secrecy does not reflect God's nature and character, as God is not hidden from anyone. Furthermore, Christians should operate in light, not darkness. He writes, "Any indication that we live more in fear of secular governments and hostile world forces than in God also injures our witness of his glory."[67]

Harris specifically cites Morris's and Tebbe's arguments for shrewd disclosure, strongly disagreeing with their conclusions:

> I disagree with their concepts of integrity which seem to justify intentionally deceiving people by telling partial truths. Note that when Jesus outsmarted the religious leaders (e.g. Luke 20:1–8) he didn't deceive them. They knew he had avoided their question. Of course we don't always have to spill everything we know, but if my heart (and newsletter) says, "My primary reason for being here is to share the gospel of Christ," that's what I say with my lips.[68]

Even in RANs, Harris advocates for "shouting from the rooftops" in order to proclaim Christ, noting that all secrecy, withholding, and concealment are rooted in fear of persecution and a poor theology of suffering. He argues that while missionary activity may bring down persecution and even death on local believers, "martyrdom is part of our Christian birthright" and that Jesus prepared his followers to suffer and die.[69] He concludes,

> Let me be perfectly blunt. If the model of the New Testament church were practiced in closed countries today, it would most likely mean a lot of shed blood, imprisonments, revoked visas, and numerous other trials and sufferings.[70]

Harris thus rejects any missionary concealment and security protocol as unbiblical and theologically untenable, even to protect others. The biblical pattern, he argues, is one of bold proclamation and persecution, rather than

67. Harris, "Theological Critique of Security," 329.
68. Harris, "Theological Critique of Security," 329–30.
69. Harris, "Theological Critique of Security," 332.
70. Harris, "Theological Critique of Security," 332.

fear and avoidance of suffering, as he interprets these security practices. Harris does not address how such a missionary might live in the RAN long enough to learn the language and culture, develop relationships, or disciple new believers.

Patrick Lai also discusses challenging issues of dual identity and concealment among tentmakers and the tremendous stress this puts missionaries under. Living in a RAN can lead to experiences of "living a double life," as a missionary cannot share parts of themselves with certain social circles:

> Living a double life can be exhausting—mentally, emotionally, and spiritually. It is important to prayerfully reflect on whether we and those we are recruiting will be able to withstand the incredible pressures of living a double life. Many tentmakers will immediately respond by saying, 'I have never lived a double life!' But I question how honest they are being with themselves. Most of us, those who have formal theological training, tell only part of our story to our close local friends. For example, on a job application we omit our years at Bible college and/or seminary. The time serving on staff with our churches back home is also tactfully redefined. When we attend missionary meetings outside our place of service, we tell others we are going on a holiday. In each of these cases we are not lying; we are simply not filling in the blanks. However, some brothers and sisters feel they are lying if they know the answer but do not provide it. Though we may be under stress due to ministry struggles, the pastor and a close friend resigning in anger back at our home church, or our team is battling some financial issue, we cannot share any of these things with our best friends who are devout Muslims. In addition, we cannot share with our close friends back home about our visits inside the mosque, our practicing Muslim prayer forms, and the struggles we have in choosing a school for the kids. Well, we may try, and we may get some sympathy and prayer, but ultimately we stop sharing those things with our former best friends as we know they do not understand. Thus, there is a feeling of living a double life. We have one life we reveal to friends overseas and another life we reveal to friends back home.[71]

Even with a credible position in a vocation, those sent by churches and mission organizations with the express intent to evangelize may withhold aspects of their identity, funding, and motivations. As Lai notes, withholding

71. Lai, *Tentmaking*, 348–49.

much of this information can feel like lying or living a double life for many missionaries.

Lai also expresses concerns that missionaries sometimes use deceitful practices to protect their missionary identity. Lai briefly addresses tentmakers' ethical issues using deceit and "being undercover." Twenty percent of his survey respondents said they had to lie to hide their missionary identity, which he finds inexcusable. Instead, he suggests following Jesus's example of "answering a question while not answering the question."[72] When missionaries are asked direct questions about being missionaries and are caught off guard or asked probing questions about their finances, they may lie to protect their missionary identity or become embarrassed and react suspiciously. He writes, "People can often feel it when we are not answering fully or truthfully. This lack of openness creates a feeling of distrust."[73] Tentmakers who have legitimate work and do what they say they're doing can help alleviate these problems and reduce the opportunities for uncomfortable questions.

Lai, who has experienced deportation in RANs for his missionary activity, discusses the complexities of disclosure and security.[74] Despite saying that people can discern when tentmakers are not answering fully or truthfully, Lai also argues for "being economical with the truth" rather than complete openness—using redirection or misleading answers while avoiding a direct lie.[75] He writes:

> Jesus did not answer every question he was asked. We need not tell every official our life story. Yet, if the full picture of our activities is revealed, we should have spoken and acted in ways that no one could accuse us of having deceived them. We should never, ever, have to lie or feel a need to lie.[76]

Lai also suggests answering questions with another question. One example he gives is that if someone asks him, "Are you a missionary?" he replies, "What do you mean?" This allows the inquirer to define "missionary," and it can lead to a helpful discussion about what the tentmaker is and is not. In addition to carefully navigating disclosure to authorities, he also advises considering whether local churches, local believers, or other missionaries

72. Lai, *Tentmaking*, 37.
73. Lai, *Tentmaking*, 77.
74. Lai, *Tentmaking*, 337.
75. Lai, *Tentmaking*, 338.
76. Lai, *Tentmaking*, 338.

need to have certain information. If they know less, they have lower chances of being interrogated or indicted if the missionary is involved in a security incident. Lai reveals some cultural or personal boundaries and definitions of truth telling and deception here. He considers direct lies as deception ("I am not a missionary"), which should always be avoided. However, Lai does not consider misleading information or withholding information as deception, even if these actions prevent someone from discovering the truth by leading them to a false conclusion. This qualitative study builds on Lai's tentmaking surveys by focusing on the experiences of dual identity and how tentmakers narrate their self-concept when managing their missionary identity in RANs.

Thomas Hale III also addresses the issue of missionaries maintaining a hidden identity in RANs. Hale describes the stories of missionaries in RANs and the "hidden identity approach" they must use in order to conceal their missionary identity and their affiliation with sending organizations. This hidden identity creates inner tension as missionaries navigate secret keeping, feelings of dishonesty, and withholding or bending the truth, especially for those with a "scrupulously high view of honesty."[77] In addition, he describes the strains on relationships that secrecy and concealment bring. He argues that keeping a secret identity is no longer as easily done in today's world. In light of this, Hale contends for "sent ones" to "modify the mission so that you can be sent openly."[78] The mission modification requires sending Christians (not missionaries) for "service" to RANs in their vocation, so that their private identity in their home country is the same as their public identity in RANs.[79] Modifying the mission for Hale also includes modifying language to be less offensive, focusing on "blessing," "dignification," or even "interfaith dialogue" rather than evangelism, church planting, or making disciples.[80] In these ways, the need for the hidden identity is eliminated, allowing the believer to maintain the same "core message" in all locations.[81] Hale clarifies that changing the core message should not be a cover for alternate underlying purposes, but must be a deeply held core belief. It is unclear whether Hale's suggestion to "modify the mission"

77. Hale, *Authentic Lives*, 58.

78. Hale, *Authentic Lives*, xiv.

79. Hale, *Authentic Lives*, 63.

80. Hale, *Authentic Lives*, 66–68.

81. Hale, *Authentic Lives*, 61. Hale quotes Love, "Blessing the Nations," extensively throughout his argument. Love's article is reviewed in the next section.

proposes a moratorium on evangelism, discipleship, or indigenous church planting in countries where such activities are illegal.

Hale describes the ethical complexities in these matters, noting that culture, personality, sense of calling, and many other factors influence a person's conscience in navigating these tensions.[82] While holding high values of humility and non-judgmentalism for those who choose differently, he affirms his conviction that Christians should seek as much as possible to reduce hidden identities. To this end, Hale describes practical suggestions for going to restricted nations without affiliation with missionary organizations. He notes the difficulty in leaving missionary organizations behind. Organizations provide cross-cultural training, allow for tax-deductible donations for language learning and the expenses of expatriate life, and support for fellowship and member care. Hale is honest about the tremendous challenges an intercultural worker might face without the benefits of a sending organization. Still, he argues that integrity and transparency are worth the extra effort.[83]

Stephen Bailey addresses the ethics of dual identity in his article "Is Business as Mission Honest?" He considers the ethics of tentmaker dual identity from his experiences as a development worker in an unnamed RAN. He frames the question thus: "The basic question is whether it is ethical to present yourself to a local government as a businessperson without disclosing your missionary agenda when the government is clearly opposed to the propagation of Christian faith by foreigners."[84] Rather than addressing the ethical issue of deceit in tentmaking and BAM as an abstract concept, he contextualizes it within his own experiences. While living in the RAN, Bailey always communicated his Christian identity and that Christians had sent him to help with development in the nation where he resided. He argues that the government of a RAN likely knows the missionaries' intentions. However, governments allow Christians to come and work because of the perceived benefits to their nation in development work. In addition, Bailey believes governments are more likely to deport missionaries for issues of honor and respect rather than for disobedience of laws related to proselytization. Bailey concludes that the tentmakers with an identity crisis are those with a poor theology of work, who do not see

82. Hale, *Authentic Lives*, 38.

83. Hale, *Authentic Lives*, 105, 158.

84. Bailey, "Business as Mission," 369.

all of the Christian's vocation as work done to glorify God. He refers to the sacred-secular dichotomy as the source of this identity crisis:

> Tentmakers who do not understand Christian vocation almost always have an identity crisis when serving in so-called secular roles. They have something to hide. But when we embrace the idea of a Christian vocation we are free to see ourselves as Christian businesspeople. We are in mission because all Christians are to be in mission and to live by the principles of the Kingdom that require Jesus' disciples to care about their neighbors.[85]

Bailey found that as he viewed his work in a silk business as worship to God, his inner tension over identity dissipated. Here again is the argument that having a biblical theology of all work being sacred unto God will resolve identity crises or the split sense of self. However, missionaries, even those with a legitimate vocation and a biblical theology of work, also engage in evangelistic activities in locations where proselytization is illegal. They *do* "have something to hide." A robust theology of work as sacred is important. Still, it may not resolve all the inner turmoil or crises a missionary may face resulting from their daily practices, which this study seeks to explore.

Missionaries of the wealthier Gulf Cooperative Council (GCC) countries are less frequently engaged in poverty alleviation or development work than missionaries may be elsewhere. However, they may bring significant financial benefits that compel governments to allow missionaries to stay. Missionaries and mission agencies may not have accurate information regarding what governments do and do not know about their identity or activities. Such information is difficult to prove. However, their perceptions of how much governments know may impact their security practices and identity management, which this study explores.

MISSIONARY INTEGRATED IDENTITY

As the realities of a globalized world make secrecy and hidden identity more challenging to maintain, missiologists and practitioners are increasingly writing about integrating this dual identity into one unified identity. This unified identity is often based on vocational identity. Rick Love, former international director of evangelical mission agency Frontiers, was one of the most prominent voices regarding missionary identity in RANs. Rick Love's book *Glocal: Following Jesus in the 21st Century* details concerns

85. Bailey, "Business as Mission," 370.

about communicating the church's core identity and mission in an interconnected, pluralistic world.[86] Love describes his journey since journalist Barry Yeoman published an exposé on his classes on evangelism to Muslims at Columbia International University. The article, written only one year after the 2001 terrorist attacks on the Twin Towers in New York City, describes the evangelistic teachings of Love as covert, undercover, and militaristic efforts to "wipe out Islam.[87] While even Yeoman admitted in a personal email to Love that the article mischaracterized Love's teachings,[88] Love considers globalization and technology's impact on Christian communication. He argues for Christians to have an integrated identity—being the same person and having the same core message in private (or Christian) spheres and the public sphere. This is especially relevant for church-planting missionaries in RANs, who are often known as missionaries in their home context and as vocational workers in their ministry context.

In *Glocal*, Love criticizes church-planting organizations' "old models" of ministry in which tentmaking operates as a cover for church-planting activities.[89] The dual identity of a missionary in the home country and a business professional in the host country creates a sense of duplicity and fear of being discovered.[90] With the internet constantly threatening to reveal the missionary identity, Love argues that church-planting organizations should rethink their paradigms and strategies for mission to reflect an interconnected world impacted by globalism, terrorism, and pluralism. This reassessment includes aligning vocation, calling, gifting, and motivation into one "integrated identity" that does not have to be hidden.[91] For Love, this integrated identity is as a Christian vocational worker, leaving the missionary identity and associated vocabulary and organizations behind. Love argues that the word "missionary" is misunderstood in Islamic contexts as militaristic and colonial and should thus be discarded. He also argues for changing the word "churches" to "Christ-centered communities";

86. See also Love, "Blessing the Nations." In *Glocal*, Love describes his changing views over the years regarding Christian duplicity and communication, which can also be traced in his writings over the course of his ministry.

87. Yeoman, "Stealth Crusade."

88. Love, *Glocal*, 4.

89. Love, *Glocal*, 12.

90. Love, *Glocal*, 11, 17.

91. Love, *Glocal*, 59.

"church planting" should likewise become "gospel planting."[92] Love also argues against the sacred-secular divide, which he believes acts as the foundation for contemporary mission praxis:

> We don't just want to train a select group of people, historically known as missionaries. We want to train everyone in our churches to model excellent work and effective disciple making. The glocal paradigm of ministry believes the whole church is sent into the world, not just a few missionaries.[93]

In the article "Integrated Identity in a Globalized World," Rick Love co-writes with Patrick Lai about the dual identity of those serving in the Muslim world.[94] The article addresses their claim that few missionaries have been able to be both effective disciple makers and tentmakers. In addition, Love and Lai address the challenges of an increasingly digital and globalized world, which makes the separation between the "home world" and the "ministry world" difficult, if not impossible. This creates a sense of having a double identity, which impacts tentmakers' integrity:

> They [tentmakers] feel as though they are hiding their true identity and face the nagging fear they may be found out. It also makes it hard for some cross-cultural disciple-makers to maintain a clear conscience before God and others (cf. Acts 24:16). The result is a lack of integrity and lack of boldness to share the Gospel.[95]

Lai and Love call this dual identity "work-ministry schizophrenia," which causes anxiety for some missionaries. As Love argues in *Glocal*, he and Lai contend instead for moving beyond the contemporary missionary paradigms of support-raised missionary funding towards an "integrated apostolic identity" for greater integrity.[96]

Much of Love's criticisms focus on "tent fakers"—tentmaking missionaries who hold fake jobs as "consultants" or own shell companies that require few working hours to allow flexibility for ministry. Lai and Love contrast "tent faking" with Paul's tentmaking practices, calling tentmakers to greater integrity. Lai and Love view full-time vocational tentmaking with no organizational ties to mission agencies or church funding as the

92. Love, *Glocal*, 20, 43, 117.

93. Love, *Glocal*, 119.

94. Lai and Love, "Integrated Identity," 337–53.

95. Lai and Love, "Integrated Identity," 338.

96. Lai and Love, "Integrated Identity," 337–38.

way forward—replacing the identity of "missionary" with "Christian businessman" as their new integrated identity. They also cite the sacred-secular dichotomy as an underlying issue in dual identity among missionaries. They note that Paul's theology was not infused with this dichotomy as missionaries may be today.[97]

Gary Taylor expresses his frustrations with his experiences as a tentmaker and missionary, abandoning both identities for a singular identity as a businessman only. Taylor had started a "kingdom company" to serve as a platform for church-planting missionaries to have a legitimate identity in the RANs in which they served. The company also provided financial support to national church leaders. In addition, he helped found Frontiers, the US Association of Tentmakers (now Intent), and Strategic Ventures Network, a creative-access facilitating ministry. However, he grew weary of the tentmaker model:

> I have lost thousands of dollars in real money along with multiple hundreds of hours fruitlessly trying to serve wonderful, sincere, visionary, but inept missionaries and tentmakers. This has more meaning if you remember that lost time is lost money and opportunity, especially to an entrepreneur who has mortgaged the ranch, literally.[98]

Taylor says that for all the talk about tentmaking, he has seen very few examples of tentmaking producing church plants or fulfilling any major ministry objectives. In addition, the business practices are often fragmented and unprofitable.

Taylor writes that his frustration led him to do a "fresh survey of how God communicated His will and His Good News to mankind." He says in his survey of the Bible, he found "not a TESOL instructor, a 10-year 'student,' and 'consultant,' or a bootstrap 'importer-exporter'" among them, referencing the plethora of "tent faking" missionary platforms.[99] Taylor decided to position himself as a genuine and successful business owner, where he shares the gospel in the marketplace. This identity, he argues, is in line with "Abraham the landowner, Daniel the statesman, [and] Peter the fisherman." Taylor also references the sacred-secular divide, arguing that missionary organizations are slow to abandon "clergy-based missions."[100]

97. Lai and Love, "Integrated Identity," 347.

98. G. Taylor, "Don't Call Me a Tentmaker," 23.

99. G. Taylor, "Don't Call Me a Tentmaker," 25.

100. G. Taylor, "Don't Call Me a Tentmaker," 25.

He elaborates, perhaps putting missionaries and marketplace professionals in competition with one another until one prevails: "I say it is not 'missionaries' to the unreached and inaccessible frontiers of the Gospel, or even missionaries as extemporaneous entrepreneurs who will prevail." In place of seminary-trained missionaries, Taylor argues marketplace identities are the key to reaching the unreached in RANs: "I say it is skilled businessmen, professionals, teachers, even skilled laborers deciding to locate their factory, their (true, professional-based) consulting, or teaching where it will make the most sense, among the lost of the world."[101]

Taylor argues for a new paradigm in which normal laypersons "marketplace the Gospel."[102] It is unclear whether his new paradigm might include seminary-trained theologians and Bible scholars, cultural anthropologists, linguists, or other skills useful to cross-cultural missions that might not be strong producers in a capitalist market. Taylor expresses strongly negative sentiments regarding seminary-trained or traditional missionaries and concepts surrounding tentmaking throughout his article, often pitting them against businesspeople and perhaps reinforcing the sacred-secular divide he decries: "Given a standard, well-qualified seminary-trained missionary and a crusty but godly man with a vision and real performance-based work experience, I would race toward the latter whether in my business or in my role as a sometime counselor in church-planting."[103]

Proponents of BAM often argue for a seamless integration of the missionary and business identities, but the reality may not align with the theories. David Bosch conducted a small (n=11) phenomenological study on BAM practitioners in an unnamed RAN that is among the least evangelized in the world. He aimed to understand the gap between best practices in BAM literature and actual practices on the field. The best practices Bosch focused on were: (1) having a mission statement, (2) understanding the language and culture, (3) having a business and ministry plan, (4) having a team, mentorship, and accountability, and (5) having measured "triple bottom-line" goals (economic, spiritual, and social). He found that in many categories, there were significant gaps between best theoretical practices and actual practices on the field.

Overall, Bosch found that few were achieving a "holistic model" of BAM that integrates the economic, spiritual, and social goals—the "triple

101. G. Taylor, "Don't Call Me a Tentmaker," 26.

102. G. Taylor, "Don't Call Me a Tentmaker," 26.

103. G. Taylor, "Don't Call Me a Tentmaker," 24.

bottom line."[104] For instance, 64 percent of participants had a mission statement, but only 18 percent included any spiritual element.[105] Only 45 percent of participants had developed a business plan and annual budget, and only 36 percent had completed any market study for the business.[106] Although 64 percent of participants had a ministry plan, Bosch notes that many of these ministry plans were not integrated into the business. Participants often indicated that business took time away from evangelism and language study, and that ministry and business were "separate."[107] Bosch concludes from this data, "It appears that there needs to be some research done on how the BAM practitioners' theology of work impacts their understanding and application of multiple bottom lines."[108] These findings also demonstrate that while best practices of BAM literature argue for integrating business and mission into one unified strategy, missionaries may face many complex contextual obstacles in achieving this integration. This present study contributes to a growing body of research on tentmaking missionaries and the frameworks through which they integrate mission and vocation as they construct their identities in RANs.

In 2014, the BAM think tank produced a report on fruitful practices in BAM and church planting that also raises questions about integrating the vocational and missionary identities into a single identity. The authors affirm that any Christian running a business can do so to the glory of God without having church planting as a goal. However, they recognize that many missionaries engage in BAM in order to facilitate church planting among UPGs. This can create some of the perceived tensions between the missionary and business identities for church planters, as businesses do not naturally facilitate church plants:

> On one hand, if they are running a business, they should do that for the glory of God and therefore be excellent and profitable. Yet church planting is not a natural byproduct from the mere presence of believers; rather, facilitating church planting requires particular strategy and focus. A Christian business simply conducting business honorably without a church planting strategy is not intentionally engaging in church planting. What is needed is at least

104. Bosch, "Gap Between Best Practices," 42–44.
105. Bosch, "Gap Between Best Practices," 39.
106. Bosch, "Gap Between Best Practices," 39.
107. Bosch, "Gap Between Best Practices," 40.
108. Bosch, "Gap Between Best Practices," 43.

> one gifted and a "sent-out" individual, akin to Paul or Titus, who understands what a church is and will patiently gather, teach, and encourage until a local church is formed.[109]

The authors emphasize the need to define clear goals in BAM for both profitability and spiritual impact, though noting the possibility that considering "church planting the main thing" recreates the sacred-secular duality.[110] But for church planters trained in church planting and sent by missionary agencies with the express goal of church planting, church planting *may be* the "main thing." The authors are honest to say that many of the participants of their study on fruitful practices have not actually seen a church planted yet, so these realities limit their suggestions of fruitful practices:

> There are correspondingly few successful businesses that have helped facilitate church plants. Certainly, there are many examples of businesses that have enabled evangelism and discipleship and many that have launched Bible studies. However, a church is different from a Bible study. Even for the businesses that have seen fruitful church planting, often such results are tangentially related to their operations. Therefore, there is much theory on BAM and church planting but few actual examples, and even fewer replicable models.[111]

The authors conclude that while there is much evidence of fruitful evangelism and witnessing accomplished through BAM, there is a strong need for more case studies of BAM companies that have successfully facilitated church plants among the unreached.[112] While there is much in the BAM literature on how business and mission should be fully integrated rather than separated, the relative dearth of successful case studies points to some potential issues with realities on the field. The realities of integrating business and church planting into unified goals may be easier in theory than in practice. This BAM think tank report showcases the potential tensions between a business identity and a missionary identity. The "bottom lines" may not always be integrated, despite the best practices espoused by BAM literature.[113] This present study is not concerned with best practices

109. Plummer and Tunehag, *Business as Mission*, 8.

110. Plummer and Tunehag, *Business as Mission*, 9–10.

111. Plummer and Tunehag, *Business as Mission*, 10.

112. Plummer and Tunehag, *Business as Mission*, 22.

113. These BAM bottom lines include economic, spiritual, social, and environmental outcomes (Plummer, "Business as Mission?").

in BAM or church planting. Rather, it explores issues in experiences of a potentially bifurcated identity among CP-focused tentmakers in RANs, which may impact self-concept.

Noting the dearth of case studies on how BAM practices work out in reality, Mark Russell studied the BAM practices of missionaries among twelve businesses in Chiang Mai, Thailand. Russell presents two contrasting models of BAM businesses he found in Chiang Mai. The BAM practitioners who reported a higher spiritual impact were open about their missionary identity, partnered with local ministries, and emphasized language learning and understanding the local culture. They held a more integrated identity as Christian business owners who sought to bless the world. Those who reported a lower spiritual impact had a hidden missionary identity that led to suspicion, worked independently from local churches, and placed a much lower value on cultural adaptation. They expressed more characteristics of having a dual identity as undercover missionaries. The table below summarizes Russell's findings.[114]

Table 4: Russell's Two Contrasting BAM Models Practiced in Chiang Mai

Higher Spiritual Impact	Lower Spiritual Impact
Blessing orientation (we are here to bless the people—which includes conversion but also holistic blessing)	Conversion orientation (we are here to convert people to Christianity)
Openness regarding missionary purpose and identity	Covert missionary purposes and identity
Partnership with local churches and ministries	Independent operations from local churches or ministries
High cultural adaptation	Low cultural adaptation

Thailand is not considered a RAN, as missionary visas are still legally available, and one Thai Buddhist told Russell that missionaries were very respected in Thailand.[115] Locals sometimes suspected tentmakers of pedophilia or drug trafficking when they were not open about their missionary purposes. Criminals in this context often use the same concealing practices as undercover missionaries, such as setting up businesses that take few hours to run. Russell reported that those who were open about their missionary identity saw more conversions to Christ.[116]

114. Russell, "Business in Missions," 247–48.

115. Russell, "Business in Missions," 250.

116. Russell, "Business in Missions," 250–51.

BAM practitioners in Russell's study also reported positive social relationships achieved through their businesses. These included the integration of prayer and Bible studies into work environments, as well as opportunities to proclaim the gospel in work events.[117] Russell does not report any church planting, however. In fact, Russell remarks on BAM goals and their potential conflict with the missionary identity:

> The bottom line is many missionaries are more qualified and gifted to be a pastor, evangelist, or full-time church planter, whatever is reflective of who they are and who they really want to be. These missionaries should not pursue operating businesses, which will be a drain to them, their mission agency, and somebody's finances. Many missionaries explained that their mission agency was pushing them to be innovative and pursue entrepreneurial strategies. In these cases, the mission agency needs to understand that business ventures require a mix of gifting, commitment, and unique context to make them work effectively. Not just anyone can do it or should do it.[118]

Russell argues that BAM may not always be a good fit for church-planting missionaries, as the goals and measurements of success in BAM may not align with their sense of personal identity. In contrast to other BAM proponents, Russell does not list a "poor theology of work" or the sacred-secular divide as issues contributing to low success in BAM in any of his case studies. Rather, he describes a misalignment of personal identity with the roles and expectations of BAM. This prevents tentmakers from achieving a fully integrated identity around the vocational identity.

Live Dead global leader Dick Brogden also argues for an integrated identity for missionaries serving in RANs. However, Brogden emphasizes that the missionary's integrated identity should be centered on being an ambassador for Christ rather than around a vocation. In "Identity, Security, and Community," Brogden acknowledges the complexities of living as ambassadors of Christ in RANs and the context-specific reasons missionaries are careful with wording, digital security, and identity. However, as a church-planting missionary who has lived in various Muslim RANs for nearly three decades, Brogden makes a case for some missionaries presenting identities that openly declare spiritual or even missionary intentions. Brogden's identity as a founder and leader in the Assemblies of

117. Russell, "Business in Missions," 277–78.

118. Russell, "Business in Missions," 276–77.

God church-planting organization Live Dead is easily discovered through a simple internet search, even though Brogden lives in one of the most restricted-access nations in the world.[119]

Brogden acknowledges that the Holy Spirit may lead to variations in praxis based on context. He nuances his advice about identity and security as his own experience, which may yield different results for some. Throughout his ministry, he has shifted his practice of concealing his spiritual identity to openly sharing it as a pastor, as a person affiliating with and even funded by a particular church and denomination, or even as a missionary in certain circumstances:

> When I started in missions, I was much more careful/cautious about my spiritual identity but quickly realized the problematic nature of a veiled identity (for me, my calling, my personality, and my own emotional health) and so migrated to an openly declared church/pastor (and sometimes even missionary) identity.[120]

This public identity as pastor and even as missionary arises from his conviction that the people of God are "proclaimers, not concealers." Brogden assumes that security forces in the country know he is a missionary, and Brogden says it is best not to hide things from them. Brogden thus maintains his missionary-pastor identity and even places it as primary and public. His businessman identity is secondary, though it is highly important as it lends credibility to his Christian identity. He argues, "When we add tangible value to society through legitimate business, employing locals, paying taxes, providing services, physically improving our natural surroundings, and integrating into culture it empowers a church-based identity."[121] Unlike Love, Brogden argues for not changing terminology—such as missionary, church planting, or Christian—simply because Muslims may misunderstand these words. Instead, he argues for relationally correcting these misunderstood terms, and even connecting them with Muslims' own experiences of being misunderstood with terms such as *jihad*.

Brogden challenges the notion of missionary longevity in a country as the highest importance, noting that many missionaries are too cautious in their witness out of fear of losing their visa. At the same time, he notes that being unwise can lead to leaving too soon. He concludes,

119. Worldwide, "Dick Brogden."

120. Brogden, "Identity, Security, and Community," s.v. "Background."

121. Brogden, "Identity, Security, and Community," s.vv. "6. Credible services to communities we live among empower church/missionary identity."

> We can leave too soon because we were injudicious, and we can stay too long—never fruitful because we were too cautious or our identity was too clouded. But in either case we must remember the goal is not longevity, the goal is God's glory exemplified in our obedience to Him (and longevity in the Biblical examples is rather elusive).[122]

Brogden strongly emphasizes suffering and embodying boldness rather than fear—especially for the sake of BMBs, who may imitate either the fear or the boldness they perceive from missionaries. A spectrum of views and practices regarding security and identity exists among missionaries in the GCC. Brogden acknowledges that his approach to identity and security in RANs is unusual in the church-planting community on the Arabian Peninsula. In fact, he recognizes that other missionaries or BMBs may not want to be associated with him because of the potential security risks of his public missionary-pastor identity. He adopts an approach that considers the security concerns and practices of the other person as more important than his own, honoring their boundaries and comfort levels. Brogden's article touches on many complexities of missionary identity management in a variety of social fields, which this study explores further.

CONCLUSION

Missionary identity management in RANs has been a prolific topic since the rise of tentmaking as an entry and ministry strategy in the 1970s. The literature shows how the issue of the criminality of seeking conversions can cause Evangelicals to attempt an incognito approach. However, this approach is not without consequences or concerns. Ethical, emotional, and relational issues surrounding dual identity, covert missionary practices, the sacred-secular divide, and deception are frequent topics in tentmaking and BAM literature. However, there is a dearth of qualitative studies on the experiences and practices of identity management and their impact on missionaries' self-concept in RANs. This present study seeks to contribute valuable data concerning missionary identity management in contexts where missionary activities may be illegal.

122. Brogden, "Identity, Security, and Community," s.vv. "9. The goal is not longevity, the goal is the glory of God and an indigenous church."

3

Identity Construction and Management

THIS CHAPTER DESCRIBES A framework for the study regarding modern Western identity construction and management. As the ideas of self-concept and identity are integral to this study, this chapter explores a philosophical framework of individualistic experiences of identity from a modern, Western perspective. This chapter also considers emerging social psychology research from identity theory, especially pertaining to personal identity, role identity, identity verification processes, navigating multiple identities, and concealable stigmatized identities. These concepts are related back to the research questions of this present study throughout the chapter.

CONTEMPORARY WESTERN IDENTITY

As defined in chapter 1, identity is a complex set of meanings that includes a person's characteristics, memberships in and allegiances to social groups, roles they play in society, and the meanings applied to all of these categories.[1] While enduring and stable elements of the self exist, identities are also characterized by fluidity and multiplicity, evolving throughout an individual's lifespan within diverse social contexts and roles.[2] Burk and Stets define *identities* as "internalized sets of meanings that can be found in culture that define who individuals are, and these meanings guide their behavior within and across situations."[3] Identity formation is a social process

1. Burke and Stets, *Identity Theory*, 1.
2. Brubaker and Cooper, "Beyond 'Identity,'" 6–7.
3. Burke and Stets, *Identity Theory*, 3.

that occurs in "conversation with others."[4] Through their social networks, individuals seek to "verify their identities"—to have the way they interpret their own selves be the way that others interpret them.[5] Therefore, social interactions and relationships shape self-concept as a person is embedded within a community.

Because of the complex interplay of the individual and society, culture plays a significant role in the development and expression of a person's identity and the meanings attached to elements of their identity. In his book *Individualism and Collectivism*, social scientist Harry Triandis explores the differences in self-concept and identity between individualists and collectivists. Every culture has elements of both individualism and collectivism, but social norms often trend toward one category or the other. Individualists conceptualize their identity as independent entities with personal attributes, and are "primarily motivated by their own preferences, needs, rights, and the contracts they have established with others."[6] Hazel Markus and Shinobu Kitayama describe individualism as an "independent construal of the self."[7] This is distinct from more collectivistic cultures, in which the primary self-concept is embedded within group membership, and in which the motivations are more based on the group's needs or preferences.

Charles Taylor's *Sources of the Self: The Making of Modern Identity* provides an intriguing perspective on the historical development of the individualistic conception of selfhood in Western civilizations. He defines this modern identity as having three primary characteristics: (1) inwardness, or the sense that identity is "deep inside" a person, (2) the affirmation of the ordinary life, and (3) the inner self as the source of morality.[8] Taylor traces these three factors, which developed over centuries through philosophical thought and cultural movements. Their development has resulted in a modern experience of autonomous individualism, an emphasis on the individual's freedoms and rights, and avoidance of suffering as a primary goal.[9] Since the research participants have all been influenced by the Western framework of modern identity, Taylor's three factors—inwardness, affirmation of the ordinary life, and morality—will be further explored below.

4. C. Taylor, *Sources of the Self*, 37.
5. Burke and Stets, *Identity Theory*, 8.
6. Triandis, *Individualism and Collectivism*, 2, 12.
7. Markus and Kitayama, "Culture and Self," 226.
8. C. Taylor, *Sources of the Self*, x.
9. C. Taylor, *Sources of the Self*, 11–13.

Modern Inwardness

According to Taylor, the modern individualist sees the inner depths as where the true self is—the inner workings of the mind and heart, which can often be revealed to the world through expression in words or actions. Outward circumstances or community life exist but are considered separate from the person, who primarily consists of the inner being. Taylor credits Augustine with the Western turn to "radical reflexivity"—the gaze is turned inward to discover the self and truth.[10] However, in Augustine's view, truth itself arises from outside the person from God and the cosmic order rather than from within. Augustine writes, "But we must seek and pray to God in the innermost court of the rational soul which is called the 'interior man,' for it is here that He has wished to make His temple."[11] Augustine describes a person going into the "inner sanctum of the soul," where prayer takes place, finding God there.[12] In this inner sanctum, a person may also discover the "inner light of truth," which comes from God rather than the self.[13] While God is separate from his creation, Augustine argues that humans receive instruction from God by turning inward.[14]

René Descartes's *cogito* further developed this idea of inwardness in Western thought, placing the source of morality and existence within the interior human self rather than an exterior source.[15] Taylor describes Descartes as the "founder of modern individualism," as his philosophies placed the responsibility for finding order, truth, and identity on the individual as he or she turned inward.[16] Taylor contrasts the inward experience with an older, mimetic experience of the world in which identity and morality were provided externally through traditions and authorities. Thought, feeling, and the very self became localized within the mind in the individualist experience, resulting in the emergence of a psychological experience of reality that separated mind and body.[17]

Summarizing Taylor's historical outline of philosophical developments of inward identity, Carl Trueman further describes the shift from

10. C. Taylor, *Sources of the Self*, 130–33.
11. Augustine, *Teacher*, 8.
12. Augustine, *Teacher*, 9.
13. Augustine, *Teacher*, 53–54.
14. Augustine, *Teacher*, 60.
15. C. Taylor, *Sources of the Self*, 143, 156–57.
16. C. Taylor, *Sources of the Self*, 182, 184.
17. C. Taylor, *Sources of the Self*, 186–89.

a mimetic view of the world to a modern, Western poiesis. In a mimetic view of the world, an external order exists and humans must find their place within that order and conform to it. In a poietic conception of the universe, the universe exists as "raw material" from which an individual creates meaning and purpose.[18] In this way, the basis of understanding shifts from external structures and authority to an internal experience. This poiesis is the foundation of what Taylor calls "expressive individualism," in which individuals must discover their authentic selves within, and then express those authentic selves in the world.[19] According to Taylor, the highest goals of expressive individualism are "self-expression, self-realization, self-fulfillment, [and] discovering authenticity."[20] The individual's uniqueness in the world is paramount for discovering meaning and purpose in life. In postmodern society, poiesis is also expressed in the rejection of an overarching metanarrative of meaning or truth applied to all people, as the "truth" of the individual is upheld as primary, and a metanarrative structure may be viewed as systemic oppression. Individualists may therefore value authenticity to one's inner self above notions of fulfilling one's duty or acting properly.[21]

The Affirmation of Ordinary Life

Taylor's second factor in the development of modern Western identity is what he calls the "affirmation of ordinary life," which emerged following the Protestant Reformation. Taylor defines this ordinary life as work, reproduction, marriage, and family life.[22] Ancient Greek philosophers such as Aristotle and the Stoics viewed these activities as necessary to the infrastructure and continuation of humanity. However, they articulated a distinct hierarchy between the "lower" masses who engaged in these matters, and the "higher" sages and philosophers who refrained from them. The ordinary life was distinguished from the "good life," which included the pursuit of moral philosophy, meditation on the order of the cosmos, and debate in politics and law.[23] These distinctions are the ancient seeds of the sacred-secular divide.

18. Trueman, *Rise of Modern Self*, 39.
19. Trueman, *Rise of Modern Self*, 49; C. Taylor, *Sources of the Self*, 507.
20. C. Taylor, *Sources of the Self*, 507.
21. Triandis, *Individualism and Collectivism*, 33.
22. C. Taylor, *Sources of the Self*, 211.
23. C. Taylor, *Sources of the Self*, 211–12.

The Catholic Church sealed this hierarchy between high and low pursuits in the Middle Ages, constructing cathedrals as sacred spaces by which the church acted as a mediator of salvation between God and humans. The Protestant Reformers rejected the church as mediator, claiming only God can mediate salvation. This rejection of mediation was also a rejection of the categories of what defined sacred and secular. Taylor, a Catholic, describes this Protestant demolition of the division between sacred and secular:

> Along with the Mass went the whole notion of the sacred in mediaeval Catholicism, the notion that there are special places or times or actions where the power of God is more intensely present and can be approached by humans. Therefore Protestant (particularly Calvinist) churches swept away pilgrimages, veneration of relics, visits to holy places, and a vast panorama of traditional Catholic rituals and pieties. And along with the sacred went the mediaeval Catholic understanding of the church as the locus and vehicle of the sacred.[24]

By "sacred," Taylor means the belief that God's power is especially present in particular places, times, people, or actions.[25] Taylor credits the Protestant Reformation as a partial but significant cause of the rise of modern secularism, since it flattened any distinctions of sacred space, time, vocation, or objects. The Protestants, in their theology and praxis, affirmed the value of the ordinary life as a means of glorifying God, removing much of the sacred-secular divide. All can be sacred, if rightly ordered. This flattening of the divide between sacred and secular also impacted views of soteriology. Salvation shifted from a collectivistic notion to more individualistic. If the church no longer mediated salvation, it was granted (or not) to individuals who stood before God alone in judgment. This soteriology led to an emphasis on personal commitment, as well as a leveling of the hierarchy of human vocation.[26] No longer were monks and priests viewed as higher or more sacred in vocation than farmers or businessmen. All stood before God equally in need of mercy. As a result, all Christians could also participate in the "priesthood of believers," maintaining access to God only through the mediation of Jesus Christ. The Reformation thus denied the distinction between sacred and secular which had long been the foundation of Western societal organization.

24. C. Taylor, *Sources of the Self*, 216.
25. C. Taylor, *Secular Age*, 76.
26. C. Taylor, *Sources of the Self*, 217.

Without this hierarchical system of holy and profane, Westerners viewed the "ordinary life" as a platform by which humans could honor and glorify God. Marriage, parenting, farming, and selling could all be part of the labor and calling that God bestows on people. Taylor notes the shift in the vocabulary of "vocation," which had been used exclusively for priests and monks in Catholic society. The Puritans co-opted the word for any normal employment that brought good and flourishing for humans, and through which people could glorify God by a spirit of obedience and service to him.[27] Contradicting Protestant missiological literature presented in chapter 2, Taylor argues that the division between the sacred and the secular is *not* a feature of modern, Western society. If anything, Taylor argues, the *absence* of a clear sacred-secular divide is a modern, Western cultural feature.[28] In his landmark book *A Secular Age*, Taylor describes the removal of these divisions between sacred and secular as problematic, contributing to factors which have led to an increasingly secular society, in which there is no sense of the sacred.[29] This flattening of the sacred and secular together into an immanent frame has far-reaching consequences for what Taylor calls the social imaginary—the assumptions about existence that we make before thinking about it. Taylor describes modern Western secularism as an age where a sense of the transcendent has been lost, and all meaning and significance must be found in the naturalistic world.[30]

These developments, over time, led to a withdrawal of the individual from the authority of society and institutions, particularly the institution of the Church. These developments also led to a more internal experience of identity as the role of personal commitment, rather than institutional allegiance, became central to how one stands before God. Personal prayer, introspection, private Scripture reading, and journaling arose as markers of spiritual maturity and devotion.[31] Mass attendance, the administration of the sacraments by the clergy, and sacred feasts and prayer to the saints were reduced in this "disenchanted" world.[32] Personal feelings thus became more important in the Western experience as sources of authenticity and

27. C. Taylor, *Sources of the Self*, 223–24.
28. C. Taylor, *Secular Age*, 226, 556–57.
29. C. Taylor, *Secular Age*, 266.
30. C. Taylor, *Secular Age*, 14–18.
31. C. Taylor, *Secular Age*, 70.
32. C. Taylor, *Secular Age*, 266.

truth.[33] These personal sentiments became especially important for issues of morality, which is Taylor's third factor for modern Western identity.

Identity and Morality

Taylor identifies the third factor in the modern self as the "expressivist notion of nature as an inner moral source."[34] With such an inwardly localized view of identity, moral action in the individualist experience is primarily centered around a concept of personal morality. In fact, Taylor describes personal identity primarily in moral terms: "My identity is defined by the commitments and identifications which provide the frame or horizon within which I can try to determine from case to case what is good, or valuable, or what ought to be done, or what I endorse or oppose."[35] Studies in individualistic Western cultures show that there is a positive correlation between moral identity and moral behavior.[36] That is, if a person has a strong self-concept that includes moral codes such as honesty, justice, or compassion, that person will usually behave in alignment with their perceived moral identity. Philosopher Alasdair MacIntyre decries the modern development of moral reasoning based on inner feelings and notions, which he terms "emotivism." He defines *emotivism* as moral judgments which arise from inward personal preferences, attitudes, or feelings.[37] This kind of vacuous moral reasoning, he argues, lacks any external evaluating criteria. Modern individualists often act out of a sense of who they feel they are deep inside, rather than by external standards or institutions. For both Taylor and MacIntyre, identity and moral behavior are strongly correlated.

Culturally focused research corroborates the correlation between identity and morality. Ethical decision-making often expresses cultural values, the shared understanding in a society of what is good and how a person should be and act. Values are prioritized differently in various cultures, leading to expressions of morality that vary widely from one social group to the next.[38] Bernard Adeney writes, "Our lived morality is a result of the way we perceive reality. People usually act in relation to their interpretation of the way the world really is, far more from a set of beliefs or

33. C. Taylor, *Sources of the Self*, 292.

34. C. Taylor, *Sources of the Self*, x.

35. C. Taylor, *Sources of the Self*, 27.

36. Jia and Krettenauer, "Recognizing Moral Identity."

37. MacIntyre, *After Virtue*, 13, 31–32.

38. Adeney, *Strange Virtues*, 15.

principles."[39] Morality is deeply embedded within cultural stories and myths that members are socialized into from birth, guiding them to act in ways that benefit that society. These cultural myths interact with individualist or collectivist tendencies, resulting in differing cultural values. Priorities emerge in moral decision-making in order to achieve the greatest good, reflecting cultural norms and taboos. In one culture, valuing a relationship may take priority over a value of complete truthfulness, and a "little white lie" is acceptable in their ethical reasoning. Collectivists will generally value maintaining relationships over honesty if the two must conflict. Lying may be viewed as proper or even mature behavior in many instances.[40] However, individualists often perceive lying as a breach of social contract, which is a severe transgression and misaligned with their inner sense of self.[41] They may feel strongly committed to the truth, even if they or others must suffer. A value of justice may override a value of a single human life; a value of loyalty to family member or close friend may override loyalty to a community. A person's identity, forged deeply by culture, forms the framework for moral reasoning and decision-making.

This internal moral reasoning also interfaces with expressive individualism in modern Western civilization. This can perhaps be seen in the contemporary impetus to locate truth within the individual rather than in an external frame of reference, such as God or the cosmos. Truth and moral reasoning in a poietic universe must be constructed from within the authentic core of a person, and then expressed to the world.[42] "Live your truth" has become the anthem of expressive individualism, by which people make moral decisions from inner emotive or personal desires. This allows them to be true to their authentic core selves.

As the Westerner experiences the inner self as the source of morality, the loss of identity is a significant psychological threat for the modern individualist. Because Taylor frames identity in terms of morality, he also describes an identity crisis as an existential loss and profound disorientation, especially in moral space:

> It's what we call an "identity crisis," an acute form of disorientation, which people often express in terms of not knowing who they are, but which can also be seen as a radical uncertainty of where

39. Adeney, *Strange Virtues*, 86.

40. Triandis, *Individualism and Collectivism*, 32, 78.

41. Triandis, *Individualism and Collectivism*, 78.

42. Trueman, *Rise of Modern Self*, 71.

> they stand. They lack a frame or horizon within which things can take on a stable existence, within which some life possibilities can be seen as good or meaningful, others as bad or trivial. The meaning of all these possibilities is unfixed, labile, or undetermined. This is a painful and frightening experience. What this brings to light is the essential link between identity and a kind of orientation. To know who you are is to be oriented in moral space, a space in which questions arise about what is good or bad, what is worth doing and what not, what has meaning and importance for you and what is trivial and secondary.[43]

For Taylor, moral identity is crucial for orienting a person to the world. Losing moral bearings can cause a person to lose all bearings and a sense of meaning and purpose, resulting in an identity crisis.

In 1980, Geert Hofstede's research identified the United States as the most highly individualistic culture in the world. Over twenty years later, Hofstede's updated metrics of the individualism index published in 2001 showed the United States still holding the top rank for individualism.[44] The Western conception of identity and selfhood in individualistic terms is an important discussion in this study, as American missionaries' experience of negotiation and managing their identities occurs through this cultural lens. The experience of the inner "authentic self," and the need to express it, may lead to a sense of identity crisis or dissonance among American missionaries who must hide their authentic missionary identity. If they cannot express their Christian moral identity of truthfulness, it may lead to the disorientation that Taylor describes as an identity crisis. However, there may be mitigating factors at play for a missionary that reduce or eliminate these negative outcomes. This study seeks to discover the impact of the concealment of identity on missionaries influenced by this cultural and philosophical milieu.

Taylor argues that modern Protestants, of which American Evangelicals are a part, do *not* generally hold a strong distinction between the sacred and secular. This is an interesting contradiction of evangelical missiological literature presented in chapter 2. The evangelical affirmation of ordinary life as sacred can be demonstrated by evangelical church-planting methods emphasizing lay leadership and de-emphasizing formal theological education and institutions. These practices are consistent with the Reformation emphasis on the priesthood of all believers. Current popular missiological methods

43. C. Taylor, *Sources of the Self*, 27–28.

44. Hofstede, *Culture's Consequences*, 215.

such as disciple-making movements (DMM), discovery Bible studies (DBS), church-planting movements (CPM), Training 4 Trainers (T4T), and others hold similar tenets that flatten any demarcation or hierarchy between an ordinary Christian and a minister.[45] The goal is often the rapid reproduction of disciples that spreads through a geographic area quickly in a network of cell or house churches. The leadership of these churches may form quickly with little formal education or ordination processes, reflecting the values of Protestant denominations. Since missiologists often point to the sacred-secular divide as the source of problems surrounding dual identity in tentmaking, gaining a clearer picture of tentmakers' experiences through qualitative research may elucidate other potential underlying problems.

IDENTITY THEORY

Modern identity theory, from the field of social psychology, grew out of structuralist symbolic interactionism, a sociological field pioneered by George H. Mead. Structuralist symbolic interactionism focuses on the interplay between the self and society to construct meaning, especially through language, which gives form to symbols.[46] This interaction also includes a person seeing themselves as others see them, creating a reflexive stance through social interactions.[47] Mead argues that self-concept is therefore constructed relationally through interactions with others.

Sheldon Stryker, building on Mead, argues that a person's role identity within society mediates meanings that guide behavior. George McCall and J. L. Simmons are also prominent researchers in identity theory, providing many of the foundational concepts surrounding role identities, role partners, and the concepts of identity prominence and salience explored below. Peter Burke is another key researcher in the field of identity theory. His research primarily focuses on identity verification by self and society, and how people react when there is a discrepancy between how others perceive them and how they view themselves.

Modern identity theory studies the experiences of the self in interaction with society in various ways. It classifies identities into four main categories: personal identity, role identity, group identity, and categorical

45. See D. Watson and Watson, *Contagious Disciple Making*; Smith and Kai, *T4T*; Garrison, *Wind in Islam*; Shipman, *Any-3*; Garrison, *Church Planting Movements*.

46. Stryker, "Structural Symbolic Interactionism," 14–15.

47. Hogg and Williams, "From I to We," 83.

identity.[48] *Personal identities* are the meanings arising from the person conceptualized as a unique self. This unique self has particular character traits, morals, qualities, and descriptions distinguishing that individual from others. *Role identities* are the meanings that arise from an individual fulfilling a particular role, which carries expectations for behavior shared by a culture. Role identities may include vocational roles, familial roles, or friend roles. *Group identities* gain meaning from the social groups people belong to—a religious community, a political party, or a family, for instance. The group's boundaries and goals define these group identities, and people are embedded within the group as they interact with one another. People develop a strong self-concept from belonging to groups and distinguishing themselves from those not in the group.[49] *Categorical identities* refer to broader social categories, such as gender, class, ethnicity, citizenship, or race.[50] A person's identity is embedded within these layers of social and personal interaction, and multiple identities can be expressed or activated in any given situation. This present study will focus especially on personal identities and role identities, as they are the categories most significant to the research questions for tentmaking missionaries.

Personal Identity

Personal identities are the qualities, characteristics, and traits that make a person unique, differentiating them from another person. John Locke is a key figure in developing the concept of personal identity in his *Essay Concerning Human Understanding.* On personal identity, John Locke wrote:

> This being premised, to find wherein personal identity consists, we must consider what person stands for—which, I think, is a thinking intelligent being, that has reason and reflection, and can consider itself as itself, the same thinking thing, in different times and places; which it does only by that consciousness which is inseparable from thinking, and, as it seems to me, essential to it: it being impossible for any one to perceive without perceiving that he does perceive. When we see, hear, smell, taste, feel, meditate, or will anything, we know that we do so. Thus it is always as to our present sensations and perceptions: and by this every one is to himself that which he calls self: it not being considered, in this

48. Burke and Stets, *Identity Theory*, 166–67.

49. Iyer et al., "More the Merrier," 709.

50. Burke and Stets, *Identity Theory*, 166–67.

> case, whether the same self be continued in the same or divers substances. For, since consciousness always accompanies thinking, and it is that which makes every one to be what he calls self, and thereby distinguishes himself from all other thinking things, in this alone consists personal identity, i.e. the sameness of a rational being: and as far as this consciousness can be extended backwards to any past action or thought, so far reaches the identity of that person; it is the same self now it was then; and it is by the same self with this present one that now reflects on it, that that action was done.[51]

For Locke, consciousness and memory are key elements of personal identity and sameness of self as distinguished from others, even if the "particles" of a person change over time. In modern identity theory, personal identity is always activated, and can thus act as a "master identity" among role, group, and category identities.[52] How the individual's personal identity interacts with cultural expectations of roles may impact how they express personal identity.

Personal identity also includes moral identity. The identity theory model of morality and personal identity is consistent with that of Taylor, who links morality with identity. Identity theory postulates that if there is a discrepancy between a person's identity standard regarding morality and the feedback about their behavior, they will change the behavior to align with their moral identity standards.[53] An identity standard includes the meanings and expectations surrounding a particular role or identity—what it means to be a "good father" or a "smart student," for example. If a person believes their core authentic self to be kind, but receives feedback through interactions that their behavior is aggressive, they will change their behavior to align with the core personal identity. A failure to overcome this gap between who they are and what they do results in feelings of shame and guilt, and likely negatively impacts their relationships through which they receive feedback, compounding the internal dissonance.[54] The person wants to overcome the discrepancy so that their actions align with their moral identity, resolving the inner tension.

51. "On Identity and Diversity," in Locke, *Essay Concerning Human Understanding*, 139.
52. Burke and Stets, *Identity Theory*, 172.
53. Burke and Stets, *Identity Theory*, 112–13.
54. Burke and Stets, *Identity Theory*, 116.

Role Identity

An important aspect of identity is role identity, a central feature of research by McCall and Simmons within structural symbolic interactionism theory.[55] People understand who they are through social interactions as they perform a particular role. A person takes on attributes of a particular role, affirming and expressing their identity using symbols and behavior. In any society, there are shared understandings of particular roles and their associated expectations and behaviors.[56] This role and its expectations provide meaning, purpose, and guidance for behavior, which all contribute to emotional and physical well-being.[57] A woman occupying the mother role may behave towards her children at home in a way that reflects the mother identity, with its culturally embedded expectations and norms. She may speak softly, have a playful demeanor, and perform certain role behaviors such as cooking and cleaning that fulfill society's expectations for the mother role. When the same woman goes to her workplace as a high-status attorney with many employees below her in the hierarchy, her role identity will cause her to behave in different ways congruent with the norms and expectations of that role and context. She may speak more assertively, have a serious demeanor, and perform role behaviors congruent with her vocation. Her different roles, activated in different situations, guide her behaviors across various social settings.

Identity Verification and Dissonance

According to identity theory, people constantly seek verification of their identity both internally and externally. Because identity is performed in social interactions, identity in each role is verified through "role partners," or those a person interacts with while performing those roles.[58] Positive reinforcement of the role identity by role partners and role-affirming experiences are associated with positive physical, emotional, and psychological effects.[59] Verification of identity, the feeling of "how they see me is how I see me," leads to higher self-esteem, a greater sense of authenticity to the core self, and a feeling of competence. Identity verification leads to the experience

55. McCall and Simmons, *Identities and Interactions*.

56. Burke and Stets, *Identity Theory*, 41.

57. Thoits, "Role-Identity Salience," 361.

58. McCall and Simmons, *Identities and Interactions*, 18, 152.

59. Thoits, "Mechanisms Linking Social Ties."

of "existential security," identity consonance, and a purpose for living.[60] Having the identity reflected back by a role partner also deepens social bonds, increases positive emotions, and reduces feelings of uncertainty.[61]

However, if a person does not receive identity verification through their role partners, a disparity may arise between their self-concept and the reflected appraisals. The person then experiences a strong drive to resolve the disparity, and self-esteem may be impacted negatively.[62] This creates a distressing experience of identity dissonance. If any of these roles causes a person to behave incongruently with their core sense of self, or if role partners do not verify and reflect back the identity performed, the person may experience identity dissonance, or even crisis and existential despair.[63]

Receiving a dissonant reflected appraisal from a role partner may cause a person to initiate a process of renegotiating role identity in light of that feedback.[64] This may include changing roles or behaviors, ignoring reflected appraisals, or interacting only with people who verify the identity.[65] Primarily, a person will overcompensate their behavior to align with their identity if others give them non-verifying feedback. If a manager says that an employee is lazy, yet the employee feels a strong identification with being hardworking, the employee may increase behaviors that signal that he is hardworking in order to verify his identity.[66] If, over time, a person consistently cannot verify their identity through interactions, they may change their identity standards gradually so that the identity can be verified, or they may change their environment.[67] Perhaps the employee will begin identifying more strongly as a family man who does not put work ahead of his home life, which accounts for the "lazy" behavior. Or perhaps he will begin to view himself as lazy rather than hardworking, and will express this new identity standard in his behavior. He may also quit his job and find a new one in which his manager verifies his hardworking identity through feedback. Relational interactions are vital for verifying the identity, shaping both self-concept and behavior.

60. Burke and Stets, *Identity Theory*, 180.

61. Stets et al., "Exchange, Identity Verification," 223.

62. Stets, "Emotions in Identity Theory," 44.

63. Thoits, "Role-Identity Salience."

64. Mlotshwa et al., "Community Health Workers," 2.

65. Asencio, "Self-Esteem, Reflected Appraisals," 307.

66. Stets et al., "Exchange, Identity Verification," 223.

67. Burke and Stets, *Identity Theory*, 222.

The reflected appraisals of others are given more weight with familiarity. If identity non-verification arises from a close partner or other relationship with high intimacy, the experienced emotional distress will be higher.[68] The impact on self-esteem is much less if non-verification comes from a stranger or a more distant relationship. In fact, the negative reflected appraisal may be ignored entirely. Likewise, the impact of identity non-verification is increased if there is a power differential between the parties. A lower-status person will more intensely feel negative emotions associated with identity non-verification from a supervisor than they would from a peer or someone with less status than themselves.[69] As role partners interact, their verification or non-verification of identity can strongly impact emotional and psychological outcomes.

In a qualitative study of role identity among paramedics, researchers explored how paramedic vocation aligned or misaligned with individuals' sense of identity and self-concept. Using role identity theory as a lens for evaluating paramedics' sense of self, the researchers explored the impact on mental health for paramedics who experienced significant incongruence or dissonance between their self-concept and their role as paramedics. They found that substantial disparity between self-concept and vocational role could result in "significant emotional, psychological, or even existential distress."[70] However, sometimes this dissonance could be mitigated by renegotiating their identity by giving another role more prominence in their identity, or by dissolving their paramedic identity entirely through quitting. Others reconciled their dissonance by reframing their experiences of their work as a psychological coping mechanism.[71]

Many missionaries may take on vocational roles that are dissonant with their self-concept to gain access to RANs, as the literature shows in chapter 2. A person with no business background may be encouraged by their organization to start a business on the field in order to obtain a visa. They may be, as Gary Taylor says, "wonderful, sincere, visionary, but inept."[72] A missionary with no strong expertise may open a consulting firm, and publicly identify as a consultant. It is unclear whether the missionary identity is enough of a narrative to overcome strong incongruence between

68. Asencio, "Self-Esteem, Reflected Appraisals," 296.

69. Burke and Stets, *Identity Theory*, 141.

70. Mausz et al., "Role Identity, Dissonance," 10.

71. Mausz et al., "Role Identity, Dissonance," 11–12.

72. G. Taylor, "Don't Call Me a Tentmaker," 23.

self-concept and vocation. As this study includes participants across a wide range of vocations in the gulf, I hope to discover whether dissonance is experienced in such situations.

Multiple Role Identities

Because people hold multiple role identities simultaneously—parent, employee, church elder, and son, for example—they will recruit or diminish aspects of identity in particular situations to suit the context. Researchers in identity theory have identified three main factors contributing to identity activation in a given situation: *salience*, *prominence*, and *commitment*.[73]

McCall and Simmons define identity *salience* as the probability that a particular identity will have greater shared meaning or will be advantageous in a certain situation.[74] In various social situations, a person may activate the identity they perceive as most advantageous or salient to the context. The concept of identity salience predicts they will choose the identity that has the most shared meanings with interactants. The concept of identity salience is likely important for tentmaking missionaries who toggle between multiple social fields and must manage their identities between them.

Identity *prominence* is the level of importance that a particular identity holds for a person, which could be for various reasons.[75] The most prominent role identity may still surface across most or even all social situations, as it is viewed as more central to a person's self-concept and an expression of the ideal self.[76] Burke and Stets note that people will invest more energy into cultivating their prominent role identities, and react more negatively when others do not verify their prominent identities.[77] In her research among volunteers, Peggy Thoits found that time spent in a particular role is an especially important indicator of identity prominence. Those who spent less time in their role as volunteers viewed that aspect of their identity as having less salience and prominence.[78] The more time and energy a person puts into an identity or role, the more frequently it is activated and becomes central to a person's self-concept. The issue of

73. Burke and Stets, *Identity Theory*, 87.

74. McCall and Simmons, *Identities and Interactions*, 85–89.

75. Burke and Stets, *Identity Theory*, 87.

76. McCall and Simmons, *Identities and Interactions*, 77, 221; Thoits, "Role-Identity Salience," 362.

77. Burke and Stets, *Identity Theory*, 88.

78. Thoits, "Role-Identity Salience," 373.

identity prominence is foundational for self-concept, and a person will put great effort into verifying their prominent identities. They may become highly distressed if they receive non-verifying feedback for a prominent identity.[79] The concept of identity prominence may be especially relevant for tentmakers who manage multiple identities through their missionary calling, vocational calling, or both. The literature review discussed tensions between the vocational and missionary identity that many experience, suggesting a conflict between prominent identities. My interviews will explore these narratives of calling, as well as each participant's presentation of their missionary and vocational role identities.

In addition to salience and prominence, Sheldon Stryker adds *commitment* to the identity as a third dimension of role identity. Stryker's research focuses on the communal aspect of identity. How people conceptualize their role identities is strongly tied to the relationships formed while performing those identities. He defines commitment to identity both quantitatively and qualitatively. Quantitatively, a person will display a higher commitment to a particular role identity when they have greater numbers of personal connections and relationships because of that role identity. A person with fewer relational connections through that role will be less committed to that identity.[80] Qualitatively, the stronger relational ties a person feels in connection with a particular role identity, the stronger the commitment to that identity. A person with more close friends, colleagues, and acquaintances who know him and relate to him in a particular role identity will exhibit greater commitment to that particular identity. In addition, that person also verifies his role partners' identities, leading to a satisfying experience of mutual verification, which builds strong social ties. Burke and Stets write, "The mutual verification that occurs through person-to-person connections builds and strengthens those connections into network, groups, and organizations. Commitment is the strength of those connections. Without commitment, those connections will disintegrate."[81] This differs from prominence in that the focus is on *external* verification of the identity through relationships, rather than an internal sense of the importance of that identity.

Identity salience, prominence, and commitment are highly correlated. The more often a person activates a particularly salient identity, the more

79. Burke and Stets, *Identity Theory*, 88.

80. Stryker, "Identity Salience."

81. Burke and Stets, *Identity Theory*, 92.

prominent that identity becomes. In addition, the more time spent performing that identity in social interactions, the higher the number of relational connections made, creating a high commitment to that identity.[82] Prominent identities are likely to be activated across various social fields, increasing their salience. Both the external and the internal verifications are essential in constructing and maintaining identities.

For many Americans, one of the most prominent role identities is that of vocation. If the role in the vocation they hold is not congruent to the motivations, commitments, and values of the inner core self, a renegotiation of job identity may be important as an affirmation of the person's core identity.[83] High commitment to a particular vocation, as well as positive feelings about the work or the future of the work, typically leads to a greater sense of coherence with identity and a reduced experience of anxiety and depression. Likewise, a low commitment to a vocation or negative feelings about the work or its future, often leads to higher experiences of mental distress.[84] One study on job identity also found that those with a stronger group identity within their job identity—such as high coherence with their organization, company, or team—reported higher job satisfaction, lower burnout rates, and lower attrition rates.[85]

Tentmakers in RANs navigate multiple role identities, especially the missionary identity and the vocational identity. These distinct role identities may hold differing salience, prominence, and commitment, which may impact tentmaker self-concept. In addition, the concealment of the missionary identity in RANs may lead to non-verification of the missionary identity, which may negatively impact missionaries. My research with tentmakers in RANs will explore whether their prominent identities and vocational identities are congruent and sufficiently verified by those they interact with. The impact on self-concept of presenting differing identities across social fields will be measured and evaluated in terms of identity verification. Identity dissonance and consonance are crucial elements describing impact on self-concept used in this study.

82. Burke and Stets, *Identity Theory*, 90–91.

83. Crocetti et al., "Job Identity," 283.

84. Porfeli et al., "Vocational Identity Status."

85. Crocetti et al., "Job Identity," 296.

Hierarchical Control System

Researchers have found that having a higher number of role identities that do not overlap leads to more positive psychological outcomes and lower overall stress.[86] This is likely due to greater opportunities for identity verification. In addition, a person with multiple role identities may have access to more social support through group memberships if verification fails in another role. Burke and Stets describe the hierarchical control system, which conceptualizes how multiple identities coalesce within one individual and manage their behavior output.[87] If two identities are activated simultaneously in a social situation, the person must adjust the meanings of all the applicable identity standards to verify all identities. When people experience multiple identities that are activated simultaneously in a situation, the meanings associated with them may overlap and confirm one another. Over time, this may merge into a single identity with no dissonance experienced between them.[88]

However, having multiple role identities sometimes leads to conflict if the identities are incompatible, and this conflict must be resolved. If a conflict exists between the two identities, an "error code" is produced in the form of a dissonant emotion, and the person must work to achieve consonance somehow.[89] With multiple role identities, a hierarchy often exists to control the meanings and perceptions, so if a lower identity conflicts with a higher identity, the higher identity takes precedence. The higher identity is perceived as having greater prominence to the individual, and thus closer to the core self in that person's self-concept. When role identities conflict, the person may consciously or unconsciously invest more resources into the higher identity.[90] The person's behavior then reflects the higher identity, if both identities cannot be performed and verified simultaneously. Or if there is a significant conflict in the two identities that cannot be reconciled, the person may begin to reidentify themselves somehow.[91]

Stryker found that if multiple role identities compete, there may be a time compensation in the lower identity so that a person spends lower

86. Iyer et al., "More the Merrier," 710–11.

87. Burke and Stets, *Identity Theory*, 190–91.

88. Burke, "Relationships Between Multiple Identities," 212.

89. Burke and Stets, *Identity Theory*, 190.

90. Zaman and ul-Haq, "Role Identity Salience," 51.

91. Burke and Stets, *Identity Theory*, 190.

time in that identity to achieve verification.[92] For instance, a woman's core identity as a devoted mother may take prominence over her identity as an employee who works overtime to get projects completed on time. The woman may perceive these two identities as competing, and she cannot verify both simultaneously. The higher identity controls the behavior so that the higher identity is verified. She may reduce work hours as a result, and redefine her employee identity standards so that she can also verify that role identity. Prominence and salience are extremely important concepts for managing multiple role identities, and may result in the less prominent or salient identity losing out. Alternatively, there may be a compromise position in which both identities shift so that both identities may be verified.[93] Thoits found that competition between identities increases stress in individuals, particularly if they are obligatory rather than voluntary.[94] When a person can lay down a particular identity freely if the demands become too much, then the distress experienced is much less than if the role identity is imposed upon them by life's circumstances.

The hierarchical control system is relevant to tentmaking missionaries, and will be used as a framework in the analysis of this research. As demonstrated in the literature review, tentmakers manage and present two distinct role identities that sometimes conflict—vocational worker and missionary. Missionaries may function with little identity dissonance if their identity as missionary and tentmaker is verified by their sending church, their teams, and their organization. However, in social situations on the field where both identities may need to be activated simultaneously, navigating those multiple identities may cause conflict in the hierarchical control system between missionary and vocational identities. The missionary identity may be unverified when it is actively hidden. Vocational or religious identities may hold prominence for a tentmaker, but may not be verified by the external community with whom they interact. In addition, the practices resulting from the need to hide the missionary identity may conflict with the tentmaker's moral identity.

Role identity theory is a helpful framework for understanding dual identity among missionaries across various contexts. Missionaries may activate certain role identities in their country of service, and different role identities in their home country. American church-planting missionaries may occupy

92. Stryker, "Identity Competition," 41. See also Burke and Stets, *Identity Theory*, 224.

93. Burke and Stets, *Identity Theory*, 224.

94. Thoits, "Personal Agency," 191.

several social roles, through which they negotiate their identity in society: missionary, vocational worker, committed Christian, parent, spouse, single person, discipler, church planter, language student, American, expatriate, and more. However, each of these role identities does not have the same priority in a person's self-concept; a person will rank them according to the prominence they give that role in their overall identity.[95] The higher their commitment to a particular role, the more tightly woven it is with their core identity and their sense of purpose and meaning in life.[96] Identity verification occurs when social interactions confirm a performed identity, leading to an internal sense of consonance. Identity non-verification occurs when social interactions reflect incongruence with a person's identity, leading to a dissonant experience of disorientation or even identity crisis. This study seeks to discover whether some missionaries struggle to verify their moral or personal identity when they engage in concealing or illegal behaviors for the sake of the Great Commission. If there is a discrepancy in the moral standard, this study seeks to uncover coping mechanisms for overcoming that discrepancy and tension in order to achieve identity consonance.

Concealable Stigmatized Identities

A relatively new and understudied topic of research in identity theory is that of concealable stigmatized identities (CSIs), or counter-normative identities. Society considers certain identities—such as criminality, mental illness, AIDS status, or certain sexual orientations—to have negative value.[97] Negative stereotypes or beliefs are often attached to such identities. However, these identities can often be concealed from general knowledge. It is unclear whether the normal process for identity verification occurs for stigmatized identities, as people may not want their CSI to be verified.[98]

In their review of current research on CSIs, Diane Quinn and Valerie Earnshaw conclude that there are two main factors in predicting psychological outcomes in those who carry CSIs. The first factor is the *emotional valence* of the identity—how the person feels about their CSI, and how others feel about the CSI when it is revealed. If a person has internalized the stigma about their identity that society holds, believing they are untrustworthy or unclean, they are more likely to suffer from depression, anxiety,

95. Thoits, "Role-Identity Salience," 363.
96. Burke and Stets, *Identity Theory*, 43.
97. Marcussen et al., "Mental Illness as Stigmatized."
98. Burke and Stets, *Identity Theory*, 249–50.

and stress.[99] Anticipating stigma from others also predicts stress and anxiety for those with CSIs, even if discrimination has not yet occurred.[100] However, a person may feel positive about their CSI, even if their social world does not. One way of fostering this positivity about the CSI is finding role models and positive information concerning the CSI, deflecting the stigma from becoming internalized.[101] Another method is through "meaning making," or constructing a narrative that puts the CSI within a story with a positive trajectory and purpose.[102] The second factor that Quinn and Earnshaw identify is the *magnitude* of the CSI, which is the level of centrality and salience that CSI holds for the person's self-concept. Centrality is analogous to prominence, defined as how central the CSI is to one's overall core identity. The higher the centrality that the CSI has to self-concept, the more isolated or misunderstood the person may feel when hiding this identity from others.[103] While there are few studies on salience for CSIs, the more frequently the person was reminded of their CSI across situations, the more negative impact it had on their self-concept if they anticipated stigma or had to carefully think about maintaining secrecy.[104]

The perceived authenticity of the CSI to a person's core self is impacted by the enactment or concealment of their identity. CSI researchers Megan Crabtree and David Pillow argue, "To the extent that an identity is considered personally meaningful, enacted more often, concealed less, and is more motivationally satisfying, individuals will come to see that identity as more authentic relative to their other identities."[105] They link together Burke's identity verification process and the Western individualist's need for authenticity to the core self. If a person frequently disguises a particular identity so others cannot verify it, there may be an increasing sense of inner dissonance and inauthenticity. The more a person conceals an identity, the lower the perceived authenticity to the core self.[106]

The role of "missionary" certainly has a negative stereotype among many Muslims, and is stigmatized to the point of being an illegal role in

99. Quinn and Earnshaw, "Concealable Stigmatized Identities," 40–42.

100. Quinn and Chaudoir, "Concealable Stigmatized Identity."

101. Quinn and Earnshaw, "Concealable Stigmatized Identities," 44.

102. Quinn and Earnshaw, "Concealable Stigmatized Identities," 45.

103. Quinn and Earnshaw, "Concealable Stigmatized Identities," 45–46.

104. Quinn and Earnshaw, "Concealable Stigmatized Identities," 46–47.

105. Crabtree and Pillow, "Consequences of Enactment," 1229.

106. Crabtree and Pillow, "Consequences of Enactment," 1228.

the GCC countries. It could therefore be considered a CSI. However, as with some CSIs, a missionary is likely to have positive emotions towards that identity as it was a freely chosen identity, or one to which they felt divinely called. Thus, the missionary identity is embedded within a positive narrative of the self, providing the needed trajectory and purpose in the process of "meaning making" with a CSI. The missionary identity is verified and viewed positively by social interactions in home churches, organizations, and teams. "Missionary" is likely integral and central to the person's self-concept, causing the person to endure hardships and discomforts to move and live internationally. However, because of this centrality and prominence of the missionary identity, this study explores the impact of concealing such a prominent part of the core self.

CONCLUSION

Contemporary Western perceptions of identity and individualism, combined with modern identity theory, provide a framework for analyzing how American missionaries manage multiple role identities. The concepts of identity salience, prominence, and commitment are fundamental as a conceptual framework for this study. These concepts describe internal and external experiences of identity, affirmed or denied through relational interactions across various social fields. As they see themselves through the eyes of those they interact with, missionaries experience identity verification or non-verification, resulting in either identity consonance or dissonance. The management techniques and behaviors arising from non-verification may impact their self-concept. These interactions vary widely across many social networks—supporting churches, mission organizations, employers and colleagues in their tentmaking vocation, their children, friends and family back home, and those they evangelize and disciple. The hierarchical control system is also a significant concept in this conceptual framework, as the multiple role identities that tentmakers present sometimes conflict. Adding complexity to managing their multiple role identities is a potentially stigmatized identity that may be prominent but hidden. The following chapter describes the qualitative methodology used in this study to explore these concepts among American tentmaking missionaries in RANs.

4

Methodology

THE AIM OF THIS study is to understand the impact on self-concept of having a missionary identity in some social fields and having a non-missionary identity in others. This research also seeks to understand the experiences that tentmaking missionaries have of navigating their identity. This includes concealing, misleading, or even deceptive practices used to protect the missionary identity from being discovered among certain social fields, as may be necessary in restricted access nations (RANs). These practices include digital behaviors that seek to circumvent detection online or through other surveillance modes. Finally, this study seeks to discover tentmakers' strategies to reconcile possible illegality, hiddenness, or deception with their moral identity. The result is a clearer understanding of the potential impact of the management of the missionary identity in RANs. These research questions guide the research methods.

ETHNOGRAPHY

I employed qualitative methods for this study on identity among missionaries in RANs. Qualitative research is uniquely focused on social or human issues and experiences. Qualitative research places people within their context at the center of the study, and data is analyzed both inductively and deductively, revealing patterns or themes.[1] Qualitative research thus allows for a rich, descriptive analysis of a complex situation from multiple perspectives. Qualitative research is especially valuable when a topic has

1. Creswell and Poth, *Qualitative Inquiry*, 44.

not been thoroughly researched yet, or when existing theories do not adequately explain the nuances and complexities of the situation.[2] Findings from qualitative studies can form the foundation for further qualitative or quantitative research. As there remains a dearth of research on missionary experiences of identity in a context of high security, qualitative research is the best way forward for this study.

I have chosen ethnographic methods to explore the impact of concealing practices arising from security concerns on tentmaker self-concept in RANs. Researchers often use ethnography to study a community with a shared culture—shared understandings of belonging, beliefs, practices, and assumptions.[3] This study examines American evangelical church-planting missionaries in Gulf Cooperative Council (GCC) countries as a cultural group. Evangelical American church-planting missionaries living within the particular context of the GCC often share similar beliefs and assumptions about their missionary and vocational calling, the urgency for church planting among UPGs, and the necessity of faith in Jesus Christ for salvation. In addition, new missionaries are socialized into their community of practice before and upon arrival in the GCC. These socialization practices include security protocols, identity management and disclosure, language learning, and cultural adaptation in dress and behavior. Evangelical missionaries in GCC countries have also created formal and informal inter-agency partnerships. These partnerships meet together for information sharing, fellowship and support, worship, and training in missionary methods and practices. Thus, evangelical American church-planting missionaries form a group that could be considered a distinct subculture within the larger Arab cultural context, and ethnography is an effective method for researching issues and practices surrounding their identity.

Ethnography combines the subjective experiences of identity revealed through interviews with the observations of the social environment and cultural realities in which the participants are immersed. Ethnography is frequently employed to examine a particular context holistically, seeking an understanding of complex social systems, motivations, behaviors, language, and symbols.[4] This sociocultural environment, combined with internal narratives and religious convictions, yields particular patterns of behavior and assumptions arising from a person's self-concept. In addition,

2. Creswell and Poth, *Qualitative Inquiry*, 46.

3. Wolcott, *Ethnography*, 251.

4. Creswell and Poth, *Qualitative Inquiry*, 90.

the broader communities participants belong to impact meanings and behaviors. Bourdieu argues that socialization into a community occurs primarily through nonconscious and unspoken practices, resulting in the *habitus*—the outward embodied practices that hold meaning and symbolism. He writes,

> Body *hexis* speaks directly to the motor function, in the form of a pattern of postures that is both individual and systematic, because linked to a whole system of techniques involving body and tools, and charged with a host of social meanings and values: in all societies, children are particularly attentive to the gestures and postures which, in their eyes, express everything that goes to make an accomplished adult—a way of walking, a tilt of the head, facial expressions, ways of sitting and of using implements, always associated with a tone of voice, a style of speech, and (how could it be otherwise?) a certain subjective experience.[5]

Thus, outward behaviors, practices, and habits may act as symbols of identity-related meaning. The personal sense of identity and social identity may be revealed in both the words and the *habitus* of the subject. Therefore, ethnographic methods that include participant observation of missionaries in various social fields may yield more insights into perceptions of their identity construction and management than interviews alone.

CONFIDENTIALITY AND DATA COLLECTION

As this study involved participants disclosing personal information that could potentially lead to deportation, imprisonment, or other legal risk, I obtained full board approval for my confidentiality protocols from the institutional review board (IRB) at Columbia International University. To protect the confidential information of the participants, I used security protocols that were in line with current security policies of each participant's organization, such as using a virtual private network (VPN) during online interviews or using substitute words for potentially troublesome words like "missionary," "church planting," or "evangelism." I let participants know they could do the interview with their camera turned off if they preferred. Before the interview, I assured participants that I would start with conservative vocabulary and then adapt to their ways of speaking. I followed the participant's lead in the interview, noting their use of particular words or code words, and imitating their word choices throughout the interview.

5. Bourdieu, *Theory of Practice*, 87.

I emailed participants a copy of the informed consent form the day before the interview. I sent an initial recruitment email (see appendix A) to potential participants, which gave information about the study, anticipated time allotment for the interview, the consent process, details of the interview, and security protocols. I provided my contact information, using secure platforms often used by missionaries in the GCC for communication. I obtained permission from my mission organization to conduct the study, and also from field leaders in other organizations to interview their field members.

I obtained verbal consent at the beginning of each recorded interview to use interviews for research purposes, a protocol approved by the IRB. Verbal consent minimized risk to the participants, as having a signed document linking their name to the study posed an increased threat to their confidentiality. Participants were informed that they could withdraw from the study anytime, even after their interview. In addition, participants were informed before the interview that they maintained control over what information they would like to divulge; they were allowed to skip any question they desired or withhold or disclose as much information as they were comfortable with. Before beginning the interview, I allowed participants to ask questions about the study or the security protocols, and I asked whether they had additional protocols they would like me to take before proceeding. In the findings chapters, I have obscured or changed identifying details of participants, such as number of children, gender, employment details, country of service, places of origin in the US, and other details. I also do not extensively describe any one participant's story in order to protect participants' confidentiality.

Interview data was separated from identifying information immediately following the interview, and I applied a pseudonym to the participant's interview and notes. I transcribed interviews immediately using transcription software, which I then edited for accuracy alongside the recording. Information from the interview that could help identify a participant was edited in the transcript to obscure their identity, including specific cities, family member names, friend names, or specific job titles or descriptions. I made notes on embodied responses that did not show up in the transcript and wrote those in brackets on the transcript. I then destroyed both the audio and video recordings, so that the participants' voices and images would not be attached to the study. I kept the transcripts in an encrypted, password-protected file on my computer. Any paper notes were quickly transcribed, depersonalized, and saved into the encrypted file. Then the paper notes were destroyed. To protect the confidentiality of participants, no one else had access to the data.

Participants

Thirty-eight participants took part in this study in twenty-nine interviews. I employed purposive sampling in this study: all participants are Americans affiliated with an evangelical church-planting organization and currently live in GCC countries as missionary tentmakers, or have moved away from the GCC within the previous three years. Five participants were not currently living in the GCC. However, one of these five was in the process of moving back to the GCC after a few years in the US. These participants who had moved away from the GCC yielded insightful reflections on their navigation of identity, having renegotiated their identity after ministry in a GCC country. Thirty-three participants were currently living in a GCC country. To qualify for the study, participants must have lived in the GCC for at least two years to allow for the process of navigating identity issues in their roles. Tentmakers on tourist or student visas were excluded from the study, as their issues of identity management may differ from long-term tentmakers. Time lived in the GCC ranged from just over two years to thirty-nine years, with an average of nine and a half years lived in the GCC and a median of seven and a half years.

Nineteen participants had lived in two or more GCC countries as tentmakers, and could compare the security issues and their practices across those different contexts. This study included twenty males and eighteen females. Four of the women were wives of tentmakers who were not currently working in professions, and their local identities were as stay-at-home mothers. However, all four were significantly involved in roles within their missionary organizations and made valuable contributions to the interviews alongside their husbands. The other fourteen women were tentmakers themselves. The minimum age for participation in the study was set at twenty-one; however, the youngest participant was twenty-nine. Engagement with technology is a significant factor in this study, and age can influence how missionaries engage with technology.[6] In addition, younger participants are likely constructing and processing their identities in different ways than older participants.[7] Participants ranged in age from

6. See Dunaetz, "More Harm Than Good."

7. Erikson, *Identity Crisis*; Dunkel and Harbke, "Stages of Psychosocial Development."

twenty-nine to sixty-nine; those in their thirties were significantly more represented than other age groups. The breakdown of the ages of the participants can be found in figure 1 below.

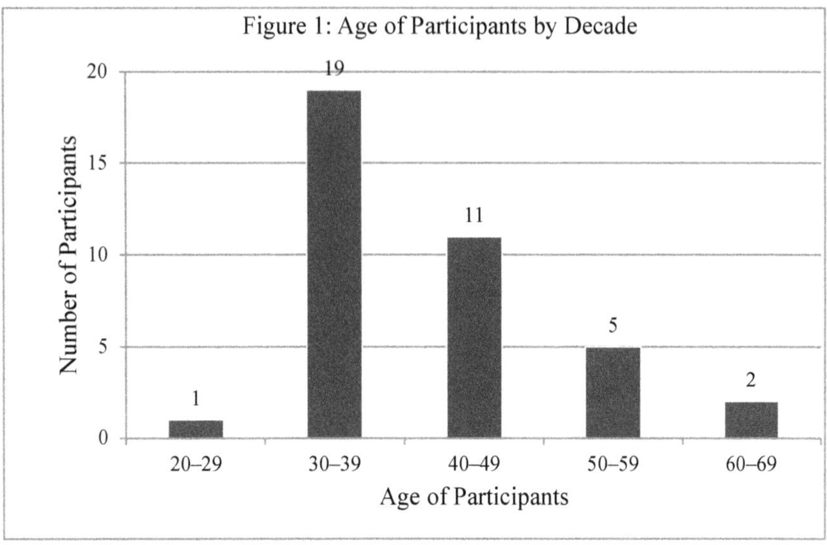

Affiliation with missionary church-planting (CP) organizations is a key factor in this study, as members have an overt identification with the evangelical values of the proclamation of the gospel and for Muslims to convert to faith in Christ. Further, missionaries associated with these organizations have received training and support for forming indigenous, Christ-centered faith communities among the UPGs of their host country. These factors contribute to the construction of a missionary identity. Whereas non-evangelical Christians or non-missionary expatriates employed in the GCC might feel at peace simply living quiet and faithful lives as a "light" in Muslim nations, Evangelicals affiliated with these organizations will be motivated to proclaim the gospel and make disciples. This may lead them to conceal, withhold, or even lie about certain aspects of their identity in a context where such work is illegal.

As a former missionary in the GCC, I knew that the general social contract among missionaries in the GCC regarding their organizational affiliation is "don't ask, don't tell." I did not gather names of organizations that participants were affiliated with, but I did send the parameters ahead of the interview to let them know that only those affiliated with an evangelical CP organization qualified for the study (see appendix A). Some participants volunteered their organization name, and I knew or could guess at others based on prior relational connections or who had given them my contact information. In two interviews, participants asked whether they qualified based on their organizational affiliation. One participant was a member not of an official missionary organization, but a tentmaker/BAM network. However, I looked at the network's mission statement, which specifically mentions both professional goals and evangelistic goals such as evangelism, church planting, and discipleship among UPGs. I included this participant in the study based on the organization's stated goals. The second situation was a couple with a missionary organization that did not explicitly have CP in their organizational vision. However, the organization used the language of evangelism, discipleship, and multiplication of spiritual groups. The couple identified indigenous church planting as among the goals they were aiming for as missionaries, and thus I included them in the study.

Access and Researcher Positionality

As security issues and trust were significant concerns for this population, I began recruitment through my personal contacts who met the study's criteria or could recommend potential participants from their networks. I identified field leaders of various organizations on the Arabian Peninsula, who approved of the study and then permitted their field personnel to participate if they desired. In addition, field leaders posted recruitment materials for the study on online partnership forums for specific GCC countries and in the broader Arabian Peninsula partnership. I identified myself to all participants as a doctoral candidate through Columbia International University studying identity and security among tentmakers. I also explicitly identified myself to the participants as a missionary with an evangelical CP organization who had lived in a GCC country. In fact, many of the participants already knew about me because of my husband's imprisonment described in chapter 1. In this way, I established quick rapport as an insider to the missionary-tentmaker community on the Arabian Peninsula and as someone who knew how to manage potentially compromising information in a RAN, and who understood the consequences of failing to manage that information.

One benefit of my positionality as an insider was that I could ask difficult questions about concealment, misleading, or outright deception without being perceived as judgmental. Further, I possess a shared language and shorthand codes with the participants that an outsider may not clearly and easily interpret. These codes arise from Arabic terms for which there is no easy English equivalent (such as *hosh*, the word for a walled-in yard area around a person's home, or *shela* for a woman's hair-covering scarf). Shared codes also arise from standard missionary language to replace words such as "evangelism" or "Muslims" in RANs. Sometimes, my body language responding to what participants described indicated a shared experience and understanding.

A limitation from my experience as an insider is that I likely share some assumptions with the participants that could go unchallenged in ways that an outsider may not share and could identify more easily. I attempted to limit this bias by seeking out participants from mission organizations with varying security protocols and practices from my own organization. In addition, I engaged in reflexive practices discussed below. Several participants shared feelings of guilt, shame, or regret relating to past experiences as they reflected on them. Reliability depended on what participants chose to divulge or how they presented themselves in interviews. Building rapport through relationships and trusted networks was critical to mitigating these limitations.

Semi-Structured Interviews and Narratives

I collected data from March through October 2023. I began data collection by conducting semi-structured interviews on a secure online meeting platform. I also conducted in-person ethnographic fieldwork among participants for three weeks. I traveled to the GCC, employing participant observation and informal conversations, which I recorded as field notes. During fieldwork visits and online, I used semi-structured interviews to ask specific questions pertaining to the research questions. Interviews averaged one hour and seventeen minutes in length. All interviews were recorded with the participants' verbal consent. A list of potential questions for the semi-structured interviews can be found in appendix B.

Semi-structured interviewing is a guided conversation using open-ended questions, which allows the interview to be adapted and shaped in the process rather than adhering to a rigid, preconfigured list of questions.[8] This allowed me to explore various aspects of the research questions as they applied to individual participants, allowing their experiences and perceptions of navigating their identity to drive the conversation. Such an

8. Wolcott, *Ethnography*, 56.

approach allowed for the questions asked to shift depending on what data emerged. For example, in the ninth interview, stories emerged of the participant's home and ministry worlds colliding, revealing fascinating data on managing the missionary identity in a globalized, highly digital world. In subsequent interviews, I specifically asked participants about ways these two worlds had collided in their experiences or how they were fearful of that collision occurring. In this way, the conversational, open-ended, yet guided interviewing style allowed for rich data collection.

In the semi-structured interviews, many questions were framed to invite the participant to tell a narrative in response to the question. Narrative inquiry analyzes a complex problem holistically through the stories of individuals' lived experiences.[9] Margaret Somers argues that "it is through narrativity that we come to know, understand, and make sense of the social world, and it is through narratives and narrativity that we constitute our social identities."[10] Constructing a plot through narrative is how humans make meaning from the events of their lives, connecting the parts into a coherent whole.[11] David Polkinghorne argues that it is through narrative that a person can form any coherent self-concept, as narratives are "cognitive organizing processes."[12] Thus, narratives are particularly rich data sources for exploring complex questions of personal and social identity.

These narratives include the individual, personal narratives, and the wider narratives of the sociocultural world in which a person is embedded. Narratives are ideally suited for ethnography, as a person's contextual particularities shape their understanding of the self and the world. A person's cultural myths and metanarratives provide a framework of meaning, upon which an individual builds his or her understanding of their past, present, and future.[13] Narrative inquiry enriches ethnographic research by pulling together the threads of the particular context, the storyteller, the listener, and the narrative's overall interpretation and intended function. Commenting on the functions of narratives, Catherine Riessman writes that "individuals use the narrative form to remember, argue, justify, persuade, engage, entertain, and even mislead an audience."[14] Identifying the

9. Creswell and Poth, *Qualitative Inquiry*, 68.
10. Somers, "Narrative Constitution of Identity," 606.
11. Somers, "Narrative Constitution of Identity," 616.
12. Polkinghorne, "Narrative and Self-Concept," 136.
13. Saint Arnault and Sinko, "Comparative Ethnographic Narrative Analysis," 1–2.
14. Riessman, *Narrative Methods*, 8.

intended function of the narrative provided can thus give insight into how the storyteller manages and constructs their sense of self, both for themselves and those they tell the story to.

I began interviews by exploring personal narratives, asking the participants to share how they and those closest to them would describe them. I clarified that this could be related to personality, core values, or anything they thought was important about themselves. By placing this question at the beginning, I hoped to understand the participant's self-concept without the issues of concealment, deception, or even missionary or vocational identity in their minds. I also asked how they came to live in the GCC, serving in the ways they were. This narrative is a crucial aspect of identity and vocation for missionaries in the gulf, as it frequently involves calling, values, emotional and logistical obstacles to overcome, motivations, and the socialization processes involved in becoming a missionary to a RAN. A person's narrative, while not fully representing any one culture, will likely express cultural values, assumptions, and worldviews that provide meaning and coherence to their story.[15]

Further, since this study focuses on potential duplicity and deception, narrative research is ideal because it allows participants to give the full context and interpretation of themselves and their situation through storytelling. Narrative allows for richer complexity in ethical reasoning that considers how participants view the coherence of their story.[16] Much of the missionary dual identity literature declares that missionaries should never practice deceit.[17] However, this black-and-white declaration may lack the moral and contextual complexity that narrative can bring to the discussion. Narrative inquiry allows participants to express themselves as they understand themselves, rather than conforming their realities and complexities to preformed questionnaires or rigid interview questions.[18] Narrative inquiry and ethnographic methods yield rich results by considering the complete picture of the participants' cultural worldview, embodied experiences, and interpretations of reality.

Interview questions included inquiries regarding vocation, vocational identity, and the relationship of vocation to missionary identity and calling.

15. Saint Arnault and Sinko, "Comparative Ethnographic Narrative Analysis," 2.

16. Riessman, *Narrative Methods*, 188–89.

17. Lai, *Tentmaking*, 37; Roemmele, "Cloak-and-Dagger Tentmakers"; Harris, "Theological Critique of Security."

18. Riessman, *Narrative Methods*, 8.

These were asked to determine whether there was a sense of dissonance or consonance between vocational and missionary role identities, and whether there was a sense of duality or integration between the identities, and to what extent. Extensive questions focused on how the participants managed and presented their identity, either revealing, concealing, or even deceiving among various social fields. I explored their social identity management in various environments and how they felt others perceived them. Practices concerning digital security and identity management were also investigated. I also asked about their ethical and theological reasonings or narratives that helped them think through issues of concealment or deception in their everyday activities. In addition, I explored with participants their experiences of stress and mental health problems arising from identity issues.

I maintained flexibility and responsiveness throughout the interviews, allowing their answers to guide the conversation rather than rigidly asking every question on my list. If they brought up something I hadn't expected but seemed relevant, we would explore that topic. I concluded the interviews by asking the participants whether they had any other thoughts or experiences regarding identity, security, and vocation in the GCC that I had not asked about but they thought was important. I encouraged them to share further thoughts via email or an additional online meeting if they thought of something later. A few participants sent follow-up emails with additional thoughts, and I included these follow-up emails in my data for analysis.

Participant Observation and Field Notes

Immersive participant observation is one of the hallmarks of ethnographic research.[19] Michael Agar describes participant observation as being "directly involved in community life, observing and talking with people as you learn from them their view of reality."[20] Together with interviewing, participant observation is an essential aspect of ethnographic research. The researcher uses these methods to write a "thick description" of a complex situation.[21] Firsthand experience and observation in the setting yield insights through the senses that interviewing alone does not produce.[22]

19. Creswell and Poth, *Qualitative Inquiry*, 90.
20. Agar, *Professional Stranger*, 163.
21. Creswell and Poth, *Qualitative Inquiry*, 94.
22. Wolcott, *Ethnography*, 49.

Over three weeks in 2023, I traveled throughout the GCC to observe tentmaking missionaries in various situations that required identity management. The observations made in the field were combined with my years of immersion experience as a missionary in the GCC. Participant observation through long-term residence "helps the researcher internalize basic beliefs, fears, hopes, and expectations of the people under study."[23] My experiences allowed me a deeper understanding of the issues faced by tentmaking missionaries of identity and concealment and helped me understand which questions to ask. During the fieldwork, I stayed with tentmaking missionaries. I observed them in various social environments: team meetings (formal and informal), in their homes with their children, on visits to homes of local Muslims, one visit with a BMB, in expatriate and house churches, and where appropriate and possible, in their workplace.

On the day I had scheduled a meeting with two field leaders, they were managing an active security crisis as a pastor of a local underground BMB house church had been arrested, interrogated, and was facing deportation. I entered into participant observation in an interesting way. I helped coordinate some of the logistics for these field leaders, supplying contact information and advice from having gone through a similar security crisis myself. Another couple I had planned to interview that weekend had to cancel, as they were some of the few Westerners involved in that house church. Nearly every participant mentioned this security incident to me throughout the three weeks of travel across the GCC, as news travels fast in the missionary community. Contextualizing the data within the participants' lived experiences provided a fuller picture of the meaning and interpretation of the data.[24] Many participants were processing this particular security incident in their interviews as they considered the potential implications for themselves, the wider missionary community, and Arab BMBs.

My role as a participant observer gave a unique angle to the research, as I had to manage my own identity through concealment and careful disclosure. I applied for tourist visas, and I identified myself as a tourist visiting friends in the GCC. I prepared a "short legitimate statement" (SLS) to use with various people should they question my trip to the GCC, especially if the missionaries I was with were not actually my friends. An SLS is a way of telling the truth, but not the whole truth—a strategy missionaries are often taught in pre-field security training. My SLS was that I was a

23. Fetterman, *Ethnography*, 48.

24. Fetterman, *Ethnography*, 25.

doctoral student in intercultural studies, researching American expatriates in the Arabian Gulf. If needed, I had prepared ways of elaborating on this research topic without revealing that my research participants were missionaries, but non-missionaries were satisfied with my answer and did not press further. When conversing with missionaries' Arab contacts, often in Arabic, I had to explain how I knew the missionary, why I had learned Arabic, and why I no longer lived on the Arabian Peninsula. As the fullest answers to all these questions were related to my missionary identity, I carefully disclosed truth but not the full scope of information to protect the participants' missionary identity. Another way I participated in the management of participants' identities was by traveling with my husband throughout the gulf. This allowed me culturally appropriate access to male tentmakers that might not have been possible had I been a woman traveling alone due to cultural gender norms. In these ways, I managed my participants' social identity in their countries of service.

I kept running bullet-point field notes on my mobile phone when it was not distracting to those present in my fieldwork, whether missionaries or others. Later in the day, I filled in details and elaborations in my field notes on a secure computer document and deleted the memos from my phone. Field notes included descriptions of locations and scenes of observation, how missionaries presented themselves physically, and language used in conversations to reveal or conceal identity. I also observed relational dynamics between missionaries and those they interacted with across many social fields. When possible, I asked questions about my observations with the participants in private afterward to verify what I had observed.

DATA ANALYSIS

Following David Fetterman, I began data analysis while gathering data in an iterative process with many layers of analysis. This allowed me to "test hypotheses and perceptions" as data collection progressed to construct a more accurate picture of the missionaries.[25] I transcribed interviews and typed field notes into an organized body of data that I could then code. As interviews progressed and unexpected data emerged, I triangulated emerging themes between participants as a way of detecting what were shared cultural values or beliefs or behaviors and what were personal idiosyncrasies, to test and validate hypotheses formed during data collection.[26]

25. Fetterman, *Ethnography*, 100.

26. Fetterman, *Ethnography*, 101.

I manually coded transcribed interviews using MAXQDA software, using both a deductive and inductive approach. Creswell and Poth acknowledge that one benefit of coding software is the ability to store, manage, and access large amounts of data.[27] Interview transcripts, field notes, and memos were uploaded into MAXQDA and manually coded line-by-line using a color-coding system and highlighting software features. A priori codes were formed from the literature review, the research questions, and my previous experiences as a tentmaking missionary in a GCC country. However, new codes also emerged from the interview data, and I coded these data segments, often using in vivo codes. The software allowed me to link codes across all the imported data to discover patterns. I then organized codes into emerging themes and an organizational schema presented in chapters 5 and 6.

I wrote a description of the data, including details about the setting, observations, events, participants, and other actors, to generate a description of the meaning of behaviors in their context. Clifford Geertz defines *thick description* as the essence and object of ethnography, including structures and their meanings, productions, perceptions, and interpretations as cultural categories.[28] Fetterman explains thick description as "a written record of cultural interpretation," which includes the actors' perspectives through verbatim quotes and a portrayal of the "scene" and episodes.[29] Chapters 5 and 6 present these findings, describing the themes that emerged from data collection to present an overall ethnographic image of how missionaries navigate issues of identity in the context of security in RANs, and the impact of these practices on their self-concept.

In quotes from the interviews, I have sought to maintain the exact wording as much as possible for accuracy and to maintain the voice of participants. However, in some quotations, I edited the transcript for clarity to reduce the obfuscation of the participant's meaning, following the recommendations of Sally Thorne.[30] I removed filler words such as "like" or "you know" when their presence obscured clarity in the interviewee's meaning. My additions or clarifications were added to the transcript in brackets. For example, if a participant described a previous conversation, they might say colloquially, "He was like, 'Where are you from?' And I was

27. Creswell and Poth, *Qualitative Inquiry*, 208.
28. Geertz, *Interpretation of Cultures*, 7.
29. Fetterman, *Ethnography*, 134.
30. Thorne, "Verbatim Quotations."

like, 'Texas.'" I edit such a statement to, "He [asked], 'Where are you from? And I [responded], 'Texas.'" Additionally, when participants stumbled over a word and repeated it, and where they were not repeating for emphasis, I removed the repetitions. I indicated long pauses with the word "pause" in brackets. When the participants spoke in Arabic, I transliterated those words, retained them in the quotes, and included a translation in brackets. Italicized words indicate the participant's emphasis during speech. If participants gave identifying details in their quotations, I indicated a change of those details in brackets in order to maintain participant anonymity. I also included somatic responses in brackets when they were relevant to the context to provide a more accurate sense of the participant's holistic response. I edited participants' quotations only where necessary to emphasize their precise meaning rather than participants' authentic speech patterns.

Chapters 5 and 6 begin with narratives to introduce the data. In chapter 5, I describe the day of one participant using data from her interview and participant observations. This narrative grounds the chapter's data in the field context, giving the reader a deeper understanding of the environment in which the research was conducted. Narratives also convey "emotional truth," which describes authentic experiences, essences, and feeling states that abstract data cannot convey.[31] In chapter 6, I present the story of Randall. Much of Randall's story is based on one participant, but in order to protect his anonymity, the narrative is a composite of multiple participants. Composite narratives are sometimes used to present interview data from several participants as a single, compelling story. Creating composites to present qualitative data requires rigorous practices to ensure accuracy and reliability. I followed Rebecca Willis's process for composing this composite narrative: (1) Basing the composite on transcripts from interviews, (2) deriving all quotations from interview transcripts, (3) taking other details only from source interviews, and (4) avoiding imposing judgment on participants' opinions, motivations, or feelings, only taking such comments from the participants.[32] Using this method, I present Randall's composite narrative as an accurate and complex depiction of the experiences not only of Randall, but of multiple participants with similar experiences.

In order to maintain a high ethical standard and reliability in representing the voices and experiences of participants, I emailed participants the sections of the findings chapters in which I told their stories, used their

31. Willis, "Use of Composite Narratives," 472.

32. Willis, "Use of Composite Narratives," 474–75.

pseudonyms, or quoted them. I asked participants to read these excerpts and notify me of any concerns they had or changes they would like me to make, so that I accurately convey what they shared with me. This also ensured that the final draft of this research meets the participants' standards of confidentiality.

Reflexivity and Researcher Positionality in Data Analysis

Qualitative research assumes that the researcher's positionality shapes and becomes part of the analysis.[33] My experience and positionality as a Caucasian female Evangelical who previously lived in the Arabian Peninsula cannot be entirely separated from this study. These aspects of my identity shape my thinking and how others perceive and respond to me. Wolcott argues that in modern qualitative research, total objectivity is no longer viewed as required or possible; subjectivity should be noted and acknowledged as much as possible so that researchers can "maximize the potential of fieldwork as personal experience rather than to deny it."[34] This is a process called reflexivity. In reflexivity, researchers acknowledge the interpretations, biases, values, and positions they bring to the research.[35] Fetterman argues that because ethnographers themselves are instruments in qualitative research, ethnographers shape the research through assumptions and preconceptions, impacting the research outcomes significantly.[36] These preconceptions and assumptions lay behind the research questions, the study design, and the data interpretation methods.

Following V. Valandra, I engaged in reflexive questioning at every stage of the research process to interact with my preconceptions and biases, recognizing my experiential and sociological setting as a significant factor in the interpretation of data.[37] I approached this study while processing my own experiences of identity and security in the GCC as a CP missionary who still had many close friends and colleagues in that community. As I researched and interviewed participants, I found myself wondering what I would or should have done differently in managing and presenting my own identity—questions to which I find no easy answers. Robert Yin writes, "Researchers cannot in the final analysis avoid their own research lens in

33. Creswell and Poth, *Qualitative Inquiry*, 49.
34. Wolcott, *Ethnography*, 49.
35. Creswell and Poth, *Qualitative Inquiry*, 261.
36. Fetterman, *Ethnography*, 38–39.
37. Valandra, "Reflexivity and Professional Use."

rendering reality. Thus, the goal is to acknowledge that multiple interpretations may exist and to be sure that as much as possible is done to prevent a researcher from inadvertently imposing her or his own (etic) interpretation onto a participant's (emic) interpretation."[38] This study strives to maintain a balance or even tension between the emic and etic aspects by including participants whose organization, experiences, approach to security, and vocation were quite different from my own. This approach included multiple voices, experiences, and interpretations that exposed my internal biases and challenged my assumptions and preconceived ideas.

CONCLUSION

This chapter has described and argued for the qualitative methodology used in this study on the impact of tentmaker identity management practices in RANs. The ethnographic methods and narrative-based inquiry yielded rich data regarding missionary identity on the Arabian Peninsula. The following two chapters present these findings as an ethnographic description in thick detail of missionaries in their context. Chapter 5 describes the ways in which participants manage and present their identities in the context of heightened security. Chapter 6 describes the impact of these practices on participants' self-concept.

38. Yin, *Qualitative Research*, 12.

5

The Practices of Managing a Missionary Identity

INTRODUCTION

THIS STUDY EXPLORES HOW managing multiple identities—especially missionary and vocational identities—impacts tentmakers' self-concept in RANs. This chapter and the following chapter present the findings of this study. This chapter focuses primarily on answering two research questions from chapter 1: How do tentmakers present their identities across various social fields? What concealing practices do tentmakers use to manage their missionary identities in RANs and online?

According to the interviews, tentmakers shift their identity management and presentation strategies to the social field they engage in. Each role partner holds a differing set of meanings and expectations for behavior, to which the participants adapt the presentation of their role identity. In some contexts where security is a concern, the tentmakers conceal the missionary identity and present the vocational identity. In other contexts, the salience of the missionary identity is high, and the tentmakers present that identity openly. Though tentmakers do not conceal the vocational identity in any social field, they often diminish the prominence of vocational identity in certain contexts. This chapter describes the practices of managing multiple role identities, organized by the role partners with whom the tentmakers interact. These role partners act as verifiers or non-verifiers of identity as a tentmaker performs a particular role identity. The story below demonstrates how tentmakers shift their identity presentation across various social contexts.

A DAY WITH CHRISTY

Christy pulls her car up into the dusty parking space of her workplace, Al Hikma Institute of Education.[1] Stepping out into the oppressive heat, she readjusts her long skirt and quickly fishes a pale blue scarf from the backseat. She wraps it loosely around her neck. "Just in case!" she says with a smile, though the odds of needing to cover her hair at the institute are slim. The students are primarily expatriates, and the few locals attending are familiar enough with Westerners not to be shocked by the sight of long female hair.

Christy is a member of Advance, a church-planting organization that has been present on the Arabian Peninsula since the gulf states started forming in the 1970s. Members of Advance founded Al Hikma Institute, a relatively new venture for the organization. One of Advance's senior leaders, Glen, has lived in the gulf for over forty years. Glen had long ago formed a friendship with the local sheikh, the tribal leader for that city. Glen told the sheikh his plans to open an education institute to serve the needs of the local and expatriate communities. Glen had also explained to the sheikh that a group of Christians wanted to create the school. He openly described how they would establish the institute on Christian values, running it in a way that would honor God and bless the community. The sheikh heartily approved, and his blessing proved invaluable to the formation and flourishing of Al Hikma Institute.

Christy, a single mathematics teacher in her thirties, came to work with Glen after she finished two years of Arabic school. She held a master's degree in mathematics and had several years of teaching experience in the US before her arrival. Throughout her education, she sensed God's calling to go to the unreached who have never heard the gospel. Through her internships and student teaching, Christy saw how teaching was a powerful platform for forming deep, trusting relationships that could bear fruit for the gospel.

1. Christy's character is based on a participant from this study. I interviewed her for nearly two hours, and also stayed with her for several days in her home in the GCC. She was kind enough to allow me to follow her into many situations. However, details of her story are conflated with others' stories in order to protect her confidentiality. All the names used in this narrative, including the names of the institute and the organization, are pseudonyms.

We walk together into the institute, relieved as a blast of cold air greets us from the foyer. Inside sits a simple but vacant desk for a receptionist in the center of the room, and bookcases line the walls. On the bookcases are a wide variety of books—many are textbooks, the type you would expect to find in an institute. But others include Bibles in many languages, theological commentaries, Koine Greek grammars, and books on the Christian life in English and Arabic. Christian artwork hangs on the walls, displaying the life of Christ. It is surprising how overtly Christian this reception room is, situated in the heartland of Islam.

Christy leads me upstairs to a small office with a few desks and a printer. Over the next few hours, she works on some tasks for her upcoming courses, prepares lessons, and reconciles payments with the accounting books. The New Zealander secretary in the next room is friendly, but I am unsure whether she is also a missionary or simply an expatriate working part-time in the office. She asks how I know Christy. I smile and comment vaguely that we were friends from way back and that I am visiting her from where I now live in Europe. In truth, I do know Christy from way back—because we had been on a multiagency missionary team together during language school in another GCC country. Since I do not know what level of information this secretary has about missionaries or Christy's identity, I avoid mentioning my time in the GCC. I know that if we follow this line of conversation, the reasons why I lived there and why I left will inevitably come up, and I do not want to navigate those waters with such little information about this woman. I figure Christy can fill her in later with more details if she wants to. I intentionally shift the conversation away from my past with Christy, and toward my current work with refugees and asylum seekers in Europe. Conversation shifting is a skill I honed while living in the Arabian Gulf.

Later that afternoon, when most gulf Arabs are napping in the heat of the day, Christy drives me to her weekly meeting for the Advance team. She pulls her car into Rick's *hosh*, the walled yard around the flat-roofed house. Rick comes out to greet us, waving from a respectful distance in case curious eyes are watching over his *hosh* wall from second-story windows around the neighborhood. His landlord and next-door neighbor, Kareem, pops his head out from a window in his house as Christy and I walk toward Rick's entrance. "Ah! Another *hefla* today?" Kareem shouts to Rick with a playful smile. "No, no party, *ya sheikh*! Just friends for dinner!" Rick laughs back as he ushers us inside. Rick and Beth have the largest home, making it ideal for hosting the team's weekly meetings. Still, the presence of additional vehicles every Monday at four—long before the dinner hour—also causes questions that are getting harder to dodge in their small neighborhood. Rick and Beth are the only expatriates in their neighborhood. They had chosen to live here because of the proximity to locals, rather than living on the expatriate compounds like most other Americans in their city. However, as the only foreigners in a tight cluster of homes, Rick and Beth feel constantly surveilled by their neighbors.

Inside, team leaders Glen and his wife Patricia are already waiting on the couch, along with Rick's wife Beth. Two toddlers cling to Beth's knees. Glen, Rick, and Christy all work for Al Hikma Institute, doing various part-time jobs. Beth, a former teacher, homeschools her and Rick's five children. Glen welcomes us to the meeting, and mentions that their teammate Rhonda will be late. She works for a local law firm, and cannot get away until seven that evening. Rick and Beth shoo their children into the TV room, where a movie and some popcorn await them. The children enjoy their parents' weekly "tea time" with their friends, because it means they get to eat take-out shawarma and watch a movie. They are unaware that this "tea time" is an organizational meeting among missionaries.

In the meeting, the team first slowly works through a New Testament story. They take turns reading in Arabic, translating tricky words, and discussing how they would teach this passage in Arabic to a new believer. Glen and Patricia, with over forty years of Arabic experience, patiently let the rest of the team wrestle through pronunciation and translating. They are particularly patient with me, as my reading skills in Arabic have diminished from my years living outside the gulf. Next, the team discusses both joyous and challenging issues that various team members are experiencing with the BMBs they are discipling. A local underground group, one of the country's very few indigenous churches, has formed in the past few years. However, a few Arab seekers want to join the group to see Christianity among Arabs up close. The BMBs have expressed some anxiety about this idea. While they want to reach Muslims who are seeking Jesus, they also want to feel safe when they gather together. They had been betrayed before by Muslims who feigned curiosity to infiltrate the group. The missionaries discuss how best to shepherd this young group through security issues, fear, and the desire to proclaim the gospel among Muslims. During the meeting, the team also forms a strategy for finding seekers through social media ads and other internet ministries. They assess the risks and benefits of this strategy, and consider how to protect their own identities in that process. We also discuss the team's security experiences, including deportment, imprisonment, and interrogations. I am highly conscious of our phones sitting out in the room; other teams and missionaries often take phones out of the rooms for these kinds of meetings. Though they take precautions, this group seems relaxed about security overall compared to other missionary groups I've observed and participated in.

That changes when Rhonda arrives. She smiles at me when she enters the meeting, recognizing me from when we both lived in another GCC country. The team meeting is finishing, but they are gathering prayer requests when Rhonda enters. She becomes reticent as she raises a prayer concern, lowering her voice and drawing her body smaller. Even though she is only two feet away, I must lean in to hear her say, "We need to pray for our neighboring country." Glen furrows his eyebrows in confusion and asks her directly, "Which neighboring country is *that*?" Rhonda darts her eyes around the room, registering the cell phones on the couches and the coffee table. She is visibly uncomfortable and asks if we can move the phones to another room. The whole group readily complies without a word, offering their phones to Beth, who holds out a basket to collect them. Beth tucks the basket off in another room of the house. With the phones safely out of range, Rhonda clarifies which neighboring country. The pastor of a local underground church has been arrested, and the church is fearful of what may happen next. We pray for that situation, as well as others mentioned. The team meeting ends at eight that evening.

During the meeting, Fatima had texted Christy to ask if she could meet her that evening—there was an emergency, Fatima said. When we arrive at Christy's house at eight thirty, Fatima and her mother, sister, sister-in-law, and younger brother all await Christy. Christy hosts her unexpected guests for dinner—a quickly ordered fried chicken delivery. After two polite hours of exchanging pleasantries and surface-level news, Fatima and Christy huddle together in a corner of the room to discuss a sensitive situation. Fatima is a BMB, as is her father, but her mother and sister-in-law are not. Christy is Fatima's primary source of Christian support and friendship. In addition, as a fellow single woman, Christy is someone Fatima strives to imitate.

By the time the house empties, it's after midnight. Christy's head hurts from the Arabic. Even after five years, it seems like every day brings new vocabulary she has not encountered before. Christy is thankful that the institute demands only part-time hours and that her boss is Glen—her mission team leader, who understands how time-consuming and energy-consuming discipleship relationships with Arabs can be. The institute allows her to have an identity as a math educator in the community—which she enjoys, even if only for part-time hours—without concealing her missionary identity and activities from her employer. But her job also gives her flexibility to do what she believes is her first and primary calling: "For the unreached to be able to have a chance to hear the truth about Jesus."

MANAGING THE MISSIONARY IDENTITY ACROSS SOCIAL FIELDS

According to identity theory, role partners act as verifiers of identity as various role identities are performed in social interactions.[2] Six main role partners that require significant identity management emerged from interviews and observations of participants. These role partners are: (1) the Muslim community, (2) the missionary community, (3) believers from a Muslim background, (4) the expatriate community, (5) the children of tentmakers, and (6) the world back home. Identity management strategies include openness, avoidance of specific social fields, discretionary navigation of information and withholding, misleading, and even lying, which are discussed below. Complications in managing the missionary identity sometimes arise when the social fields overlap, and missionaries must adjust their self-presentation as multiple audiences collapse into one context. A final section explores these collisions of social fields and the complex navigations of identity presentation that occur as a result.

Role Partner 1: The Muslim Community

Muslim Friends/Neighbors/Locals

Among Muslims in their host countries, all participants emphasize that they openly identify themselves as Christians or followers of Jesus.[3] They assert

2. Burke and Stets, *Identity Theory*, 42.

3. Missionaries in the GCC have differing practices on how they identify with their Christian faith. Many choose to distance themselves from institutional Christianity by not using the word "Christian" in Arabic to describe themselves, and instead use the phrase "follower of Jesus." However, many missionaries in the GCC openly use the Arabic word for Christian, and many identify with the public churches, even if there are misunderstandings among Muslims about what a Christian is.

this Christian identity in various ways—praying for people, sharing stories of Jesus in conversations, or publicly identifying with expatriate churches. Their vocational identity is highly salient in Muslim social fields, as their job is usually the reason expatriates relocate to the GCC. All thirty-eight participants report that among Muslims, they intentionally do not identify as missionaries or as Christians sent by churches or organizations to share the gospel. While this is a prominent aspect of their identity, the participants perceive that sharing this identity openly would disrupt relationships through misunderstandings or unnecessary offense, as the Arabic terms for "missionary" and "evangelism" have connotations of coercion in the GCC.

While full-time language students were excluded from this study, participants often identify their time during language school as one of the most stressful concerning their identity in the gulf. Language school typically consists of two years of full-time Arabic study; missionaries rarely hold paying jobs during that time, as language study is intensive. This often made the salience of vocational identity a source of tension in relationships with Muslims. Families especially proved confusing to the local community, and the topic of money often arose in their interactions with locals. This issue of funding during language school was where most participants felt like they came closest to deception, or where they had to engage in concealing behaviors the most. Many confessed to avoiding their neighbors so they would not have to answer financial questions. William, trained primarily in pastoral ministry, describes an uncomfortable conversation with his neighbor during language school. In this conversation, he tried to maneuver around questions that might reveal his missionary intentions, such as finances and even vocational background:

> There was an older gentleman, [and we had] a normal conversation on the road [by] our house. He was very pointed.
>
> [He asked], "So why are you here?"
>
> I [said], "Oh, I'm learning language. You know, it's hard to learn Arabic in [Ohio]."
>
> And he [asked], "Okay, how do you get your money?" Which was also a normal Arab question.
>
> And I [replied], "I get it from family and friends, and we've saved." You know, all true statements, but all deceptive, right?
>
> And then he [asked], "Okay, when do you go back to America?"
>
> And I [responded], "I don't know. I don't know that we will."
>
> He [asked, with a forceful tone], "So what is your profession? What do you do?" He was obviously confused.

> And I [said], "Oh, you know, I'm mostly a teacher." And I told him, "Hey, listen, I gotta get back for dinner. My wife is waiting on me. It was such a pleasure meeting you." I just had to back out, but that was probably the most pointed [conversation] where it was "Where do you get your money? How long are you staying here? What are you trying to do here?"
>
> He didn't believe any of [my answers].

William notes paradoxically both the truth and the deception behind his statements about funding. Truthfully, he was relying on family, friends, and personal savings. However, he also purposefully omitted where most of his funding came from—churches and supporters who made donations through a missionary agency. He intended for this omission to lead his neighbor to a different conclusion from "missionary." His stated vocational identity as "mostly a teacher" also evaded his church connections as a pastor, not fully revealing his vocational identity. However, William was not truly a teacher as his neighbor understood the term; he had never worked at a school or in a typical educational capacity beyond preaching or teaching the Bible. William confessed about his neighbor, "I found myself avoiding him" to prevent getting into a situation where he might need to lie to conceal his missionary identity.

After language school, the priority for missionaries is to secure a residential visa through vocation. Two general options exist for Americans in the GCC, which are only available to some nationalities: starting a business or taking an existing job. Both options provide a role identity in the community, giving the tentmaker a legitimate reason for being in the GCC without being suspected as a missionary. In addition, each option has the potential to provide a platform for living out and proclaiming the gospel to Muslims. Each choice offers benefits and drawbacks, and interviewees often wrestled between the two options. Many had even switched categories at some point in their career, changing the visa type that allowed them to remain in the GCC. The findings describe tentmakers as either "business owners" or "job takers," the two main categories that emerged from interviews.[4] Table 5 below shows the number of participants currently in

4. Some participants considered "business owners" in this study do not actually own the small businesses they work for. Other missionaries may have established the business, and the participant is one of the employees. Such is the case for Christy at the beginning of this chapter. However, for simplicity, I refer to these participants as business owners, since they enjoy the same benefits of establishing a vocational identity in the community and time flexibility as business owners. In addition, their legal visa category

each employment category, or the category they were in when they left the GCC. The table also shows how many participants changed employment categories over the course of their careers.

Table 5: Participants' Employment Categories			
Number of Job Takers	**Number of Business Owners**	**Number of Participants Who Switched Categories**	**Currently Unemployed Participants (All Stay-at-Home Mothers)**
12	22	10	4

For many, the primary reason for choosing the business-owning path is that this option generally provides more time flexibility, which job takers employed by local companies often do not have. Without the oversight of a local manager keeping track of hours worked, business owners perceive that they can invest more time into developing deeper relationships with locals, evangelism, growing in their Arabic skills, discipling believers from a Muslim background (BMBs), and nurturing young church plants. In addition, business owners can often devote more time to fulfilling organizational obligations, including participation in team meetings, administration required for leadership roles, conferences and training, and interagency missionary partnerships.

However, business owners often feel they have a weaker role identity in the community, since locals may not understand their vocation as clearly as they do for job takers such as nurses, teachers, or engineers. Furthermore, only some business owners draw a meaningful salary from their businesses. Therefore, business owners still sometimes face the same questions about finances that they received as language students. None of the participants operate a shell company, where a business is faked and makes no profit, sometimes called "tent faking" in missiological literature. One couple came close to tent faking, working only two to four hours per week; their story is discussed in chapter 6. All business owners interviewed provide actual services to clients and maintain the legal requirements for a business in their country of service. They also work towards generating a sustainable profit to pay business expenses, pay salaries to the missionaries, and hire local employees. However, among participants of this study, most businesses and consultancies still made such small profits that their existence in the country would not make sense financially if their income became known to locals.

---

is identical to that of the business owners.

For business owners, this inability to draw a living wage from their vocation emerged from the interviews as the most frequent aspect of their identity that they need to conceal. Many discovered that it is culturally appropriate and common for Arabs to ask about their yearly salary. Many tentmakers answer indirectly in a way they perceive as equally culturally appropriate: religious deflection. They respond, "God has been generous," or "God has provided everything I need." Others tell half-truths, perhaps referencing another source of income, such as working online as a travel agent or receiving book royalties from a prior publication. These are often actual sources of income for the participants, but rarely are they significant sources of income. Some tentmakers intentionally use misleading statements with locals to deflect questions about their small businesses' financial success and sustainability so that locals will not discover their missionary identities and church funding. In his interview, Blake describes how he intentionally led curious locals to a false conclusion about his income:

> Blake: I made no money from that business. I did run all the logistics, but it was always a word game. And always intentionally leading people to a conclusion. I could walk people to the conclusion that I wanted them to reach with no problem after a while.
>
> A. G. Smith: So you didn't have to outright lie and say that you made a lot of money, but they would assume?
>
> Blake: They would assume.
>
> A. G. Smith: And you'd let them assume?
>
> Blake: I would not correct their false assumptions. So they would [imply], "This is a small-time gig that you have going here." [And I would say], "Yes, but I have another [business] as well." And I intentionally led them to the conclusion that we were being financially supported by these endeavors, when that was not the case. I was never paid. I was about to be paid before we left and had finally grown one of the businesses to a profit. But I was never paid for any of my work.

Blake said he never told any direct lies about the two businesses he owned. Still, he would word things in such a way to lead locals to falsely conclude that his second business was financially supporting his family, rather than churches or supporters. Blake did not directly say that his second business was more financially successful and supported his family, but he implied it so that locals would conclude that the second business was his primary source of income. Misleading without telling direct lies about finances emerged as a frequent strategy for missionaries to avoid revealing their funding through a missionary agency.

In contrast to business owners, job takers report that they rarely lie or evade questions about finances in order to conceal the missionary identity. Nearly all job takers interviewed retain support funds through their missionary agency to supplement a lower income or pay for ministry costs. However, since their income and vocational identity match their lifestyle and their perceived status in the country, they receive fewer questions about money from locals.

In their relationships with Muslim locals, participants sometimes hide or minimize their relationships with other missionaries. Many interviewees identified questions about knowing other missionaries as potential relational minefields with locals, especially if the other missionary lives in another city or country in the GCC. Denying knowledge of a missionary colleague would be lying, and they might be caught out in their lie. However, admitting to knowing them could lead to further questioning about how or why they know them. The truthful answer might be because they are on the same missionary team or organization, or that they met at a missionary conference for GCC missionaries. If Muslim locals discover the missionary identity of one person, this knowledge could compromise the security of those associated with that missionary. When Arab friends ask Steve whether he knows another American who is a missionary, it is never a simple answer. He calculates why they are asking, whether the other missionary has already claimed to know Steve, whether the inquirer knows more than they are letting on, and whether the connection to that person will unveil his missionary identity:

> When people ask if I know other people, "Oh, do you know this other American guy?" Typically, I have to think through it, and it would be helpful if I was a little bit more calm in those situations. But when they ask, "Do you know this guy?" I'm trying to deduce why they want to know if I know him. What has this friend of mine or other [missionary] said to him? Do I want to connect myself to that person? But I found that to be less and less of an issue when we moved to [a city, as opposed to the smaller town where he lived previously], because the assumption [here in the city] is that Americans know all the other Americans. So until I understand what the person's angle is, I may not express the level of my relationship with that [missionary]. I may have known him for years, and he is one of my closest friends, [but] I may not actually

> say that. I may just say, "Yeah, I do know them." Which is not untrue. I just haven't shared the level of my relationship with that person, until I deem it necessary or relevant to the conversation.

By withholding the fuller picture of his association with other missionaries, Steve avoids potential consequences of disclosing too much information. Participants frequently employ the strategy of saying the truth but not the full picture of truth to locals, in order to protect the missionary identity. They explain or reveal minimal information to prevent locals from gaining a clear picture of their relationship to other missionaries, in case secure information has been compromised.

Another frequent situation in which missionaries carefully navigate the disclosure of truth with Muslim locals involves travel for organizational conferences or home ministry assignments (HMAs). Several team members, or even organizational members spread throughout a country, might have several overlapping relationships with locals. When their organization holds conferences in other countries, their local friends may notice that several people are simultaneously going to one specific country for a "holiday." Rosemary recounts that she once took an Arabic class, and most of the students were from one particular mission organization different from Rosemary's. The teacher asked Rosemary, "Are *you* going to Greece next week?" Rosemary laughed and said no, but then the teacher remarked, "Oh, that's strange. I feel like every foreigner I know is going to Greece next week!" Rosemary shared that the teacher was confused and perhaps suspicious.

Another situation requiring careful identity management in Arab social fields is evangelism. Evangelical missionaries in the GCC often do evangelism with friends through story-telling and by making connections between everyday situations and the Bible or teachings of Jesus. Blake describes his identity among Muslims as a "high-profile Christian, low-profile evangelist." In other words, he seeks to make it clear to everyone through his words and lifestyle that he is a committed Christian. However, he takes more calculated risks in evangelism, a practice many participants share since proselytization is illegal, and locals may report them to police. Luke, a teacher who has left the GCC, explains that he navigated the security risks of evangelism by sharing the gospel and stories of Jesus only with close friends with whom he had developed trusting relationships. However, when visiting the owner of the school he taught at for Eid al-Fitr, a Muslim holiday, he never mentioned Jesus or Christianity. He notes the calculation that went into this decision:

> That was not one of the things I was really willing to take a risk on. So with each relationship, there was definitely a conscious, calculated risk because I knew every conversation was going to be risky to a certain degree.

Luke calculated that sharing his faith with his employer put him at greater security risk. As a result, he managed his missionary identity by only displaying his vocational identity in that social context. In addition to friendship evangelism, a few participants regularly engage in street evangelism once a week, though this was not common among participants. Their practice includes visiting the local parks in the evenings, making new contacts, and engaging interested Muslims in conversations about faith. Other than one incident where a Muslim man became aggressive towards the evangelist, the participants describe these evangelistic excursions as generally well received by Muslims, who enjoy discussing religion with foreigners.

Most missionaries in the GCC focus on having a clear *vocational* identity that makes sense to locals and provides at least the appearance of a reasonable income. However, Monica and her husband are shifting their lifestyle to project a more apparent *spiritual* identity in the GCC. After struggling with lingering and debilitating long-term COVID symptoms, Monica's husband found that he could no longer maintain the pace of balancing his full-time job, ministering to local Muslims and BMBs, fulfilling organizational leadership responsibilities, and being a good husband and father. Burnt out from his health struggles and multiple role identities, he and Monica stepped into a sabbatical season with their organization to realign their vocational identities with their ministry goals. They were in the midst of that transition at the time of the interview, considering various vocational possibilities focusing less on income and "making sense financially" to locals and more on "making sense spiritually" to them. During the interview, Monica explained her idea for a spiritual retreat center, a vocational option that would allow them to present an openly spiritual identity to Muslims as people who value prayer and spiritual practices:

> I like this idea of where the Lord is helping me become used to an idea of having a clearer spiritual identity. Because I feel like, in some ways, it really is our passion and who we are. And I'm always looking to live more authentically, like who I am. And I share these [Bible] stories with my friends, and I pray for them. And they know I spend time praying. So if I have something that looks more official in those ways, could that aid in the gospel?

By creating a business centered on Christian meditation, prayer, and other spiritual practices, Monica and her husband hoped to present their vocational identity and Christian identity in a more unified manner. This feels more aligned with their core authentic selves. Rather than avoiding being identified as a religious professional, a frequent practice among GCC missionaries, Monica wants to present this as her primary identity to Muslim locals. When I followed up with Monica several months after her interview, she and her husband had worked with a coach in their organization to come up with a different solution in presenting their identities:

> Even as we seek to have a clearer spiritual identity—pursuing prayer and worship and figuring out how we can communicate that part of our life to local friends—we actually have decided to open a [specific type] business and realized we couldn't have a visa by only having a spiritual identity. The choice of opening a [specific type] business came after coaching with our org[anization] to find a way forward which included our strengths, interests, ways of connecting with people, gifts, and passions.

Her ideas for tying their vocation to their spiritual identity did not work out as they hoped so that they can maintain a visa. However, Monica and her husband will open a type of business that aligns with their aptitudes, personalities, and interests while still communicating their spiritual identity to local friends.

Many of the participants have never been directly asked by locals if they are *mobusher*, the Arabic word for missionary. Some had been asked, and the most common response to this direct question was to answer it with the clarifying questions, "What do you mean by *mobusher?* What does a *mobusher* do?" The Arab would frequently respond with an Islamic understanding of *mobusher*—someone sent by a government to forcefully coerce conversion to fulfill colonialist agendas of their home country and religion. The missionaries could then truthfully say, "No, I'm not *mobusher*." When faced with these questions, many participants would also use the opportunity to describe their Christian identity and activities openly. Several would transparently explain that all Christians should share about Christ out of love for their neighbors, and that they sought to glorify God in everything they did. Even as they denied being *mobusher* according to the Muslim definition, the tentmakers would demonstrate openness with what they believed about being ambassadors of the gospel, using the accusation as a platform for sharing about Jesus. While they continue to conceal their organizational affiliations, they openly affirm a better-defined understanding of Christian ambassadorship and proclamation.

Government

The government in the GCC is another role partner within the broader Muslim community, but missionaries interact with the government in ways that differ from personal contacts and relationships. Participants hold varying perceptions of whether the government is aware of their missionary identity. This impacts their practices of managing their missionary identity. Those who hold to more strict security protocols tend to assume that the government does not know their missionary identity. Many of these participants intentionally moved their mobile phones out of the room during interviews, team meetings, or informal conversations involving missionary activities, especially when discussing BMBs. Blake and Derek had previously been interrogated by the police and were deported from GCC countries for ministry activities. Through their experiences with the government, they are convinced that while the government does know some things about missionary identities, they do not always know who all the missionaries are, or the BMBs with whom they are connected. Derek's approach to security is to do everything possible to avoid giving the government additional information about missionary or BMBs' identities, but not being fearful about what the government does know.

Others entered their country of service assuming the government *did* know their missionary identity. In online or in-person interviews, these participants tended to be looser in their security protocols. Their phones often remained in the room, and they used words such as "missionary" or "evangelism" in our conversations rather than code words. However, these participants emphasize the need for wisdom, still taking some security precautions and not flaunting their missionary identity to cause authorities to lose face. Layla, who matriculated at an evangelical missions-oriented college program for her undergraduate degree, describes how she believes the government knows she is a missionary because they have seen her transcripts, which include several missions-focused courses:

> I'm under no illusion; the government definitely knows why I'm here. If the Lord still wants you to be in the country, he's going to protect you from [being deported]. [All] my undergraduate transcripts have gone through the government, it is all there in black and white. There are two scenarios in my mind. One, they

> really don't care as much as we think they care. Because we went through a lot with our whole process [of gaining employment in one location, and starting a business in another]. [My transcripts] have gone across a lot of desks.
>
> Or [the other scenario is], they know exactly what I'm doing here. And they're waiting until it becomes a problem. "She hasn't been causing problems for anybody that we feel we need to react to. And so when she becomes a problem, then we have all the evidence we need to kick her out." That's where I'm at in my mind. I don't want to let the fear of being kicked out prevent me from doing what the Lord has asked me to do here.

Layla describes how she relies on God's sovereignty to manage anxiety about the government's knowledge about her true purposes in the GCC. She feels that she will remain in the country until God, not the government, decides she should leave. In the meantime, she assumes the government knows she is a missionary, and they either do not care or they are waiting until her presence becomes problematic to locals. Interestingly, participants with higher security protocols and lower security protocols all emphasize God's sovereignty and the importance of not being fearful when it comes to security.

For most participants, much of the anxiety surrounding security lay in the risk of having their missionary identity exposed through technology. In Oman and Saudi Arabia, many missionaries assume that the government can and does listen to private conversations through their mobile phones, even when not in use. During team meetings or other missionary gatherings, missionaries often remove phones from the room where discussions take place to prevent government eavesdropping. Many participants use VPNs when checking email or accessing their organization's websites to protect their missionary identity from being discovered by the government, as well as to protect their private information from being targeted by hackers. Most participants use an encrypted email service. Several participants laughed at the older practice of using certain codes in emails, such as "pr@yer," noting that if a child could crack that code, so could anyone who managed to access the email in the first place. However, they avoid using terms like "evangelism," "discipleship," or "church planting" over the internet or on phones, and use pseudonyms for Muslims, BMBs, or other missionaries they interact with.

Four of the thirty-eight participants had been interrogated about their missionary activities in the GCC. Deportment from the country quickly followed for all four, along with a lifetime ban from reentering the GCC country. Blake and Derek faced pressures in their interrogations to reveal other missionaries and BMBs associated with their ministries. They engaged in various tactics to protect others, including withholding information, giving unhelpful information such as names of missionaries who had already been deported, or even direct lying. Blake, facing threats to his family and years of imprisonment for a charge of forced conversion, eventually named his organization in interrogations in an attempt to appear as transparent as possible. Chapter 6 describes Blake and Derek's stories further.

When police interrogated Jude, he did not feel he had to lie, as he spent much of the interrogation asking the police to define their terms. His approach to the government about his identity was to be transparent about the sharing of his faith as a normal Christian practice, carefully distinguishing that from the coercive practices that Muslims expected:

> I could have easily just said [we did] *tabsheer* [Arabic: evangelism]. That means telling good news. Yeah, we do that, that's evangelism. But instead, I asked [the police officer], "Will you tell me what [*tabsheer*] is?" Because his definition of it was something that we wouldn't have done. I could very easily be truthful and say, "No, we don't do that kind of thing.'
>
> And I even said, "You know, on my way here [to the police station], there was a guy on the side of the road who was trying to get a ride. And I had seen him before, so I picked him up on my way to the police station, and gave him a ride somewhere. And as we're talking, he asked me where I was from, and if I was a Muslim. And I said, 'I'm a believer in God, but a follower of Jesus. And I follow the *Injeel* [Arabic: New Testament, or Gospels].' And so he then said, 'Do they have an *Injeel* in Arabic?' And I said, 'Yes, [there is an *Injeel*] in Arabic.' And so he was asking me for one."
>
> So I could easily say to the guy there at the police station that even on the way over here, I had a guy asking me for *Injeel*. [So I asked the police officer], "Now am I supposed to tell them, 'No, I'm not allowed to give that to you?'" And [the police officer] said, "No, no, don't say that. Don't say that. If he wants one, you can give it to him, no problem." And I said, "Well, what if they run down here afterwards and say, 'See, he's doing *tabsheer*. He gave me this Bible!'" And [the police officer] said, "No, no, I'll ask him, 'Did you ask for that?' And then if he says, 'Yes,' then I'll say, 'Okay, that's all right.'"
>
> Different people [have] different definitions [of *tabsheer*], and this [police officer] was really nice. So I'm sure there would be

> others that wouldn't have been quite as open as that. But in the end, they never really asked me directly anything [about missionary activities]. When I did eventually get kicked out, it was all being done [by] them talking to other people, not really to me directly. But I didn't feel like I really had to falsify anything. You know, I obviously didn't fess up to everything, saying, "Oh, yeah, I'm here with a mission organization, trying to share the gospel with people, helping them come to Jesus."

Jude's strategy in police interrogation was to clarify meanings about what police meant by *tabsheer*, even openly describing an incident where he had given away an Arabic Bible that he kept in his car on the way to the police station. Jude was transparent with police about his Christian witness, and described how he shared his faith without coercion. However, he intentionally withheld potentially harmful information such as organizational ties, and his overarching purpose of "helping [Muslims] come to Jesus." Jude feels he clarified and revealed much more about his role identity and activities than he concealed.

Local Arab Muslims comprise the primary role partner that missionaries are concerned with managing and presenting their identity among, as this is the UPG they feel called to share the gospel with. However, tentmakers carefully navigate the tension of presenting their Christian identity and commitment without disclosing their missionary identity or organizational affiliations. Concealment occurs around funding and organizational ties, travel for organizational meetings, relationships with other missionaries, or protecting BMBs. Tentmakers perceive that Muslims would misinterpret their missionary identity as being subversive agents sent to coerce or forcefully convert Muslims. As a result, participants conceal their missionary identity from local Muslims, even as they openly perform their Christian identity. Tentmakers primarily present the role identity of Christian vocational workers in Muslim social fields.

Role Partner 2: The Missionary Community

The missionary community is another significant role partner that participants interact with, performing their identity differently than with the Muslim community. With the missionary community role partner, the missionary identity rather than vocational identity is salient. Participation in missionary networks and partnerships increases commitment to the missionary identity. For the participants, missionary identity often centers around organizational teams and interagency partnerships. The missionary community, as a subculture in the GCC, forms a system of mutual identity verification for tentmakers. Tentmakers verify one another's identities in ways the Muslim community cannot, as missionaries conceal their missionary identity from the Muslim community.

Teams and organizations in the GCC quickly socialize new missionaries into the accepted security practices of the missionary community to protect the missionary identity from being revealed. When communicating with one another over text messages about missionary activities, many missionaries in Oman and in Saudi Arabia do not trust the end-to-end encryption of WhatsApp. Instead, they use messaging apps advertised as more secure, with servers located outside the GCC. Participants in Bahrain were the least security-conscious participants. During his interview, one participant in Bahrain laughed as he checked his email without a VPN on. Having previously served in more restrictive contexts, he felt a new sense of freedom in Bahrain and said, "I would have *never* done this anywhere else we've lived."

Despite growing interagency partnerships, missionaries in the GCC often have a "don't ask, don't tell" policy with other missionaries about their organization affiliation. The primary reason is for "plausible deniability," should the other missionary be interrogated. Because of this dynamic, I usually did not ask participants to name their mission organization. However, one couple I met in Bahrain kept referring to my mission organization and our mutual contacts through the organization, and they seemed much less security-conscious than previous participants. Since Bahrain also tends to be less restrictive than other GCC nations for missionaries, I asked them which organization they were with while in the privacy of their home. I immediately sensed from their body language that it was an unexpected and uncomfortable question. They never said the organization's name aloud, but instead told me with a smile that they were "friends of [name]," the organization's founder. Even among those with lower security protocols and concerns, missionaries rarely share their organization affiliation openly with one another.

Another reason participants frequently give for concealing organizational ties within the missionary community is that organizations often have differing approaches to security. Those adhering to more strict protocols sometimes avoid missionaries with looser protocols. Missionaries often wait to disclose information to other missionaries until they trust their ability to handle secure information with discretion. Likewise, those with looser security protocols sometimes avoid those with more restrictive protocols. Brooke, a highly evangelistic missionary who often engages Muslims in spiritual conversations in public spaces, says more security-conscious missionaries stress her out with their carefully coded words, even in their homes. She acknowledges that her approach stresses them out as she may take risks they are uncomfortable with. As a result of these differences in approach to security, missionaries sometimes avoid one another. However, it is essential to note the sentiments behind the avoidance. Participants frequently expressed that they avoided other missionaries to honor the other missionaries' security concerns and spiritual convictions, rather than create unnecessary friction.

When they chose not to avoid missionaries with differing security protocols, participants sometimes withheld information about ministry projects, BMBs being discipled, or indigenous house churches from other missionaries to prevent security breaches. Mike and Lydia, who had previously worked in Muslim RANs in Africa, were surprised at the perceived distrust between missionaries in their city when they arrived in their first GCC location. The government in Yemen had deported several of the missionaries living in their city after interrogating missionaries from other organizations and discovering their missionary networks. A sense of betrayal remained with these missionaries after leaving Yemen. Mike remarked that these missionaries carried memories of real dangers from others having too much information, and that these experiences may have bred some distrust and insularity between organizations and missionaries. During Mike and Lydia's time in that GCC city, however, they saw growing partnerships and information sharing across missionary organizations.

In interviews, participants frequently mentioned managing the collective security of the missionary community as a particularly complex subject. The practices required to manage collective security often involve concealment, misdirection, or even deception. As noted above, missionaries manage their collective security by explaining connections to other missionaries to locals, expatriates, or police. The connection would often be from a missionary organization or an interagency partnership, which the missionaries concealed. Some told half-truths or withheld information in order to protect the missionary identities and information about the missionary community. Luke recalls that for weekly team meetings, his mission team rotated whose house was used as the meeting location, because neighbors would ask about the cars parked outside. Luke said that when his neighbors inquired, he would reply that he had hosted a dinner party with friends—a partial truth, he said, but not the whole truth.

Monica, now in the GCC but with experience across several Muslim RANs, recommends a thoughtful and considerate approach for new missionaries entering a RAN, recognizing how individual missionaries identify themselves publicly can impact the entire missionary community:

> We were more conservative at the beginning, because you're trying to understand your new world, and you're trying to engage and read what new context you're in. We've come to this medium ground [after several years in the GCC]. I don't think it's very wise or honoring, and it does bother me when people just overtly don't care and want to make a statement [by openly identifying as missionaries]. Because I'm mindful that I'm in a community of people. So we need to honor and respect the other people who are here, whether they're connected to us or not.

Likewise, Mike and Lydia hold more loosely to certain security protocols themselves for managing their own missionary identities. However, for managing the identities of others in the missionary community, they "follow the law of love, and letting that guide how we do security consciousness, whatever is best for expressing the love of Christ in community with other believers." They describe that this sometimes entails adopting practices they would not normally use to manage their own identities, such as withholding information in certain social contexts or putting phones out of the room for meetings.

The role partner of the missionary community is vital for verifying the missionary's identity. However, as there are many organizations and teams across the Arabian Peninsula with varying security protocols, there is sometimes concealment or secrecy between missionaries until trust has been established. In a context of high security, tentmakers acknowledge the complexity of managing not only their own missionary identities, but also that of the other missionaries in the region. This may lead them to enact concealing practices to manage other missionaries' identities that they may not have normally adopted for managing their own missionary identity.

Role Partner 3: Believers from a Muslim Background

The third role partner with which missionaries manage their missionary identity is the community of believers from a Muslim background (BMBs).

Most of the participants say the BMBs they are associated with are not aware of their missionary identity. The participants reason that they withhold their missionary identity from BMBs primarily to protect the BMBs, should police interrogate them. Instead of presenting a missionary identity to BMBs, participants almost always present their identities as American Christians who moved to the GCC for work. Thus, the tentmakers seek to present a consistent identity to Arab friends both before they come to faith and after. Only one participant had a BMB friend who knows he is a missionary with an organization. The BMB, an Arab not originally from the GCC, only discovered his friend's missionary identity after many years of close friendship, and when the BMB permanently relocated to Europe. At one point, the participant began sending the BMB his family's prayer newsletter, which describes the missionary's evangelistic and church-planting activities in the GCC. The BMB even financially supported the participant through his mission organization when the GCC company he worked for downsized. However, the other BMBs this participant knows do not know his missionary identity or organization.

Amy says that her Christian identity is apparent to her local Arab BMB friends. However, the BMBs are not aware of her ties to an organization, or that she intentionally chose her location to reach Muslim UPGs for Christ. She describes her Arab BMB friends' perceptions of her missionary identity:

> I'm not sure what they would say. I feel like their understanding of a believer is someone who shares their faith, and someone who loves people and loves God and wants other people to know God. And that's something we talk about very early on, sometimes even before [they] are believers. So I think that general understanding of the role [of Christian evangelism] is clear. That's something that all believers do.
>
> I wouldn't say that they would think that I chose this place because of that. I don't know that any of them would know that or would think that. Maybe some of them do and they just don't say it, or they don't [pause]. They don't maybe want to know the answer. But I would say that they have an understanding of what I'm doing [sharing about Jesus]. That's clear to them; that's not hidden to them.

Amy openly discusses with BMBs that all Christians should be sharing about Jesus with others, and she models this in her life. Still, she withholds her organizational ties to conceal her missionary identity from these BMBs. This is the most frequent approach to managing the missionary identity with BMBs among participants.

While tentmakers usually conceal their *missionary* identity from BMBs, several participants openly present their *pastoral* identity to BMBs. Casie, an ordained minister in her denomination, discovered one unexpected challenge when she withheld her pastoral identity from BMBs early on. She and her husband Cory had originally presented their identities as Christian business owners, and they were known in the community as such. However, when discipling new Arab believers, Casie found that BMBs wanted someone with theological credentials and church authority—not an entrepreneur—to disciple and guide them. Cory, her husband, recalls this situation where concealing that part of her identity had been detrimental to her discipleship purposes, the primary reason they came to the GCC:

> [The BMB] started having questions, and she said, "Look, I really need someone who's an authority figure to speak to these [questions], like a pastor or a priest at a church." And finally, Casie was at a point in their relationship where she [said], "I'm just going to tell her I'm an ordained minister," which she is. And it didn't really seem to make a difference to [the BMB].
>
> She [said], "Okay, great, but who works at a church that I can talk to?" And so we ended up connecting her with an Anglican priest. And she talked to him on the phone and [he] kind of answered the questions. But what we saw is, maybe because of the Islamic understanding of what an authority figure is on doctrine, [concealing our pastoral identity] didn't seem like it was helping us to develop mature, fruitful disciples. Even though we do believe that you don't have to be an ordained minister or have theological education to make mature disciples who can establish the church, we found that it was more helpful with people who genuinely want to know, "How can I grow? Can I trust this person to help me do that?" It seemed to be really important. So we're experimenting in this season, trying to figure out what we can say about ourselves or be more open about, that both of us have continuing education in theology.

Cory perceives that because Casie originally concealed her pastoral identity in her relationships with a BMB, suddenly presenting it later on in the relationship had very little impact. As a result, the BMB wanted to speak to someone in an official clerical role rather than to Casie about her spiritual questions. Having since relocated to a new GCC country, Cory explained that he and Casie are experimenting with how they present their identities as ordained ministers with theological education. They are currently exploring how they might present their pastoral identities and theological education credentials in association with the expatriate church.

Leslie, an ordained minister and businesswoman elsewhere in the GCC, has also found that presenting a pastoral identity to BMBs is important for developing trust as she teaches Scripture:

> I don't know that I would call myself a pastor. But it has helped in some instances when we're teaching, or we're doing theology or we're doing [Bible] study. It's helpful, especially for Arabs in this culture, to know there's some authority behind [me]. [There's] some study, there's a degree or certification or something. I think people tend to respect that and trust that. That helps people learn more, I think.

Leslie doesn't feel like a pastor, and resonates more with her business owner identity. However, she has also found that presenting this clerical aspect of her identity among BMBs provides a needed sense of authority when she teaches. While Cory, Casie, and Leslie all articulate that theological education and credentialing are not vital criteria for disciple makers, they also recognize the cultural expectations of authority and trustworthiness that a pastoral identity can fulfill.

Some participants mentioned that other missionaries in the GCC do sometimes disclose their missionary identity to BMBs. However, none of the participants of this study openly relate their missionary identity to BMBs, and the primary reason is to protect the BMBs themselves, rather than the missionary. This creates some internal tension for the tentmakers as they grow closer to BMBs, which will be further discussed in chapter 6.

Role Partner 4: The Expatriate Community

For many missionaries in the GCC, the expatriate identity is a complex role identity to navigate. In the expatriate community, the missionary is usually known by their vocational identity. However, expectations, behaviors, and roles come with the expatriate identity that are distinct from the vocational identity. Arabs frequently hold stereotypes of American expatriates as being wealthy, drinking alcohol in hotel bars, and keeping themselves separate from the local community by living on compounds. Most non-missionary expatriates do not learn Arabic, as the companies that hire them usually function in English. Expatriates may dress how they would in their home countries, though many try to respect the local culture by dressing modestly.

Many participants emphasize that one of the most stressful situations in navigating security is with other expatriates who are not missionaries. Participants agree that managing a missionary identity with expatriates is often more difficult than with locals. Again, finance emerged as a prominent stressor for business owners if their businesses were not yet financially sustainable and successful. Non-missionary expatriates would express surprise that tentmakers chose to live in the GCC without taking a job with a high salary. Those who are consultants or business owners, but have never done consulting or business in the US, are particularly suspicious to other expatriates. Steve, a job taker and missionary field leader with his organization, discusses some of the ways this has impacted missionaries he knows in the GCC, and how it comprises a significant security risk for business owners and consultants:

> People are typically thinking that the area that they will get tripped up is in speaking with locals. But I find that your biggest security risk is engaging other expatriates, Western or Eastern. I think that is where your life, depending on what you do, makes less sense and is so much more easily exposed. Because if you move to [the GCC] for a job, you have a specific skill set. And you've been able to get that job because [of] that specific skill set.
>
> When you are at a restaurant or a sports club, and you bump into a fellow American, and [they ask], "What do you do?" [And you say], "Oh, I run a consulting business." If someone has moved from their home country, they're doing it for financial benefit. So they would have to be looking at you saying, "Can you make more money in [the GCC] running your own business than you could in America? If so, then you must have some special skill; what's your background? Oh, you're a pastor? That doesn't make any sense." Or, "I used to work at a church." That doesn't make any sense to them.

Steve describes how identity presentation among non-missionary expatriates can cause suspicion when the vocational identity does not match the tentmaker's educational and vocational background. For example, presenting a business consultant identity is incongruent with a pastoral work history or theological education. Steve articulates that while most tentmakers preparing for the field think carefully about how they will present their identity to locals, they may not realize that the most challenging social field to navigate with security may actually be other expatriates. Many participants describe similar experiences, perceiving that other expatriates could discern the missionary identity more easily than locals.

Expatriates, living as foreigners apart from their usual support structures, often seek one another out for friendship. However, many participants express that security concerns about their missionary identity and activities sometimes leads them to avoid non-missionary expatriates. For Holly, avoiding other expatriates is necessary because they can sometimes identify her missionary identity, and she does not want to be dishonest with them:

> I tend to avoid those people [expatriates]. Honestly, I tend to not get involved in those communities, just partly for matters of time. And partly because I don't one hundred percent see the point, if I can't be super honest with them. Very early on, and I'm quite embarrassed to admit this. But this was very early, within my first year. There was a situation where I outright lied about whether or not I was a [missionary], because [a Western expatriate] asked me directly, and I had not learned yet how to respond to that appropriately. And there's quite a bit of guilt surrounding that. But I had to learn. I hadn't really learned yet how to deal with that; it was something new.

Holly found that Western expatriates could more easily identify missionaries than locals, and she still feels some remorse years later over a quick lie she told to cover her missionary identity when an expatriate directly asked her. Learning to "respond appropriately" here probably indicates an answer that is a partial truth but not the whole truth—the "short legitimate statement" (SLS) that explains a missionary's presence in the country without disclosing their full agenda. Holly also articulates in her interview that time spent with other expatriates conflicts with time spent with locals. Her full-time employment already takes much time and energy, so she focuses on building intentional relationships with local Muslims rather than with expatriates after work to fulfill her calling to the unreached. She does not want additional friendships where she has to hide, tell partial truths, or lie to protect her missionary identity from being revealed. This leads to a general avoidance of the wider expatriate community, a strategy several participants share.

For Kyle, his avoidance of the expatriate community has less to do with security, and more to do with cultural bonding and learning. He responded to a question about why he avoids most non-missionary expatriates:

> One [reason] is to stay focused in bonding and understanding the [locals]. Especially in your early months in a new country, the more you rely on the expat community for your relationships or your friendships for getting things done, the harder it is to really learn and go deep [with locals]. It's harder to understand the language and culture and build those lasting relationships. So we really focused on [bonding with locals] as much as possible. I want to bond with [locals], and I want to ask [locals] for help when I need help.

Kyle and his family have only been in the gulf just over two years, but their high value of cultural adaptation would likely make them very strange in the expatriate community. His wife and daughters wear the black *abaya* and *shela* to cover their clothing and hair as local Muslim women do, and Kyle sometimes wears the long, white garb worn by the local men. Kyle and his family's non-Western dress may lead other Western expatriates to identify them as missionaries, as their behaviors in the GCC do not conform to expatriate norms. Kyle emphasizes that his family's level of cultural adaptation serves their missional goals. They want to reduce the barriers local Muslims have to the gospel, including language and cultural forms that make Christianity seem like a foreign, Western religion. As a result of these values, Kyle and his family purposefully spend most of their time with locals rather than with expatriates.

Navigating security and concealing a missionary identity among expatriates is complex for both job takers and business owners. Job takers generally meet the expectations of the expatriate community, not raising many questions about why they would move to the GCC. However, job takers often must withhold information or conceal their activities from other expatriates in their social circles or at work when those activities include discipleship of BMBs. For business owners, navigating the expatriate social field is often described as where they came closest to lying, and avoidance was a more frequent tactic. Navigating the expatriate social field is especially complex if the non-missionary expatriates were Christians or part of the expatriate church.

Expatriate Christians and Churches

In the GCC states, being a Christian and expressing a Christian identity through church attendance is legal. In most larger cities of the GCC with high numbers of expatriates, registered churches gather for worship services on Fridays in church buildings or hotel conference rooms.[5] Some tentmakers join these expatriate churches. Others form house churches, usually comprised only of missionaries for higher security maintenance, or a mixture of missionaries and BMBs. Participants noted that house churches, even among Western expatriates, are technically illegal in some GCC states as the government wants to avoid the formation of radical religious cell groups. However, these laws are intended to prevent terrorist cells from forming outside of mosques, and participants said the police had not raided expatriate house churches in years. However, police had raided some Arab BMB house churches and pressured converts to Christianity to return to Islam.

Kyle and his family chose to form a house church with other missionaries for three primary reasons. First, he notes that government officials tend to check in on expatriate churches, who must register their members and have a high degree of video surveillance. Kyle perceives that being associated with expatriate churches may present a higher security risk to the missionary community. He believes that avoiding the expatriate church protects the missionary community. Second, he and his missionary colleagues want to model a popular CPM ecclesial structure, allowing for more rapid replication of Christians and churches across relational networks. This structure emphasizes all members sharing the gospel and a method of Bible study facilitation, rather than teaching by a theologically trained leader from a pulpit. He perceives local BMBs attending expatriate churches may work against these church-planting strategies:

> It is not, overall, helpful or strategic to encourage new local BMBs to attend expatriate churches. In doing so, the local BMB is quickly extracted and cut off from their natural socioreligious community and family as they are integrated into a foreign religious community, which is typically far removed from their deep emotional, social, and spiritual needs. They are also more likely to experience unnecessary persecution and ostracization from their natural community because of their decision to join a foreign religious group, effectively cutting off any impactful witness they may have among their people. Instead, we encourage new local BMBs to remain in their existing families and communities and begin small

5. The one exception to this is in Saudi Arabia, where Islam is the only religion that may be practiced, according to the law. There are only a few legal churches on expatriate compounds throughout the country. These are sometimes called "morale groups" rather than churches, and they are not available in all major cities in Saudi Arabia.

> Jesus-centered fellowships and/or discovery groups with their existing relationships in their homes or other gathering places.

Third, Kyle perceives that expatriate churches would not be safe places for local seekers or BMBs to attend, as video surveillance on these religious compounds is very high. His private house church provides a safer environment for Muslims and BMBs to explore the Christian faith than a public expatriate church. For these reasons, Kyle and his missionary colleagues believe a house church is the best way to manage security for their particular goals in their context.

Several participants who formed a house church comprised exclusively of missionaries experience it as a refreshing time where they can finally be themselves. Steve says he and his wife currently attend house church only with other church planters because of the openness they can experience there. They can share prayer requests more vulnerably, pray together for certain relationships or situations related to their missionary vocations, and share information or discuss complexities pertaining to church planting. He feels he could not safely do this at an expatriate church. Steve remarks that among his Arab friends, other expatriates, and his colleagues, he is not fully known as so many aspects of his life must be concealed to protect his missionary identity. Even when he visits churches or friends back in the States, he is not fully known or understood as supporters often find his dual missionary and vocational role identities confusing. But in his house church with other missionaries, he can remove his masks and be his authentic self. Several participants who chose to do house church only with missionaries mentioned that this was one of the few social fields where they did not have to wear masks. Missionaries, surrounded by other missionaries, could worship and pray openly as themselves without having to meet the expectations of multiple role identities. In a context of high security where missionaries conceal or diminish important aspects of their role identity, house church with other missionaries is experienced as a safe space where they can be themselves and have their identities verified in ways that they cannot with other role partners on the field.

In contrast, many participants feel that identifying with a public Christian church is essential for their Christian witness to Muslims. They noted that it would be strange for them to say they are Christian while avoiding the public churches. Navigating the expatriate church is complicated for these tentmakers who conceal their missionary identity from other expatriates. Concealing the missionary identity from other expatriate Christians can be inordinately stressful and sometimes leads to profound misunderstanding. Chapter 6 discusses the disparity between how members of expatriate churches perceive tentmakers and how they see themselves.

Non-missionary expatriate Christians are rarely trained to handle sensitive or secure information, making them a potential security risk among missionaries. Elyse and other missionary women had revealed their role identities as missionaries to a non-missionary Christian expatriate couple. Elyse recalls the missionary community's regret in disclosing secure information to the couple, as the wife handled information carelessly, putting many missionaries and BMBs at great risk several times. Eventually, after much painful deliberation and debate, the missionary community decided to ostracize the couple from their friend group, cutting off their access to compromising information. Elyse remarks that this experience has influenced her practice of withholding secure information from non-missionary expatriate Christians until she is confident they can handle secure information appropriately. Elyse, along with several other participants, also expresses that the decision whether to disclose information about her missionary identity is not always hers alone to make. Often, these decisions are made with the consensus of the local missionary community, as one person's disclosure may impact the wider missionary community.

Christian expatriates can sometimes guess who the missionaries are, as missionaries typically speak Arabic and often have more friendships with locals than other expatriates have. Paul says it makes him anxious when someone in his expatriate church directly asks, "Are you a missionary? What organization are you with?" He says he uses discretion, telling certain people but not others. Often, he tells people, "It's probably better that you don't know, because then if somebody asks you, you can say you don't know. So plausible deniability." Paul conceals his missionary identity from most Christian expatriates. However, it is not a firm rule for him as he does disclose his missionary identity to certain people he trusts. In telling expatriates they would be better off not knowing, Paul avoids telling a direct lie and providing more information than he is comfortable with. Yet, he and his wife are always eager to be resources to others who have relationship with locals, and to provide training which uses their expertise in the international church, even if it somewhat exposes them.

Christy also faced uncomfortable questions from a woman in her expatriate church when she returned to the US for three months of HMA (home ministry assignment) to meet with her supporting churches. The woman kept asking questions about how Christy's job let her take so much time off. She wondered aloud how Christy could afford to take such a long vacation. Christy reports that she thought, "Oh, my gosh, please don't ask these questions! It's not a vacation, but how do I explain this to someone without telling them more than I want to tell them?" Since her missionary identity is concealed from the expatriates in her church, Christy struggles to give a truthful answer that does not provide information about her missionary identity.

However, not all missionaries in the GCC conceal their missionary identity from their expatriate churches. When they first arrived on the field, Henry and Olivia's expatriate church knew of their missionary identities. At that time, a mixture of missionaries and Christian expatriates comprised the church. However, as expatriate churches often have high turnover rates, Henry and Olivia are now the only missionaries in their congregation. While they feel emotionally closer and more open with the missionary-only groups, they enjoy the diversity of the expatriate group. They do not often discuss their missionary identity with their non-missionary expatriate church friends. However, because church members know Henry and Olivia are missionaries, the expatriates often go to them with questions about how to share their faith and understand the local culture. Henry and Olivia can share with their expatriate church ways to be more intentional and bold about their faith as expatriate guest workers. They also share resources from their missionary training. However, Henry and Olivia withhold information about BMBs from their expatriate church, perceiving this as too great a risk for the BMBs. When the non-missionary expatriates ask them questions about BMBs, Henry and Olivia evade the questions with vague answers and redirect the conversation.

Tentmakers in the GCC repeatedly confirm that managing the missionary identity among other expatriates is a stressful and significant security situation. Missionaries sometimes entirely avoid close relationships within the expatriate community, choosing instead to form house churches rather than identify with public expatriate churches. Others feel that avoiding the expatriate church is a poor witness to their faith, or denies the opportunity to strengthen non-missionary expatriate Christians as witnesses for Christ. These tentmakers carefully navigate the disclosure of secure information to these expatriate Christians in various ways.

Role Partner 5: Children of Tentmakers

In interviews, missionary children emerged as significant role partners with which tentmakers had to manage their missionary identity for the sake of security. Many participants who are parents express the tension between raising their children to value mission and yet concealing their own missionary identity from their children. Most participants with older children report that when their children were small, the *m* word (missionary) was not even in their children's vocabulary. Participants were concerned their children might use this word in the wrong context. Several participants confirm it is standard missionary practice in the GCC not to use *m* words in the household around small children.[6] During a casual conversation with a tentmaker couple in their home in the GCC, I forgot this rule as we discussed how organizations might better prepare tentmakers for ministry in the GCC. I let the word "missionary" slip, and I immediately felt the weight of the word falling in the room. The mother and father's eyes darted over to their six-year-old daughter, skipping rope on the other side of the room. They waited in silence a moment to see whether the girl registered this word being spoken by the adults, but they relaxed when they realized she had not been listening to the adults' conversation. She attends an international school with many local classmates and is an extroverted, talkative child prone to repeating everything she hears. Her parents perceive that having "missionary" in her vocabulary is a security risk.

However, parents who participated in the study described how they teach and model a missional lifestyle to their children, which includes telling others about Jesus, especially those who do not have much access to the gospel. They often pray with their children for the salvation of local Muslim neighbors and friends. Two mothers say that instead of "missionary," they use terms with their children from the Bible that apply to all believers, such as "ambassador" or "witness." As children grew, they often discovered their parents' missionary identity during events that affirmed it—such as speaking in a church during HMA or attending an organizational conference. Participants note two primary reasons for concealing their missionary identity from their children: they did not want their children to be afraid, and they also did not want their children to tell others in the gulf that their parents were missionaries.

6. *M* words include "missionary," "mission," and associated words such as "evangelism" or organizational names.

Monica compares talking to her kids about being a missionary to conversations about sexual activity: as their understanding and maturity grow, so does their ability to handle a greater scope of truth. But too much information before they are ready can be harmful to them, creating fear or a burden to keep secrets that a young child does not need. Her children have grown up praying for their friends to know Jesus, watching the example of their parents sharing their faith as a normal part of life, and understanding that all believers live as ambassadors of Christ wherever they are. However, while their family exudes the missionary heart, the children do not specifically connect the word "missionary" to their family. Monica describes her approach to communicating the truth, without harming her children with too much information:

> I want to, in general, communicate with my kids [by] always giving them a truthful answer. But not maybe [everything], but what they're ready to handle. So if it's about sex, if it's about religions, if it's about, "Is my friend going to hell?" [I think], "What kind of answer can I give that's *truthful*, but then as they get older, they get the fuller answer?"

Monica's approach with her children is always to give truthful answers, but only what the children can handle at their stage of maturity, which involves withholding information. In her interview, she elaborates on how she pays attention to how her children might talk with other people about the information. Her children are still young and do not know their parents' missionary identity, but Monica plans to give them increasing access to that sensitive information as they grow—just as she does with other sensitive subjects.

Certain aspects of the missionary identity, such as fundraising and speaking in home churches about the work, prove challenging for keeping the word "missionary" out of children's vocabulary. Mike and Lydia's five-year-old son Titus discovered his parents' missionary identity on HMA, since they traveled to many churches to tell their stories and raise support. Titus became accustomed to the missionary identity as many church members talked to them and prayed with them about this part of their life. When they returned to the GCC, the couple had to act quickly to train Titus to affirm Mike's vocational identity and stop referring to their family as missionaries. Lydia tells this story about "brainwashing" her son to switch his vocabulary regarding his parents' identities:

> So we put him in local school, and the very first week of school it was Career Day. And so [the teachers] were asking the kids, "What do your parents do?" And so I asked Titus, "What do we do?" And he [said], "Well, you're a missionary." And I [said], "Noooo, Papa is a business owner." And so I basically brainwashed him. I got a cup of M&Ms, and I would say, "What is Papa's job?" And when he would say, "Papa is a business owner," I'd give him an M&M. "And so what is Papa's job?" "A business owner" [motions that she gave him an M&M]. "What does he do?" "He goes to work" [motions that she gave him an M&M]. And so I'm just feeding him M&Ms. So we did this for like, three hours of brainwashing.
>
> And then a week later, I was just in the kitchen, we were hanging out and I just got a wild hair. And I said, "Okay, Papa is a business owner," and he said, "Yes." And I said, "What does Mama do?" He said, "Oh, you're a missionary." And so then I was like, "Okay [stressed tone]." So then I got out the M&Ms again. "Mom is a stay-at-home mom" [motions that she gave him an M&M]. Honestly [laughs]. So we had to kind of brainwash him a little bit. But then it was a surprise again [that they were missionaries], when we got back to the States [a few years later].

While Mike and Lydia did not conceal their missionary identity from their son, they did manage the vocabulary he used through an unusual retraining exercise. Otherwise, Titus would immediately reveal his parents' missionary identities to his teacher and classmates. Among participants, it was highly unusual for children as young as Titus to know their parents are missionaries. For many participants, managing their missionary identity in front of their children became more complex when they performed their missionary identity in social fields where they were expected to identify as missionaries. Several parents said they tried to avoid these situations by leaving young children with a babysitter or nursery worker while they spoke at churches on HMA about their missionary activities.

Before Blake and his family moved to the GCC, other missionaries warned him not to tell his young children—ages five and three—the name of the country for the sake of security. Other missionaries had found that curious church members would sometimes question small children to discover the ministry location that the missionaries had intentionally obscured in their church presentations. In light of this advice from seasoned missionaries, Blake and his wife told their children they were simply moving to "the desert." Their children only discovered the name of their country of residence after living there for some time. Until then, they used "the desert" or the city name to talk about where they lived, but their children were small enough that they did not notice.

As children enter their teen years, however, missionaries cannot as easily conceal the missionary identity and must begin giving them more information. Silas and Tansy's teenage daughter, who had grown up in the GCC, called her parents liars after hearing them speak in an American church on HMA. She thought her parents had been lying to the congregation about being missionaries in the gulf. Her parents laughed incredulously as they realized their daughter was unaware that they were missionaries by this point. Their family was constantly sharing stories of Jesus and even discipling BMBs in their home, and had been for years. The parents had raised their children to share their faith boldly and to pray for others to know Jesus, deeply embedding missional values into their family culture. They had just never applied the word "missionary" to those activities. The daughter just thought of her father as working a job overseas, just as the fathers of her friends at schools were. She did not know there were organizational ties, or that visits from certain other expatriates were actually team meetings. Tansy noted, "It occurred to us that we had not been good about connecting all the dots for our kids so that they could reach this conclusion." Tansy and Silas then had many intentional conversations with their teenagers to help them understand this newly revealed identity.

As children get older, or when a security crisis forces them out of the country, missionaries must navigate disclosing their missionary identity to their children. Participants report that these revelations often came as a shock for their children, and they began a process of reinterpreting their history—were *these* friends also missionaries? Were *those* Arabs actually an underground church rather than adults just gathering for coffee? Was that TCK (third culture kid) camp actually a missionary organization conference? Some children accused their missionary parents of being deceptive to them their whole lives, and felt a sense of betrayal. Some children of missionaries struggled with fear or nightmares, worrying about the dangers if police discovered their parents' missionary activities. Some teens bore a new burden of keeping a secret, worried they might say the wrong thing to the wrong person and endanger the whole family.

Talise's children had been born and raised in the GCC. When Talise's family transitioned to a second GCC country, her kids were in their teenage years and had only recently become aware of their parents' missionary identity. Talise and her husband adopted a more open approach to presenting their missionary identity to their children, but with caution and care, not disclosing everything:

> We were very upfront with them coming to [second GCC country]. "Look, you guys know that we're with an organization. You know we're going for intentional purposes. We have this [missionary] role." We try to be careful about how much information they have, and try not to have them sit in on conversations like this [about missionaries and security]. Because they don't need to bear all of that. But telling them a little bit about some of the things that we're doing so that they can, in a sense, feel like there's value to us being here. But we told them ahead of time, "You can't say that we're [missionaries] when we go to [GCC country], you can't tell your friends at school that, you can't tell people at church that. There are safe people, and *these* are the safe people that you can talk to, but the people beyond that, you can't say that." So it is a burden.

Talise and her husband gave their children clear parameters on what they could and could not say, and who they could and could not talk to about their missionary identity. They identified safe adults for their children to talk to, if they needed to talk about anything related to the missionary identity to someone other than their parents. Talise notes that as the children matured, the "burden" of the missionary identity and keeping secure information safe grew. As a result, she and her husband continue to withhold secure information from them to minimize the number of things their children need to avoid talking about. In her interview, she described some of the "anxieties and weights they're carrying," including a recurring nightmare one of her children has of her parents being taken away by police.

Tentmakers in the GCC often conceal their missionary identity from their children for security until they are mature enough to handle the information. This is done to protect the security of the missionary community and BMBs, as well as to protect children from bearing burdens they are too young to handle. Tentmaker parents often enact their missionary identity with great care around their children to keep missionary vocabulary out of the family's usage. They often reframe team meetings, organizational conferences, and church speaking engagements in ways that conceal the missionary identity from their children until they are older.

Role Partner 6: The World Back Home

Home ministry assignment (HMA) is often necessary for many missionaries and sometimes required by missionary organizations. On HMA, missionaries return to their passport countries where they present ministry updates to supporting churches, meet with individual supporters to report on ministry work, raise additional funds, engage in professional development such as church-planting training, visit their organizational base, and perhaps take a vacation or sabbatical. In the GCC, most missionaries take HMA in the summer months, as many GCC companies provide expatriate guest workers with airline tickets to their passport countries as a benefit of employment. Therefore, American missionaries in the GCC can usually take a short HMA—usually four to twelve weeks—without appearing suspicious to locals and non-missionary expatriates.

HMA strengthens the missionary identity, which becomes the salient identity performed by fulfilling role expectations on HMA. Many participants express that their anxiety about security is highest on HMA, because the internet poses a threat to their missionary identity being revealed. All the participants say they refuse to speak at a church if the service is being live-streamed, and they have protocols in place to ensure they are not recorded. This has been increasingly difficult following the COVID-19 pandemic, as many churches adapted to live-streaming and continue the practice. Paul says that even though one church agreed not to record his presentation, he still caught someone taking a video of him with a phone. He says, "Our greatest anxiety is in the US and what someone will do in the US, [rather] than here [in the GCC]." Missionaries are concerned that recordings of their ministry presentations may end up on the internet, where their Muslim friends or colleagues might encounter them, exposing their missionary identity.

Many participants say that they are particularly guarded while making presentations to churches in the US, as they are uncertain who is in the audience or how they will handle secure information. As a result, many participants intentionally withhold their location, names of Arab contacts, and companies they work for. One participant had a teammate who gave a presentation in their small rural US church, where he was open about his professional identity, country name, and organization's name. He discovered later that a journalist had been present that day who was fascinated by the idea of undercover missionaries in RANs. The journalist wrote an online article about missionaries in the missionary's country of service, which a GCC newspaper in that country then published online. Speaking openly in church had compromised the security of the missionary who made the presentation, and all those in the missionary community connected to him. Multiple participants across several organizations mentioned this incident in their interviews, showing the widespread impact of such an incident on the entire missionary community.

Churches that support missionaries in RANs sometimes perceive missionaries as super-spiritual heroes who risk their lives every day, a stereotype a few participants mentioned as an uncomfortable and false perception of their identity. William says he becomes guarded when presenting his missionary identity to churches because some tend to make their missionaries into "trophies." He expressed embarrassment to even talk about it, saying it was crass to talk this way. But his experience was that the more he emphasized to churches the need to keep his family's information safe, the more people would treat them as "trophies" to be shown off and displayed with pride. The churches were proud to have missionaries in "dangerous" places. William does not like this interpretation of his missionary identity, and it sometimes causes him to diminish his missionary identity even when he is expected to perform it.

Several participants noted the struggle to balance giving churches enough information to be motivated to pray and support their ministry, while withholding enough information to keep their missionary identity safe. Holly describes this tension of sharing and keeping secure information safe, and her practices have shifted over the years with greater experience:

> It's always a bit of a tension. Because the more you can share, the more you'll connect. So there's always that tension. I tend to [pause], it very much depends on the size of the group, and if I know the people present. Less specific information gets shared in larger audiences, for sure. But that's always a tension, I would say, the longer I'm on the field. And probably within the last couple of years, the more I'm navigating to be more open and more free, and seeing that as a better trade-off than being highly secretive.

Holly shares that she is working to reduce the concealing practices with churches around her ministry information, that being "open" and "free" is more desirable than being secretive. However, she still experiences tension in navigating disclosure with groups. Along with Holly, several other participants say that at the beginning of their missionary career, they had adopted stricter security protocols with home churches, limiting how much information they disclosed. Many relaxed some of these policies the longer they were on the field and understood the context better, while maintaining some security practices such as avoiding online streaming of church presentations.

Missionaries presenting the vocational identity in the GCC sometimes baffle those in the world back home. While back in the US, some participants find they have to defend their vocation as part of the "real work" of ministry, primarily to their supporting churches. Layla had to speak with several supporters who did not understand why she wanted to start a business in her host country when she was there to share the gospel with Muslims and disciple BMBs. Layla said that as she talked with them, she realized that her supporters were not against her working a "secular" job, as she had initially thought. Instead, they lacked the understanding that she needed to gain a visa to stay in the country. Her supporters had grown up with missionaries going overseas on missionary visas; tentmaking was a novel model for them.

Cory, a business owner in the GCC, describes the tensions of his experiences of managing his vocational and missionary identity to supporting churches. Cory chooses not to draw a salary from his business so he can afford to employ local Arabs in his office. This has led to many opportunities to share his faith with local employees. As a result, his family maintains full financial support from churches and individual supporters to further facilitate this ministry alongside his business. However, Cory finds he must diminish his vocational identity to supporters similarly to how he diminishes his ministry identity in the GCC:

> Overseas, we feel like there is motive to conceal or to leave out parts of our story for the benefit of the people we're with, as it pertains to ministry identity. Whereas when we're back in the States, it's kind of the opposite, where there's motive to be very clear, upfront, [and] direct about our ministry identity. But there is some motive, and even some tension around how clear we are about our business and professional identity [in the US]. So much so that one pastor I spoke with was really concerned that they were funding people at all to do work that involved a profit-making business, because they thought, "Well, shouldn't you be paying your own salary, because you're doing this work?"
>
> And so there was this triple tension of, we're doing the [ministry] work we're there to do, with legitimate legal identity, we're trying not to pay ourselves salaries so that we can actually hire more

> local people, even though I have the right to one as an investor. And then at the same time, I need to justify to this person who's supporting the living income that we have, why that's a helpful way for us to go about doing things. And so it was tricky switching our environments, and where we felt like we had to speak more directly to how much of an identity we have either on the business side or on the ministry [side].

Cory's experiences of managing his identity, both in the US and in the GCC, involve diminishing one identity and putting another forward. He finds that some churches are suspicious of funding missionaries who work in profit-yielding businesses, as it seems they should be self-supporting if they make a profit. So Cory intensifies his missionary identity to emphasize the missional purposes behind his vocation, and finds tremendous tension in that. As a result, he sometimes feels the need to minimize his vocational identity in the US to supporting churches.

A few participants also noted that they had to carefully manage their missionary identities with their family or friends back in the US, particularly when those people were not believers themselves. Three participants had family ties to the CIA, so they tried to keep information about their missionary activity diverted from those family members. Another participant said she actively conceals information from her mother, because she is too "excitable" and not trustworthy with sensitive information. She knows her mother would tell people any details she has access to. Mike said that his family relationships are sometimes strained because of the perceived shame of their fundraising as a missionary family:

> The reputation in their eyes of what someone is who's a [missionary] is a hard burden for some of them to bear. To some of them, that means we go around with a hat in our hands begging people for money, even though that's not how we see the work of fundraising. We see [it] of course as partnership development, people we have the privilege of inviting into a shared common vision. That's super exciting. But it's not the same perspective that probably most of our family has, in terms of that aspect of our ministry identity when we're back in America.

Mike's missionary identity is perceived as a source of embarrassment to some in his family because his vocation does not provide his family's income, which causes him to manage the presentation of his identity with his family carefully. In his interview, Mike also discusses how as he presents his identity to various audiences, he must "flip-flop" between them and wear a different "hat"—either his vocational identity or his missionary identity—depending on the audience. He says he must think carefully how each audience will perceive what he communicates about his identity. He concludes, "We do long for more stability, in terms of being able to live out an integrated identity, without having to shift our emphasis depending on which audience we're interacting with."

Digital Communication with the World Back Home

Missionaries not only manage the missionary identity in their home country while *in* their home country, of course. Missionaries use digital platforms such as secure email, text messaging, and video calls to communicate with people back home. Most participants have social media accounts, but many also said they never use them. Several participants rely on their spouses, who do use social media, to keep in touch with people back home. Only a few participants actively engage online on social media with their friends back home. Most participants say they avoid social media due more to a lack of interest, rather than for security reasons. However, several participants name Facebook as a particular security concern. Their supporters—usually in older generations—who are most likely to post something that compromises missionary security often use Facebook over other social media platforms. One participant's wife joked about security breaches on social media, "It's always grandmas, and it's always Facebook." This joke was confirmed as valid in interviews, as many participants shared stories of their grandmothers posting how proud they were of their missionary grandchildren on Facebook.

Some participants change their name on social media to make it more difficult for local Muslims to find them online. Those who did this intended to reduce the amount of contact their home world has with their field world, in case someone from home posts compromising information about the missionaries. Some participants hold two separate social media accounts—one for friends back home, and one for connecting with locals. Some participants lament that their communication with many supporters or family members probably was less than it should be. This was often because supporters feared breaking the security protocols the missionary had given them. In addition, the secure phone apps missionaries most frequently use for communication in the GCC are not often used by people back in the US, making communication less secure than the missionaries are comfortable with.

Nearly all participants express concern over how their sending churches manage the missionaries' identities online. Many churches typically post their missionaries' photos, names, locations, prayer requests, and ministry details on the church's website and perhaps on a physical bulletin board in the church building. All participants require their churches not to post any of their details on the internet, and many tentmakers also frequently conduct searches online to ensure their churches adhere to their security protocols. Several participants mentioned that their church displays some of their information on a physical bulletin board in the church building. However, the information presented on bulletin boards about GCC missionaries is often much less than what the church shares about missionaries in non-RANs that the church supports.

Nathan and Brooke met on the field in the GCC and married a few years later. An interesting issue they face is that they have had to merge two radically different approaches to security, especially their disclosure of information to supporting churches. Nathan, a qualified professional in his field and a business trainer, has kept an up-to-date public LinkedIn profile that includes his professional credentials and location. Brooke, who did highly evangelistic ministry before their marriage, has never told her supporters or even several family members which country she lives in. As a married couple, presenting their missionary identity and managing security among their different home churches and family members can strain them. Brooke describes the tensions between them as a couple when they make church presentations, as they have different approaches to sharing information:

> We have big fights when we get back from church [Nathan and Brooke both laugh; she is overstating the tension experienced]. I think we just realized we're very different people and we approach it differently. And that's okay, as long as we can find a kind of comfortable normal, where I'm trusting the Lord when he does things that I probably wouldn't feel comfortable doing. And I'm like, okay, my way isn't the *right way*.

These digital security concerns make communication with the world back home a complex landscape to navigate as they manage who has access to certain information.

In email newsletters to the world back home, the participants often withhold information from their supporters, such as specific locations and names. They also ask recipients not to forward, print, or post their newsletters publicly. All participants use pseudonyms to communicate prayer needs about Muslim friends or BMBs. One couple even changes their own names in their email newsletters to friends and supporters so that their missionary work might not be associated with their real names and organization. Participants almost always use virtual private networks (VPNs) when checking their secure email accounts where supporters and churches might interact with them. Several participants had been told at some point that using a VPN made them look suspicious to the local government as people with something to hide, but they disagreed. Their local friends all use VPNs to access better movies on streaming sites; VPN usage is now a normal practice for many people. Furthermore, in an age of hackers and threatened web privacy, several participants say they would use VPNs even if they weren't missionaries in order to keep banking information safe.

As missionaries interact with the world back home in person and across digital communications, they frequently experience tension between sharing information to connect with people, and withholding or concealing information to protect security. While HMA allows them to present and verify the missionary identity, missionaries also experience challenges in verifying their missionary identity when supporters or family misinterpret them, either positively or negatively. Digital platforms for communication are a primary concern for missionaries, as the missionary identity is vulnerable to exposure on the internet.

The Collision of Social Fields

Potential complications in managing the missionary identity arise because of the flattened nature of the modern digitized world. Most participants are known almost exclusively as missionaries in their home context, but are known instead by their vocational identity in their country of service. A threat to the security of their missionary identity materializes when those worlds unexpectedly overlap. Jude describes how his missionary and vocational identities intersected suddenly years ago because of an international ministry in his hometown. He met and befriended Abdul, an Arab student from the GCC studying in the US, through an outreach to internationals at his home church while on HMA. When Jude returned to the GCC, Abdul contacted Jude's mother and asked if he could continue to attend church with her. At church, Jude's mother realized that Jude's name was in the church bulletin under the heading "Pray for Our Missionaries," which Abdul saw. When Abdul graduated from university, he returned to his home country in the GCC. Despite being aware of Jude's missionary identity, Abdul later sponsored Jude's new business venture when his family transitioned to live in Abdul's home country. Jude never discussed this incident with Abdul and did not know what Abdul's perceptions of a missionary were. Still, it was an alarming collision of his two worlds, which normally remained separate.

Steve is also concerned about his separate social fields colliding because of the globalized nature of the GCC company that employs him. The company he works for has international offices in many countries, including the city where his sending church is located. When he is with his sending church, he primarily presents his missionary identity, describing his ministry activities in the GCC among unreached Muslims. He withholds his company name from most church supporters because of this concern, uncertain of how he would handle the collision of his vocational world and his ministry world:

> Who's to say that somebody from our office in [US city] doesn't go to my sending church? I don't know, maybe they do. Maybe they don't. But you know, it's not something that I'm [pause], it's not a bridge that I'm wanting to cross if I don't have to. So if I bumped into someone and they figure out I work for the same company, and we're on home assignment, and I'm at my local church, that might be a little bit confusing. And I'm not actually sure how I would navigate that.

One couple also carefully withholds where they live from their churches and supporters at all times, as they live in Dubai. They know that many people at their church often travel to Dubai for business, and they worry about how their home world and field world might collide, compromising their security. The husband describes how they strive to keep their identities in their home and field worlds separate, a challenge they have not entirely been able to overcome:

> So in the US, we take on fully the identity of [missionary], and we lose the detail of where we are [in Dubai]. Whereas, when we get on the plane and fly here, we lose the [missionary label] and take on that we're here doing this [vocation]. And where that gets messy is when there are Arabs involved in the US, which has happened multiple times. Even in a family gathering, one of our cousins invited her Arab boyfriend. All of a sudden, our nice family vacation became not so nice. And we were just like, "Okay, we'll just be in the other room." We kind of just avoided him.

His wife added,

> Arabs are so well connected. And Arabs, especially our city that we live in, every Arab in America probably has a relative or connection or friend in our city. And they could tell them about us instantly. And Arabs know that what we're doing is illegal.

The intersection of social fields in which the couple would be known by different role identities—either by their vocation or as missionaries—makes navigating those situations so complex that this couple seeks to avoid overlapping worlds as much as possible. They are concerned that the intersection of their home world and field world will expose their hidden missionary identities.

As noted above, many missionaries do not fit the typical mold of the American expatriate in the GCC. As their primary concern is to communicate the gospel to Arabs, tentmakers often adopt behaviors that other expatriates would not. However, the expatriate community and the local Muslim community exist in overlapping social worlds that must often be navigated simultaneously, which can sometimes cause missionaries to offend one group in order to meet the expectations of the other group. Casie found that she "kicked up a hornet's nest" in the expatriate community in the GCC city where she and her husband Cory used to live. Casie and Cory highly value listening to others and learning from them, and they adapted the presentation of their identity in an effort to minimize offense among Muslims. In removing cultural barriers for Muslims, Casie collided with the expectations of the wider expatriate community, especially Muslim expatriates who became suspicious of her intentions:

> After a year of being there and doing a lot of interviews and making local friends, I really felt like I needed to cover my hair in order to gain access to more conservative situations. Just to make [Cory's] friends more comfortable, and to make my friends more comfortable. But there were so few internationals there that I stuck out like a sore thumb [by covering my hair]. And people assumed, based off my dress previously, that I was on vacation, or, you know [pause]. Bottom line, I didn't know Arabic yet, so I really was having a hard time getting into community.
>
> So anyway, when I started covering my hair, it became an issue at the kids' [international] school. Because there were a few women that were like, "Oh, she's a [missionary]." They kind of raised an alarm at one point. So it was interesting to navigate, because I didn't want to change my approach with locals. But it did bring up

> more yellow flags or red flags within the [pause]. It wasn't really [local] parents that were concerned, it was mainly Muslims from other countries that were saying, "Who is this in our midst?"

Many, but not all, American missionary women in the GCC choose to cover their hair, particularly those who live among more conservative Muslims in smaller cities or villages. Casie lived in a smaller city at the time with fewer expatriates, and decided to cover her hair. She noted in her interview that her local friends appreciated this decision. However, this is not considered a normal American expatriate practice, and Muslim expatriates immediately suspected Casie of being a missionary. By respecting the cultural norms and expectations of the group she was trying to reach with the gospel, Casie accidentally signaled to other groups her missionary identity. The collision of two social fields and their competing expectations created difficulties in presenting and managing her identity.

One evangelistic strategy uses internet advertisements to engage Muslim seekers, allowing them to ask questions about the gospel. The online ministry then connects seekers to missionaries for follow-up and ongoing discipleship. Abram had his missionary and vocational worlds collide through a media contact he received. The media contact was not a local, but a Jordanian Arab. Still, Abram was excited to study Scripture in Arabic with this seeker. However, Abram soon discovered that the Jordanian seeker had a friend who was one of Abram's colleagues at the company where he worked. Abram said the seeker stopped texting him and the relationship ended before it became a problem, but discovering the mutual contact was a jarring experience. Abram needed to carefully consider how he would present his identity to both the seeker and his colleague, and answer questions about why he would have received a media contact from Arabs interested in Christianity. The true answer was that he was connected to the missionary community, which receives such media contacts. He said in his interview that he was still unsure how he would have explained everything had the relationship progressed.

Several participants note that their Arab friends often suggest they will visit the tentmakers or their families in America—a real possibility thanks to the affordability of global travel for GCC Arabs. The Arab cultural expectations of hospitality demand that the tentmaker's family host their Arab friends and introduce to them to the tentmaker's social circle during a visit to the US. As the participants considered what that might look like, they acknowledged that this would be a challenging visit, especially if their Arab friends visited their churches. Several tentmakers have their photo displayed on the missionary bulletin board in their home churches. In addition, they are concerned about what their family and friends—not accustomed to navigating security issues—might accidentally reveal. At the same time, tentmakers recognize the potential loss of not introducing their Muslim friends to their home churches in the US, where Muslims might feel more free to visit a church without worrying about government surveillance. Leslie's Arab friends tried to connect her with an Arab relative near her hometown while she was in the US on HMA. Leslie felt torn—she wanted to strengthen this relationship with her Arab friends by visiting their relatives, but she had great concerns about navigating the security complexities it might create. In the end, she avoided making the connection. Her two worlds were coming too close for comfort.

Context Collapse Online

The internet poses a unique challenge for tentmakers' identity management as multiple audiences collapse into a singular context. For participants who do use social media to intentionally present a Christian or spiritual identity to their Muslim friends, Snapchat is a favored app. Amy says that in her area of the GCC, Snapchat is a primary form of communication, even more than texting apps such as WhatsApp. She describes what she reveals and withholds on Snapchat and Instagram to local Muslims and to Americans who know she is a missionary:

> [On Snapchat] I only add girls, [and] I post pictures of myself. I'll sometimes post Bible verses. I'm open about my life here. When I go to America, I post a lot because [Arabs] love to see my family and the kids and everything. And they know where I live [in the US]. I don't hide the state that I'm from, or anything like that on Instagram. I also share [spiritual] stuff sometimes, but I never share stuff about my [ministry] work here. Because on Instagram, I have [Arab] friends [and American friends], it's a mixture. So I would say it's kind of generic stuff in [the GCC], stuff in America, but not a lot of deep [spiritual content]. I would share spiritual stuff for sure, about being a Christian in general. And I'll even share some stuff translated into Arabic. But I wouldn't talk as if I'm talking to my [Christian] audience in America [about ministry activities in the GCC] on Instagram. It's not public.

Amy is careful to present her Christian identity on social media, but she is aware of her multiple audiences on some platforms. These multiple audiences include both Christians in the US who know her as a missionary, and Muslims in the GCC who know her as a teacher. As a result, Amy censures her content to present a Christian identity to both groups without revealing missionary intentions or activities.

However, Amy also notes that because she works with young adults, she has discovered that they are a "generation of stalkers and hackers." She says students at her school have created profiles of teachers they pass around to one another containing private information. As a result, she constantly feels surveilled in public—not by the government, but by curious young adults who can potentially expose sensitive information about her:

> I have a lot of students that are kind of like stalkers. Most of the time, it's innocent, kind of cute and sweet. But any of those people could turn into someone who [pause]. They tell me after I'm not their teacher anymore. They have a whole WhatsApp account of thousands of students. And they have a profile on every teacher. They have pictures of her from her social media, private social media accounts, pictures of her, information about her, what kind of teacher she is, things about her, personal information. They have a lot of resources, and lots of time. And they're just good at stalking. This is like a stalking generation, just for fun.
>
> In public, I can't fully be myself. When I go to other cities, [I feel nervous] even just laughing or telling stories. A couple of weeks ago, I was at dinner with a friend. And she's a really close friend, so we were having a really intense conversation. And then while we were walking out [of] the restaurant, I saw three of my previous students, all separately, not together. And they came over to me and they [said], "Oh, we saw you eating but we didn't want to disturb you." And then in my mind, I'm thinking, "What was I talking about? What was I saying? Was it appropriate? Was it [pause]. Are they gonna think this?" And I feel that way all the time here.
>
> It's almost like they're little spies watching. And it's innocent, you know, they just want to see their teacher, but they have videos of us. They have videos of us in their group chats. One time, there's this video I saw, it's me and my friends at the *souq* [Arabic: market] getting some dates or something. And it's zooming in. This girl must have been right next to us, zooming in on us, and I have no memory of this happening. But I'm [wondering], "What if I was talking about something else?"

Amy describes the anxious feeling of having her private information and personal conversations constantly surveilled by local Muslim students. Her missionary identity is threatened while conversing with friends in public places such as the market or a restaurant, where former students may be recording her every word. This information may be posted to thousands of Arabs on social media groups. The context of a private conversation with a close friend then collides with an unintended public audience.

Tansy, who has been in the GCC for over twenty years, has seen the rapid changes of technology in the gulf and how that impacts relationships with Muslim locals:

> We were here when the internet was first starting with dial-up. [It was] very slow. And it's completely different now. You have things in your phone [now], there were no smartphones in the beginning, so that piece has changed. That makes accessibility to information very quick. For example, you go to visit a local, and you've never met them before. [But] they've already Googled you. You show up, and they know all this information about you. [It's] very common for them to Google who you are, especially if they have a good command of English. So that's a huge change. Before, there was nothing like that that you could do. It [depended] on who knew you, and who you knew.

Tansy is highly cautious of what she puts on the internet, only rarely posting vacation photos for friends back home. This minimizes what her local contacts can find when they conduct an internet search of her name. In her interview, she communicated how missionaries need to be continually aware of what information is available online about them, a new issue she did not encounter when she first became a missionary.

The collision of multiple social fields is a particular concern for missionaries in RANs today. Managing multiple role identities and communicating with differing audiences and contexts sometimes creates complex situations for missionaries. These overlapping social fields sometimes cause missionaries additional stress or anxiety as they consider how to present their identities to multiple social fields simultaneously.

Conclusion

This chapter has presented the first part of the findings of this study. This chapter has described tentmakers' strategies to manage and present their identities across various social fields. These strategies include openness, but also concealing practices such as withholding information, telling partial truths but not the whole truth, avoidance of relationships, deflection, misleading people to a false conclusion using true statements, and occasionally lying. The role identity that participants present changes with their various role partners. The contexts and social fields determine how participants fulfill the expectations and behaviors of that role identity. In some social fields, tentmakers manage their social identity by presenting the vocational identity and concealing the missionary identity. In other social fields, tentmakers present the missionary identity, diminishing but not concealing the vocational identity. Where social fields collide, missionaries must adapt to present their identities to multiple audiences to avoid offense, confusion, or a security breach among their audiences.

The next chapter continues the findings of this study. Chapter 6 identifies the impact that these concealing practices have on missionaries, as well as the impact of duality sometimes experienced by the participants. This impact includes five types of identity dissonance that emerged from interviews. In addition, interviews of participants who experience greater identity integration are analyzed to reveal factors for identity consonance.

6

Tentmaker Identity Dissonance and Consonance

CHAPTER 5 DESCRIBED THE first part of this study's findings, focusing on how tentmaking missionaries in the GCC manage their multiple role identities across various social fields. Chapter 5 also described the concealing practices, in person and online, participants used to manage the missionary identity in RANs. Chapter 6 continues the study's findings, focusing on the *impact* of those practices on tentmakers' self-concept. Chapter 6 answers the three remaining research questions from chapter 1, including the primary research question: How does presenting a missionary identity back home and a non-missionary identity overseas impact one's self-concept? How do tentmakers perceive the experiences of navigating identity in a RAN? What strategies do tentmakers use to reconcile illegal, hidden, or deceptive activities with their moral identity?

In this chapter, the impact of presenting two distinct identities across social fields and concealing one identity is described in terms of identity dissonance and consonance. These categories are taken from identity theory as described in chapter 3. Interviews with participants confirm two distinct issues in managing their identities: the perceived necessity of concealing the missionary identity in the GCC, and the experience of conflict between the vocational and missionary role identities. These two issues sometimes lead to experiences of identity dissonance, a negative experience in which the multiple parts of the self conflict and compete with one another.

Five categories of identity dissonance emerged from the interviews: dual identity dissonance, moral identity dissonance, vocational identity dissonance, missionary identity dissonance, and friend identity dissonance. In the experiences of identity dissonance, participants describe theological, ethical, and cultural coping mechanisms that help them reframe their identity management practices and resist dissonance, with varying levels of success.

For some tentmakers, the discreet navigation of their identity in order to protect security is seen as unproblematic, a necessary set of skills for a complex cross-cultural life and calling. In addition, their multiple role identities sometimes do not conflict, leading to experiences of identity consonance and integration for some participants. This chapter describes the common factors of participants experiencing identity consonance. Randall's story below illustrates some of the concepts presented in this chapter related to the concealment of the missionary identity, conflict between the vocational and missionary role identities, and identity dissonance.

RANDALL'S SECRET IDENTITY

Randall trained as an engineer in the US and worked at an engineering firm in Michigan for twelve years, rising in the company quickly.[1] A mentor had been a significant part of his spiritual journey. This mentor had invested a lot of time with Randall, teaching him Scripture and helping him to live out his faith. Randall longed to do the same for others. When he and his wife sensed a calling from God to reach Muslims in the Middle East, they directed all their life goals toward becoming effective ministers of the gospel there. In addition to his engineering degree, Randall pursued a master of divinity degree. He excelled in teaching, and he envisioned being a Bible teacher to help disciple Arab BMBs.

In language school, Randall proved to be a gifted linguist, surpassing his classmates in Arabic from the start. Randall describes himself as a hard worker and driven to excellence in all he does. He demonstrated these characteristics as he spent every spare minute studying Arabic verbs, local idioms, and Scripture, dreaming of the day when he would help shepherd BMBs in the word in their heart language. After language school, Randall got a job with an engineering firm in a large GCC city. He quickly rose to the top of the company, his aptitude recognized by all. In fact, he received a

1. Randall's character is a composite primarily based on one participant, whose story is conflated with the details of several other participants to protect his identity. The quotes belong to the participant known as Randall, but the experiences reflect true experiences of several participants.

prestigious award for his excellence in engineering. However, he struggled with some aspects of his engineering job. While it afforded him a legitimate social identity in the community and a paycheck to support his growing family, Randall grappled with the lack of relationships with Arabs in his day-to-day life. In his engineering firm, he rubbed shoulders with very few Arabs—mostly other Americans, Brits, and Indians instead. The long days at the office, where he spoke only English, slowly eroded his ability to communicate effectively in Arabic. While he enjoyed engineering and firmly believed that his excellent work served as a witness to Christ, he felt his job did not contribute to his ultimate calling of discipling BMBs. Especially during major projects when he often worked fifty hours or more in a week, Randall sometimes felt his vocation conflicted with the reasons he came to the GCC, a tension he could not resolve. The better he performed his work, the more his boss promoted him—giving him more responsibilities that left little time for relationships with Muslims.

When Randall returned home to his wife and children late in the evening, the duties of family life took precedence over Arabic study. Randall felt his hard-won Arabic proficiency slipping away—along with his dream of teaching the Bible in the local heart language. Sometimes, after the kids were in bed, he met a local Muslim friend for coffee and conversation, but he had to be careful how many nights a week he did this. His wife Ellen, alone with their young children all day, struggled to connect with local women and felt tremendous loneliness. Ellen was the only woman in their Arab neighborhood who wasn't working full-time; all the women seemed too busy with life for a new friend. Randall and Ellen had chosen this neighborhood strategically, hoping they would be a light to their Arab neighbors. It didn't seem to be working that way. For both Randall and Ellen, their daily lives were not leading to relationships with locals as they hoped. The reason they moved across the world seemed a distant mirage. Randall began to wonder how he could position himself to invest more time into the local community, build trust and deep relationships, and share Christ with Muslims.

After living in the country for five years, Randall set up a web-based consultancy for engineering. He held a strong reputation in the country for his excellence in engineering. He used this reputation to gain clientele over time, then quit his job with the engineering firm. He now had a residence visa as a business owner, rather than as an employee of a company. His family spent several extra months in the US that year, raising their ministry support as their primary source of income. The new business seemed like the perfect solution: Randall retained his legitimate identity as an engineer, but now he had more flexibility as the owner of his consultancy. He could now make time for Arabic study, relationships with Muslims, and discipling BMBs. Randall could set his weekly work hours, decide how many clients to take, and report only to himself. Randall spent many hours working on his website, learning the intricacies of running a small business in the GCC, and managing clients. He could also work from home and be more present with his family. After five years, Randall found more mental and emotional capacity for growing relationships with local Muslims and BMBs than he ever had before.

Within a few years, Randall and Ellen began shepherding a small group of local BMBs in the early stages of a house church alongside another missionary couple from a different organization. The group took a lot of time and energy. One BMB, following the teachings of a charismatic Arab Christian preacher on the internet, suddenly divorced his second wife and left her destitute. Another BMB made passive-aggressive jabs at other group members' tribes; he presented them as jokes, but his comments exposed underlying tensions between the members' tribes and families that they brought into the new church. Another disciple voraciously read Scripture and wanted to preach to his imam one week, then disappeared from the Christian community entirely the following week. He went from hot to cold instantly and without warning. Another BMB became suicidal when her highly religious family discovered her hidden Bible and ostracized her from the community. The missionary women found her a safe place to stay and sat with her through many sleepless nights, praying with her and counseling her through despair. The group—one of the first indigenous churches in the country—was likely years away from having healthy, mature Arab leadership.

The weekly hours of Randall's consultancy could mostly flex to the discipleship needs that frequently arose with this young house church. Randall was finally doing what he had felt called to do—discipling and teaching the infant BMB church in one of the most unreached countries in the world. However, he couldn't reconcile himself with the hiddenness of this lifestyle, which made him feel like he had a secret identity. One way he took the burden off his overwhelmed wife was to do the grocery shopping while she homeschooled their children. When Randall left his house at ten in the morning to go to the store, his local neighbor called out a friendly greeting. Chatting for a few minutes in Arabic, the neighbor suddenly commented on the strangeness of Randall being home all day, "like a woman," as the man described it. Randall tried to explain his web-based consultancy and how this allowed him to work from home, but the older man had no cognitive categories for such a job. Over time, little comments from the men in his neighborhood about how they viewed Randall and his work ethic created a sense of dissonance for him. He saw himself as hardworking, driven, and competent. The men in his community seemed to interpret him as lazy, loafing, and doing his wife's bidding.

At the store, Randall ran into Jeremy, an American pastor who had just moved to the city to lead the expatriate evangelical church. The country's government had provided a church compound for all the Christian expatriate guest workers to worship legally. Jeremy greeted Randall, and after some small talk, Jeremy nudged Randall with his elbow and said, "Hey, we'd love to see you and your family at church on Friday. It'd be great to see you grow in your new faith." Startled by this comment, Randall suddenly realized what Jeremy must think of him. Randall claimed to be a Christian, yet he was not involved with the local expatriate church at all. The reason for this, of course, was that Randall was secretly worshipping with an illegal underground church with BMBs from the local community on Fridays. But he could not tell Jeremy this. Randall knew from the experiences of other missionaries with this expatriate church that if Jeremy discovered Randall had a degree in theology and a passion for teaching the Bible, Jeremy would likely pressure Randall into helping the expatriate church with pulpit supply and Bible studies. Randall was unsure how to answer Jeremy in a way that would satisfy both Jeremy's kind invitation and Randall's need to protect the local believers. He smiled and said, "Sure, we'll think about it," knowing he would *not* think about it.

One day, Muhammad, a young local intern working in the same engineering firm Randall used to work for, met Randall for coffee. Muhammad excitedly told Randall of his acceptance into the university in Randall's hometown in Michigan. Muhammad was excited to meet Randall's extended family and friends in Michigan. Randall considered the collision of his two separate worlds, especially since everyone in Michigan knew Randall primarily as a missionary. Randall reflected with self-contradiction on this startling news, capturing the conundrum he felt: "I was not terribly excited about that, because I didn't want his world to overlap with our church world. I *did* want his world to overlap with our church world. But I *didn't* want his world to overlap with our church world." In other words, Randall did want Muhammad to come to Christ and be part of his church community in Michigan. But he also did not want Muhammad to find out Randall's true identity as a missionary in the GCC. This situation left Randall deeply conflicted about his secret identity.

The internal conflict was greatest for Randall in interactions with people he became close friends with. He had to hide the most from his closest Muslim friends to keep his missionary identity concealed, and his concealing practices wore on him over time. One recurring and significant issue was his income, which was not a locally taboo topic. The stress of concealing that 75 percent of his finances came through a missionary organization wore on him over time as he sidestepped questions and told half-truths to manage his missionary identity. Randall describes the increasing discomfort as he got closer to someone, and they realized Randall seemed to be hiding aspects of his life from them:

> The more I got to know somebody, the more I did ministry with somebody, the more they got to know my family, the more they got to know my [work] schedule, or my lack of schedule, the more questions [they] raised. And they began to see, "Okay, you told me one thing, which was true, but it wasn't the whole truth. And now you've led me down this pathway to think one thing, and I'm realizing there's a whole other reality going on in your life."
>
> And if you're sharing the gospel with somebody, you don't want them asking questions like "What are you hiding from me? Why aren't you telling me all this? Why aren't you telling me what's true? What's being hidden about you?" And I wasn't hiding the gospel from people. I wasn't hiding that I'm a Christian from people. I wasn't hiding that I love Jesus from people. But it was still evident to them that there was something not being talked about. There were equations of my life that didn't add up to what they were supposed to add up to.

Randall also describes his growing crisis with his secret identity as a missionary, which he believes is impossible to hide in today's connected world:

> [It's] like I've got this secret identity. But it's impossible to keep it secret. We could talk about online presence and what churches put online and what churches don't put online. There's no way you can keep your missionary identity [secret], at least in this century. There's *no way* you can keep it secret. And then if you do try to keep it secret, when you get found out, you look like a fool for hiding something that you can't really hide. And you don't want

> people to find it out. Then they find it out, [it's like] you're standing there with no clothes on. That summarizes the struggle that I have. If you have a secret identity, you have to keep it secret, and I don't want to have a secret identity anymore. I understand you don't have to tell everybody everything. But my struggle was, even with sharing the truthful statements, your short legitimate statements [pause]. I felt like my short truthful statement was 100 percent truthful. But it led people to think something else.

Randall felt his missionary identity was constantly at risk of exposure. His concerns with security and keeping his missionary identity a secret led to a deep sense of disunity within himself, which he describes in his interview as a "great tearing inside." Over time, he distanced himself from many relationships to maintain his secret missionary identity. On the one hand, he desired that people see his Christian character and be drawn in by it. But on the other hand, he did not want them to see what he was hiding so that he would not lose his visa.

Randall and his family left the GCC due to several complex factors—not just identity. However, he said that if he were ever to return to the gulf, he would openly share with people that he is a Bible teacher and an engineer, though he would not use the term "missionary." He would explain that while he worked as an engineering consultant to support his family, he was primarily supported by Christians in America to be there to teach the Bible to others. The secret identity model is not one he could ever repeat.

IDENTITY ROLE CONFLICT AND CONCEALMENT

Like Randall, many participants describe conflict between the missionary and vocational role identities. For a variety of reasons, they may feel tensions between their vocational responsibilities and their missionary calling. When missionaries perceive conflict between their multiple role identities, they initiate the hierarchical control system to prioritize their internal frameworks for external behavior. As discussed in chapter 3, the hierarchical control system is a concept in identity theory in which an internal framework controls the meanings of a given role identity. As multiple role identities exist within one person, the role identities interact with one another to control the person's behavior.[2] The actions of the person, or output, attempt to make the meanings of the multiple role identities congruent and to verify all activated identities.

2. Burke and Stets, *Identity Theory*, 189.

In this study, the primary competing role identities are missionary and vocational role identities, which participants often simultaneously activate. Other activated role identities include friend, family, and personal identities, which all carry specific meanings and behaviors for those roles. The vocational identity comprises the social identity by which missionaries are known across various social fields and provides a residential visa; the missionary identity is the motivating factor for living in the GCC. For some participants, most of the meanings and identity standards of these two role identities are aligned, and tentmakers receive verification of both identities, though perhaps not from the same role partners. These participants experience consonance across the multiple role identities. However, the missionary and vocational role identities sometimes carry opposing expectations, creating a conflict between the role identities. In these situations, the tentmaker cannot simultaneously verify both role identities, and the hierarchical structuring of identities comes into play. The higher or more prominent identity controls the behavior output so that the higher-order identity is verified.

The interviews reveal that when multiple role identities conflict, tentmakers' internal framework of calling, vocation, and personal identity greatly influence the output of the participants' hierarchical control system. Based on interview data regarding calling, vocation, and identity, I categorized each tentmaker according to Ian Prescott's tentmaker identity and calling spectrum.[3] I considered using Rundle and Lee's four business and missionary identity saliency categories: explorer, faith-driven entrepreneur, evangelist, and BAMer.[4] However, the interviews revealed more complexity than these four categories, as many participants in the study were job takers. Rundle and Lee's study categorized only BAM practitioners rather than a wide variety of tentmakers. Rundle and Lee's business identity salience did not fully align with tentmakers who took other professional jobs, such as engineers or teachers. In fact, none of the interviewees met the criteria for the explorer or faith-driven entrepreneur categories, which have low missionary identity salience. Missionary identity salience, as defined by Rundle and Lee, was high for all participants since they were all members of CP organizations and valued the spiritual goals of those organizations.[5] Prescott's scale more closely aligned with the tensions in calling and role identities

3. Prescott, "Identity and Platform."

4. Rundle and Lee, "Motivations, Backgrounds, and Practices," 420–41.

5. Rundle and Lee, "Motivations, Backgrounds, and Practices," 426–28.

that tentmakers expressed in their interviews. Thus, Prescott's categories for tentmakers were more accurate for analyzing this set of participants.

Prescott's tentmaker categories include six types of identity along a spectrum, denoted as Types 1 through 5, with an additional category of Type 2.5. According to Prescott's categorizations, none of the participants could be categorized as Type 1, who openly self-identify as missionaries and who seek to reach people without using any other professional skills. In order to obtain residence visas in the GCC, missionaries must rely on professional skills or identity other than the missionary identity.[6] Additionally, none of the thirty-eight participants openly identify themselves as missionaries to their Muslim friends or to the governments in their country of service, though they present their missionary identity in social fields in the US. Types 4 and 5 are also excluded in this analysis because Prescott defines Type 4 as expatriate Christian professionals with no missionary intentions, and Type 5 as Christian professionals working in their home country with no missionary intentions. Therefore, based on the parameters of the study, I categorized participants as either Types 2, 2.5, or 3 (see table 6 below for definitions). Tentmakers' wives who were interviewed who are not currently employed in the GCC were categorized with careful consideration. None openly identify as missionaries in the RAN where they reside, though they present a missionary identity back home. They currently rely on their husbands' professional skills to reside in the GCC; all four present their identity to Muslim and expatriate social fields as stay-at-home mothers. I took all four unemployed wives' narratives of calling and work experience throughout their careers, as several had worked in professions as tentmakers on the field before having children. In addition, I considered their roles within their missionary organizations and ministry activities, which were significant for all four, confirming a prominent missionary identity. Based on thirty-eight interviewees' responses to questions about their sense of calling, vocation, identity, and ministry, seventeen were Type 2, seventeen were Type 2.5, and four were Type 3.[7] The table below sum-

6. As noted previously, limited visas are provided for clergy or hospital chaplains in some parts of the GCC for expatriate churches. One participant held such a visa for a time; his story is discussed below. However, even as he publicly presented a religious worker identity and pastoral vocation, this participant did not publicly self-identify as a missionary whose goals were to witness to Muslim Arabs so that they would become Christians.

7. Tentmaker wives are included in this number.

marizes Prescott's tentmaker categories and definitions, and the number of participants representing each type.[8]

Table 6: Prescott's Tentmaker Identity Categories for Data Analysis			
Type	2	2.5	3
Primary Calling	Missionary (Professional Calling Is Secondary)	Missionary-Professional (Equally)	Professional (Missionary Calling Is Secondary)
Relationship to Vocation	Goal is to reach a people and use their professional skills to help reach a people *if* their professional skills can be used. May switch jobs and professions over time to stay in the country or find better ministry opportunities. Tend to emphasize reaching the lost. May view a job as a means to the end of ministry.	Goal is to reach people and serve in a profession. Feel a dual calling to both roles. If there is a conflict, they may not be sure which should take preeminence.	Goal is to serve in their profession and use their professional skills to help reach a people *if* their skills can be used. If they can't reach people using their professional skills, they find another location to do so. Tend to emphasize professional excellence.
Number of Participants in Category	17	17	4

Prescott's tentmaker identity categories reflect the concept of identity prominence in identity theory. How tentmakers interpret their calling, how they self-identify, and their vocational identity all reveal the hierarchy and prominence of either the vocational or the missionary identity, or both equally. How a person presents their role identity may shift with the social field, displaying that role identity's salience for the particular role partner, discussed in chapter 5. However, their prominent identity may be different from the salient identity in a given situation. Tentmakers' prominent role identities can also reflect their commitment to a particular role identity, as the number of relational connections while performing an identity may strengthen identity prominence.

8. Prescott, "Identity and Platform."

The narratives of divine calling are important for identity prominence among tentmakers. As they shared their stories of calling, the narratives centered around a plot of God urging them as individuals, couples, or even families to share the gospel with Muslims in the Middle East. Many spoke of God giving them compassion for Muslims and providing a specific leading to the Arabian Peninsula. A significant motivator for participants moving to the GCC was that Arab Muslims on the Arabian Peninsula comprise an unreached and largely unengaged people group. Several mentioned that they wanted to go where others might not be willing or able to go, and this helped them decide on the Arabian Peninsula—known for its harsh climate, difficult language, resistance to the gospel, and persecution of believers. Some participants described a vocational calling alongside their missionary calling, knowing that a professional identity would be needed for entry and long-term service in RANs.

Tentmakers operate with two significant role identities: missionary and vocational. These are distinct role identities because each role has different goals, expectations for behavior, and standards of practice. This is demonstrated in how tentmakers approach language study in the GCC. A high value for CP organizations and tentmakers is communication in the local language for effective, contextual ministry. This value and practice is *not* shared with the vocational identity, as non-missionary expatriates in the GCC rarely study Arabic to a high degree of fluency, and do not need Arabic to perform their jobs. Where the meanings and standards of practice are not shared between two role identities, the individual uses the hierarchical control system to sort the priorities between the multiple role identities, controlling the output (behavior). All the participants except six began their time on the field in a season of exclusive language study apart from a vocational identity, whether it was in an institute or with language tutors using the Growing Participator Approach (GPA).[9] GPA is a method using local language "nurturers" who tutor students using a semi-structured approach. Participants frequently discussed the desire to share truth in the heart language of gulf Arabs, and to remove as many cultural barriers to the gospel as possible. Several participants noted the resulting gap in their resumé as a result of language study, which they had previously worried might impact their future employment after language school. This gap in the resumé presented a conflict between the missionary identity and the vocational identity. In language study, the missionary identity controlled

9. See Growing Participator Approach.

the behavior output for most participants, causing them to accept potential detrimental effects to their career and employment success in favor of gaining high linguistic proficiency. The missionary identity achieved higher prominence than the vocational identity for these participants when it came to Arabic study.

Six participants entered the GCC with a full-time vocation and did not exclusively study Arabic. Of those six, two were teachers who then suspended their teaching careers on the field for two years to attend language school and achieve high fluency in Arabic to aid their ministry. The hierarchical control system again prioritized the missionary identity over the vocational identity in these cases. Two additional participants used GPA tutoring alongside their vocation to gain fluency in Arabic. Since these tutors could work around the participants' vocational hours, participants could fulfill the expectations of both missionary and vocational identity roles simultaneously, verifying both identities without conflict. For these participants, neither the missionary nor the vocational identity had to be diminished long-term.[10]

The two participants who had not done any significant language study are Type 3s whose vocations prevent them from spending time learning Arabic. This often limits their relationships to locals who speak English with high fluency. For these participants, the standards of the vocational identity are prioritized. These participants still possess the missionary identity, but they reframe their expectations for ministry around the limitations of language. One participant in the UAE laments his limited Arabic and says it would be helpful if he knew it. At the same time, he feels Arabic is not required to minister in the UAE, as English is widely spoken. His story of calling reflects his practices; he feels called to "work in an Islamic context," and his calling is centered on location and faithfully working in his vocation, not limiting him to a particular people group. While he has few Emirati friends, he has many spiritual conversations in English with others he encounters through his job. In this way, he can verify his missionary identity along with his vocational identity.

Identity prominence, as narrated by tentmakers through their stories of calling and vocation, is an important factor in the experiences of identity consonance and dissonance. The prominence of the missionary identity,

10. Both of these participants have been in the GCC more than two decades; I do not have enough data to conclude how these two role identities may have competed in their first several years on the field.

the vocational identity, or a mixture of both impacts decisions on how to present and manage the tentmaker's identity across various social fields. Ideally, the tentmaker could verify both the missionary and vocational role identities across various situations. If the missionary and vocational role identities conflict, the hierarchical control system prioritizes one of the role identities over the other, influencing the behavior. Tentmakers often achieve consonance when prominent identities are verified by role partners frequently and do not have to be diminished. This consonance is especially achieved when tentmakers experience fewer instances of their multiple role identities conflicting with one another or their personal identity. As a result of this consonance, tentmakers experience an aligned sense of self across multiple role identities. When multiple role identities do conflict, prominent aspects of the identity remain unverified, and tentmakers experience dissonance.

In addition to conflict between role identities, concealment of a prominent identity also sometimes results in dissonance among tentmakers. Research on concealable stigmatized identities (CSIs) predicts that if a person frequently disguises a particular identity so that role partners cannot verify it, there may be an increasing sense of inner dissonance and inauthenticity. The more a person conceals a particularly prominent identity, the lower the perceived authenticity of that identity.[11] For some, the experience is mild, perhaps an ongoing annoyance that requires additional coping mechanisms. Participants often reframe their dissonant experiences using theological or cultural reasonings, which relieves the tension for many. For others, the dissonance is a significant source of distress, requiring more radical action to achieve consonance. They sometimes change their environment or their overall goals in an attempt to verify their identity. The types of dissonance, and the coping mechanisms used to resist dissonance, are described in the next section.

TENTMAKER IDENTITY DISSONANCE

Presenting a missionary identity back home and a vocational identity in the country of service sometimes leads to experiences of identity dissonance. Identity dissonance is an internal experience of conflict in which aspects of the self feel unaligned, inharmonic, and in competition with one another. From the interviews, five categories of identity dissonance emerged: dual identity dissonance, moral identity dissonance, vocational

11. Crabtree and Pillow, "Consequences of Enactment," 1228.

identity dissonance, missionary identity dissonance, and friend identity dissonance. These are discussed below, along with the coping strategies participants mobilize against these experiences of dissonance.

Dissonance #1: Dual Identity Dissonance

Many participants describe having a dual identity, as they are known by their vocation on the field while hiding their missionary identity. When they meet with other missionaries or go back to the US, they perform the missionary identity that is often hidden in other social fields. Several participants compare their lives to spies or a "007 experience," saying they often feel like they are living a double life due to concealing the missionary identity on the field. This experience is the dual identity dissonance. Silas and Tansy, a married couple who have lived and worked in the GCC for over two decades in an area of high religious persecution, have different experiences of dual identity. Tansy (Type 2.5) feels like her two lives were once separate, but they have become one integrated identity over time as she proclaims Christ through relationships in her workplace. Tansy describes the shifting experience of her double life into an integrated identity:

> We don't have it so much anymore. But in the early days, years ago, before the internet and everything, we had our jobs and worked the normal job. And then the afternoon and evening was all around the ministry, [which] didn't really relate to our jobs. And so it felt like a double life, because you had *this* life and *that* life. It's very hard to do that. And I will say, after working this particular job, and having ministry [pause]. First of all, I believe that *all* life is ministry. But just for explanation's sake, after many years, the two just kind of come together. And the truthful fact is, if you're doing what you're called to be doing, you can't hide it for very long.
>
> You can do a good job of not intentionally drawing attention to it. But as Christ shines through you, more and more people [pause]. The two lives just kind of come together [holds her hands up and brings her fingers together to interlock with one another]. And it's hard to separate them at some point. But it did take several years. I mean, we did quite well for many years, keeping them separate. But as people know you, and you're there longer, and you're in a routine, you're eventually going to have friends from one section of your life colliding with friends in the other section of your life. And yeah, sometimes it feels like a little bit of a 007 kind of thing. But not so much anymore. I don't feel that way. [To Silas] Do you feel that way? [Do] you *still* feel that way?

Silas's (Type 3) reply to Tansy shows that he is having more difficulty integrating his vocational and missionary identities, and he still experiences a dual identity:

> [Emphatically] Oh yeah. I go to work. A guy asks [me], "What did you do this weekend?" I can't tell [him], "Oh, we did this, this, or this." I just say, "We went to the desert." I've got to be very vague. I can't tell them everything or all the fun stuff. I can't show them pictures of what we're doing or stuff like that. So yes, it is like a double life. Because this expat that I know that works for me, knows other people that I know [in a ministry context]. So I've got to be careful [about] what I say and what I do around him. Whereas [with] the locals, they work and they leave. There's no meeting with them outside of work. So that's hard.

Even within a marriage, the two spouses have different experiences of living a double life. Whereas Tansy's life feels more integrated, Silas feels he must conceal more from his colleagues at work. He cannot share many aspects of his life because they revolve around spending time with BMBs or with Muslims in a ministry context. In addition, Silas notes that his relationships with locals at work are often only work-related. However, Silas also says he builds relationships with locals at work, and they call him "brother" affectionately. In the interview, Silas noted the high degree of surveillance at his workplace and a few incidents in which his missionary identity was nearly revealed through mishaps with technology. Silas's work world and ministry world are separate more often than not for the sake of security; this leads him to the dissonant experience of duality.

Casie (Type 2) and her husband Cory (Type 2.5) experience the tensions of living a double life as they navigate the two contexts of home and field. Casie describes how these two worlds sometimes collide on the internet, and she must consider how they present their identity to two different audiences in a combined context on social media:

> We always have to Google ourselves, because churches really love to put our sermons on their media. It's messy now with the internet and social media: Instagram, Facebook, Snapchat. [There are] all these different layers of, 'What do I post about myself? What do I not [post about myself]? Who knows what?' Because it's not just [about] us posting. If I have friends on both sides [home and field], I might have a well-meaning church person that will comment on a picture and [say], "Oh, God bless the work, you're doing well!" And then a local friend might see that, and it [might] cause

> tension. So I wish I could say I've figured out how to navigate the internet persona world well. But it still is challenging to know how much to share, when to share, and what makes sense to share.

Cory agrees, and then describes the exhaustion of presenting and managing a dual identity across their two separate worlds:

> I think it's an everyday tension that we carry of "Who am I? What do I represent? And how and why?" I do feel like over time [it] has become, especially in different seasons, very, very exhausting, to the point where we are trying to be more transparent on both sides [home and field] about who we are. And just take whatever risks come with it, because the tension of navigating it is exhausting over time.

Cory and Casie's dissonant experiences of managing two identities in America and the GCC have caused them to consider how they can present the same identity in both home and field contexts, even if it brings additional security concerns and risk. As mentioned in chapter 5, they are attempting to reduce the dichotomy and dissonance of living a double life by openly presenting their pastoral identities in the GCC. By doing so, they hope to place their spiritual identity and goals at the forefront of their identity presentation in all contexts, rather than presenting that identity at home but concealing it on the field.

Part of the tentmaker's burden is knowing which identity is salient for the particular role. When tentmakers meet new people in the US while on HMA, it can be difficult to assess whether that person is safe to share secure information with. Derek (Type 2.5) and Helen (Type 2) describe their tensions of duality while in the US in churches. They note the disparity between their two basic identities of missionary and vocation and not knowing which to present in a given situation. Derek describes the experience as "constantly hiding something." Helen struggles with knowing how to present their identities to strangers at church, since they may be in the same industry as Derek and might not be sympathetic to missionary purposes:

> Going back to the States and meeting people at church, do you introduce yourself as, "[We're] Derek and Helen, we live in [GCC country], Derek works for [company]?" Or "[We're] Derek and Helen, we live in [GCC country] as [missionaries]?" I have to make that decision even at church, "How am I going to introduce myself today?" With this person versus that person.

When interacting with new role partners, tentmakers may not know which category to place that role partner in and thus how to interact with them. There is a set of information given to supporting churches and like-minded Christians in the US who know them as missionaries. However, there is a different set of information given to people who know them in their vocational role only, and for whom the missionary identity may not be safe to disclose to them. The divisions between the role partners are often more clear on the field than they may be in the US, and tentmakers must quickly calculate which set of information to disclose to a new role partner, especially when they meet strangers in a supporting church. This increases the feeling of living a double life with one hidden identity.

Martin (Type 2.5), a teacher in the GCC, describes how the information he gives to people in the US differs radically, depending on whether they know him as a missionary or as a teacher. Whereas he feels his identity is more integrated when he is in the GCC, his identity feels more dichotomized when he is in the US because of the differing sets of information he gives to different role partners:

> If it's a random stranger at the supermarket where I don't know anybody [they know], and they don't know anybody I know, I just say, "I teach English over in [GCC country]." But then to other people, if they're at a church or something, I don't share those details. I share a totally different set of details about who I am and what I do. So in the US, it feels more dichotomized in terms of, this group of people over *here* might know where I live. And this group over *here* doesn't know where I live, but they know *why* I live there. So here [in the GCC], it's a little bit more blended because it's all just a little bit more interconnected.

With church role partners who know Martin as a missionary with church-planting intentions, Martin conceals his specific location and workplace. However, with strangers in the US who do not know Martin as a missionary, Martin gives a different set of information that meets the expectations of that group. It would not make sense to conceal the location of where he lives to that group, given his vocational identity there. To manage his missionary identity in the US, he presents separate sets of information to different groups, depending on the role identity he performs with them. This gives Martin a greater sense of living a double life in the US, which he doesn't experience in the GCC. However, Martin does note that he occasionally considers what his university would do if they found out how he spent his evenings in ministry activities, such as Bible studies or evangelistic conversations with locals. Several other participants agreed that their identities felt more integrated while in the GCC, and more dichotomized while visiting the US.

Coping Strategies for Dual Identity Dissonance

Dual identity dissonance brings together both issues of concealing the missionary identity and the tension between prominent role identities. Participants often perceive that concealing the missionary identity is a necessary aspect of their ministry for protecting others, reducing misunderstandings, and maintaining a residential visa. However, concealing the missionary identity frequently leads to the experience of the duplicity of living a double life, with which many were uncomfortable. In addition, several participants noted the tension with presenting their vocational identity while hiding ulterior church-planting motives and agendas.

To resist dual identity dissonance, participants primarily use theological or biblical coping strategies to frame concealment, living a double life, or having hidden purposes other than a vocation for being in the GCC. Several participants refer to the hidden agendas of the prophet Samuel in 1 Sam 16, where God tells the prophet Samuel that he has rejected Saul as king. As a result, the Lord commands Samuel to go to Bethlehem and anoint David as king of Israel. When Samuel protests that this action will put his life in danger, God replies, "Take a heifer with you and say, 'I have come to sacrifice to the Lord.' Invite Jesse to the sacrifice, and I will show you what to do. You are to anoint for me the one I indicate" (1 Sam 16:2–3). Samuel performs a sacrifice, but it is not the whole reason for his journey—or even the primary one. His primary reason will endanger his life and David's life. This biblical narrative is essential for some participants in constructing a framework for concealing their missionary purposes from locals and authorities in RANs, and in telling partial truths rather than the whole truth.

Many participants use Jesus's life and teachings as theological coping mechanisms. In situations of persecution, Jesus told his disciples, "I am sending you out like sheep among wolves. Therefore be as shrewd as snakes and as innocent as doves" (Matt 10:16). In interviews, participants quoted this Bible verse most frequently to frame the concealment of their missionary identity. Derek notes the tension between innocence and shrewdness as he shares the gospel in a place where it's illegal:

> Our philosophy is that we realize the Lord has called us to a place where it's illegal to share the gospel. It's illegal to proselytize. And we know that. But he's called us to that. So how do we do that in a wise way and not a foolish way? So balancing innocent as doves, but wise as serpents. So we take the necessary security protocols.

Derek considers his divine calling in a context where his activities of sharing the gospel and discipling local BMBs are punishable by law. He describes how opposition to the gospel requires following security protocols and concealing the missionary identity. Several participants pointed to how Jesus himself did not fully reveal all his purposes to all his audiences and how he was often cryptic with people. They felt this was a model of wisdom—a keyword in discussions about concealment. Most participants accepted that hiding their missionary identity was simply part of the call to reach Muslims on the Arabian Peninsula and that presenting a vocational identity instead was wise and necessary.

However, for some participants, the concealment of their missionary identity and presenting two differing identities at home and on the field wore on them over time. Competing demands of multiple identities increase the distress of individuals.[12] One method of coping with this distress is a radical reorientation of identity. According to the hierarchical control model, individuals desire to get all identities verified, and a discrepancy between the identities yields dissonance, requiring action to resolve. The entire identity system of a person, composed of multiple role identities, moves towards congruence as a whole.[13] When there is conflict, higher-level identities influence the lower-level identities, causing the whole system to change to bring alignment and congruence.[14] This results in a renegotiation of the identity in order to bring alignment and congruence across the multiple identities so that the identity can be verified. For Cory and Casie, their pastoral identities were higher-level identities over their business owner identities, though both identities were important to them. Over time, the higher-level identity controlled the meanings and standards of behavior. They are now working to present a more consonant and unified identity that feels authentic to that higher-level identity, which they believe will resolve the dissonance of living a double life. Several participants discussed identity reorientations they made on the field over time, often to

12. Burke and Stets, *Identity Theory*, 201.
13. Burke and Stets, *Identity Theory*, 195.
14. Burke and Stets, *Identity Theory*, 214.

present a more unified, authentic spiritual identity both in the US and on the field. This reduced the dissonance of having a dual identity.

Dissonance #2: Moral Identity Dissonance

A significant category of dissonance emerging from interviews is moral identity dissonance, in which participants act in ways that are disparate from their own moral norms. Moral identity dissonance arises particularly around the need to conceal the missionary identity. Charles Taylor wrote that when people feel unmoored from their moral identity, they experience deep existential crisis and dissonance.[15] When tentmakers feel pressured to tell half-truths, mislead people, or lie, it often creates internal disparity with their moral identity standard. Most participants report they had never been put in a situation where they felt they needed to lie directly, such an interrogation. Several said about interrogation that they are uncertain how they would handle it, and many participants expressed compassion for those who felt forced to lie in such situations. However, all participants engage in purposefully withholding information. Many say they intentionally provide true statements that lead people to a false conclusion. Some participants felt this practice was deceitful. Others did not, since they gave true statements.

The concealment of the missionary identity on the field sometimes leads to role partners perceiving the participants as immoral, as participants cannot disclose the whole truth to their role partners. Elyse (Type 2) was pregnant in the GCC but planned to return to the US to have her baby. The company where her husband worked provided health insurance in country, but not for the US healthcare system. However, Elyse's missionary organization required her to carry their healthcare plan, paid for by donor support. Another American expatriate friend, whose husband worked at the same company as Elyse's husband, expressed curiosity about how Elyse would pay for the birth. The question about insurance caught Elyse by surprise, and she had to respond quickly to keep her missionary identity concealed. Elyse told her friend vaguely that they had been grandfathered into some prior special insurance plan that was no longer available, hoping the conversation would end. Instead, the friend kept pressing for more details, desiring a similar health insurance plan to cover medical costs in the US. Elyse kept sidestepping the questions with vague answers, making her friend suspicious. Ultimately, the friend became convinced that Elyse

15. C. Taylor, *Sources of the Self*, 27–28.

was fraudulently using her sister's health insurance. Elyse could not defend her moral identity without explaining her mission organization's healthcare plan, revealing her missionary identity. While Elyse prevented her missionary identity from being uncovered, her moral identity could not be verified with her expatriate friend.

Frequently, stories of moral dissonance come from participants' time in language school, when it was difficult to explain why they had moved their families overseas and were not working—often for two years. William (Type 2) shares an experience of moral identity dissonance when another local warned his Arab friend about William. Upon meeting him, the local assessed William as a liar and warned William's friend not to have anything to do with him. William could not receive verification for his moral identity. He considers himself highly honest, and this assessment bothered him for a long time. William noted there was validity to the local's warning that William *was* hiding something.

Luke (Type 2.5) also reflects some ongoing ambivalence about his strategies to manage team security during language school. His method primarily involved carefully disclosing true but not entirely true statements, framing team meetings as dinner parties. However, he cannot fully resolve the internal tension this created:

> It was weird to say that. I'm not lying. I'm not saying things that are untrue. We *did* eat together. But the fact [is] that you're not telling the whole truth. You've been told to tell [the whole truth] your whole life, and then you're kind of *not*. You're having to be some [other] person to a certain degree. You may not realize [it] at first, but you're just leaving out some details. Yeah, it's weird, [it] doesn't feel right.

Several participants, reflecting on their security practices to conceal their missionary identity, struggle with the concealment and deception sometimes required on the field. Luke, who no longer lives in the GCC, reflects on his inner conflict with telling partial truths to protect others and ministries that he still wrestles with:

> That's conflicting. It's conflicting in that you've always been brought up to tell the truth, the whole truth. You don't want to sin in ministry. You don't want to sin at all. And that's what we're trying to strive for as believers, is [to] live like Christ did. So it's like, do I really need to do that? Do I really need to be subversive? Do I really need to be hiding something? Do I need to *not* tell the

> whole truth on this one? Is that really how God would want me to do this part?
>
> But then at the same time, you have a lot of fear about what could happen if you don't. So yeah, I'd say very conflicted. That was kind of the biggest [pause]. And at the time, it was just kind of a necessity, at least in my head, it was a necessity. It was like, "Well, if we want to stay here and survive here, that's what we have to do." And looking back on it now, it's like, no, maybe [pause]. Maybe not. So [I'm] still conflicted to this day, I guess.

For Luke and several others, partial truths and the feeling of sneaking around in ministry lead to the inner conflict that characterizes moral identity dissonance. However, as Luke notes, these practices often feel necessary. Socialization into the GCC missionary community includes receiving the advice and canon of stories from previous missionaries about security. Balancing the fear of what could happen with the desire for integrity created moral identity dissonance that Luke has not entirely resolved, even after leaving the GCC.

The secrecy required to maintain security in the missionary community sometimes leads missionaries to engage in deceit, especially when trying to protect other people. This often creates dissonance with their moral identity, even if they ultimately decide they might do it again if faced with the same choices in the future. Most participants in this study reported that they did not have to lie in their daily lives and had not been in any situations where they felt forced to lie, such as interrogation. More common were the daily practices of withholding information, or using truthful statements that did not provide the full scope of truth. Participants experiencing little dissonance over these activities often viewed them as acceptable and normal parts of relationships. However, for some participants, frequently using misdirection and not being fully open with people created a profound sense of dissonance. Chapter 5 described the story of Blake (Type 2), who used misdirection regarding his two businesses to lead locals to believe they were supporting his family. Over time, Blake came to associate this misdirection with outright deception, since it had the same end result. He became concerned about the way it was forming his overall moral identity:

> Honestly, I was starting to feel ashamed by how easy it was. It got to a point where I could meet somebody, and I could give them the version of myself that needed to be presented at that time without really having to think. I sort of felt like a chameleon, to the point where I'm not entirely sure which version of myself is the *actual*

> *one*. So that was a big struggle for me. Because I like to think of myself as an honest person. But when nobody else knows you, are you *actually* an honest person? Of my two hundred contacts, there [were] about four that had the whole picture.
>
> And I understand that you can't be full-on with everybody. That's part of life. But these were major things that I was keeping back, and it was too easy to do that, too stressful. I could play the game, no problem. But then [I had] feelings of shame and feelings of "This is wrong." I was intentionally leading people to conclusions that were inaccurate.

Blake described himself as an "open book" and highly people-oriented at the beginning of his interview. He experienced the daily practices of withholding and misleading as highly disparate to his personal identity, to the point that he began questioning which version of himself was the true one.

Blake reports that his police interrogations over his ministry activities challenged his moral identity significantly. He resorted to lying and playing word games to protect other missionaries and BMBs:

> On occasions when I was questioned at length by the police, it was [pause]. Yeah, it was lies. They told me to give a list and write down all of my associates [other missionaries]. [So] I wrote down all of my associates that had already been kicked out of the country, or had moved and weren't coming back. And due to the nature of the ministry that we had, we were connected with pretty much everybody [missionaries] in the wider gulf. When they asked if I had named all of my associates, I said yes, because if I had named all of my associates, I don't know what would have happened. But yeah, [that] didn't feel great.
>
> There was one instance where I claimed ownership of evangelistic material. And it was *not* mine, but I was seeking to take the heat off of a brother. And then when that [lie] was found out by authorities, it caused more problems than I was hoping to solve. So I would have [pause]. I would have done that differently. A lot of that is just [pause]. You start to play word games. It's like, "Well, were they your Bibles?" [and I'd say], "Well, no, but they were in my house." So, [it] depends on how you define ownership. I feel like I'd be a great politician at this point.

In interrogation, Blake sought to protect his ministry teammate and the wider missionary community by withholding information and lying. He later got caught in the lie when police revealed they knew the Bibles and evangelistic materials belonged to his friend. Blake tried to retract his previous statements with word games about ownership—the materials were technically not his, but had been in his possession. Ultimately, Blake saw himself through the eyes of his interrogators: as a liar. Blake remarks with negativity that he has gained the skills to make a great politician, using word games to dodge the truth. He added with deep emotion and tears in his interview,

> It felt awful, knowing that I am possibly the first Christian that these interrogators have ever met. And they are sitting across from a liar. I didn't feel like I was being a good representation of the person of Christ.

When I asked Blake whether he would do anything differently given the same situation again, he was still unsure. He said the missionary he was trying to protect was from a country with less political strength than the US, and Blake was worried about how the police might treat him. His desires to protect fellow missionaries and to be a truthful ambassador of Christ feel at odds with one another. Even years later, recalling this incident of being caught in a lie brought Blake a deep sense of shame.

Coping Strategies for Moral Identity Dissonance

Moral identity dissonance is the most stressful type of dissonance among participants, requiring the most robust coping strategies. Biblical narratives are the most prominent coping mechanism to relieve the dissonance between participants' actions of misleading or deception with their Christian character. Many participants referenced biblical commands or narratives focused on obeying God rather than authorities. These biblical narratives navigate the complexities of relating to governing authorities, concealment, and even deception in contexts of government pressures and persecution. Often, participants referenced the Hebrew midwives in Egypt, who lied to the Pharaoh to protect the lives of Hebrew baby boys (Exod 1:15–19). Several participants brought up Rahab, who lied to the authorities to protect the spies in Jericho (Josh 2:1–11) and whom the New Testament authors commended as an example of faithfulness (Heb 11:31; Jas 2:25). Several participants also quoted Peter and the other apostles who told the Jewish leaders that they were compelled to obey God rather than men, and would not remain silent in their witness to Jesus (Acts 5:27–33).

To cope with the moral dissonance of lawbreaking, participants referred to the lawbreaking actions of Daniel and his friends, living in a pagan nation in exile. Hananiah, Mishael, and Azariah bravely refused to comply with the law to worship Nebuchadnezzar's golden image, trusting in God's deliverance from the furnace they were thrown into as punishment (Dan 3:8–18). Daniel refused to comply with the injunction to only pray to King Darius, continuing in his faithful Jewish practice of prayer towards Jerusalem three times a day—with an open window so that all could see (6:10). This law-breaking caused Daniel to be thrown into a den of lions, but God protected Daniel. The book of Daniel describes faithful obedience to God, to the point of death, by refusing to comply with laws that go against God's commands. Kingdoms and rulers rise and fall, but God is sovereign and only his kingdom will endure. Participants often see their situation as Christians living in RANs in a similar light.

Leslie (Type 2.5) cites both Daniel and Esther as examples of God working through the lawbreaking of his people for transformation:

> In the Old Testament, you have people at the highest forms of government doing a lot of illegal things, and having favor [from God] in the middle of it. You have Esther, you have Daniel, you have people who are not in friendly situations, that God raises to a point of favor and then uses to transform the culture itself.

However, Leslie carefully notes that Daniel and Esther both broke the law in plain sight, not hiding what they were doing, accepting the consequences that may follow for being faithful to God:

> [Preaching the gospel and building the church] does expose you. It may expose you to persecution and to suffering. And if we're doing this among UPGs, it *will*. And that's just [pause]. Persecution is a biblical promise. So I don't think we should be all that afraid of it. I think we should probably try to handle [it], and that's where a lot of these discussions around security things come. We need to be handling our fear and our problem of persecution through a biblical lens of acceptance, rather than "How do I protect myself?" I think that has implications for church planting. I think that has implications for our own sense of boldness while we're here.

For Leslie, understanding persecution as a normative experience leads her to reflect on how to balance wisdom with boldness. Secrecy and fear in a high-security context may inhibit faithful witness. Though the nation's laws make missionary activity illegal, many participants see their lawbreaking as faithfulness in the footsteps of Daniel and other exiles obeying God's commands.

A few participants mentioned David's lies to the priest Ahimelech in Nob as he fled from Saul (1 Sam 21:1—22:19). When Saul feels threatened by David and seeks his life, David flees to Nob for refuge. As the priest Ahimelech is the brother of Ahijah, spiritual advisor to Saul, David may not know whether to trust him (1 Sam 14:3; 22:9). David lies to Ahimelech, saying, "The king sent me on a mission and said to me, 'No one is to know anything about the mission I am sending you on.' As for my men, I have told them to meet me at a certain place" (21:2). David also asks for a weapon, remarking that Saul's mission was so urgent that David had left unarmed (21:8). David tells outright lies to protect himself from certain death. However, Doeg the Edomite, one of Saul's shepherds, is present and tells Saul that David is in Nob. David flees to Gath, and when he hears the citizens repeating the chorus that gives honor to David and shame to Saul, David again fears for his life. His strategy this time is to fake insanity before the king of Gath by letting spittle drip into his beard and by writing on walls and gates (21:13). His ploy works, and he is not detained in Gath and escapes to the cave of Adullam for safety. Participants conclude from this passage that in extreme circumstances, deception may be permitted to protect lives.

Participants in this study report they avoid lying wherever possible, but often recognize that sometimes lying is, in extreme cases, practiced to preserve life—their own lives and especially the lives of BMBs. Duplicity and deception in the face of extreme security situations are present in biblical narratives, and missionaries apply those passages to their situations in various ways. However, the clear biblical injunction to live as people of light and truth, reflecting the God in whom there is no darkness or lie, must be carefully held in tension with these more extreme situations. These biblical narratives helped them frame these experiences when they felt they had no other options to protect themselves or others in high-risk situations.

In addition to theological coping mechanisms, participants also frequently employ cultural framing strategies to resist moral identity dissonance. One strategy to cope with concealment, half-truths, and deception in relationships with locals is framing it as "acting in an Arab way." Participants note cultural differences in perception regarding openness, truth telling, and discretion: Americans want to tell "the truth, the whole truth, and nothing but the truth," whereas Arabs often view lying, withholding, and concealment as necessary and sometimes even morally good actions to protect relationships and people. Paul (Type 2.5) explains the cultural differences in ethics:

> Arabs have, well, honor-shame culture is a hiding culture. It's a covering culture. Just recently, I was teaching on reconciliation [to BMBs]. And one of the guys was sharing this *methl* [Arabic: proverb]. Basically, "I cover you, you cover me," and how that works.

This "covering" culture, Paul explains, values discretion and saving face in relationships rather than full disclosure, which might break ties of loyalty. Holly echoes similar cultural sentiments about truth telling with Easterners and how they do not expect full disclosure as a requisite for healthy relationships:

> When you're dealing with Easterners, I feel like it's very, very natural to withhold a certain amount of information anyway. It's not just about my identity. But that's a strategy for balancing and maintaining healthy relationships. You don't say everything that's complete. Honesty is not necessarily a relationship-builder with Easterners.

Many participants said their missionary lifestyle challenges their American values of openness and telling the whole truth. By adhering to an Eastern ethic of disclosure, they frame their actions of concealing or withholding in a new way, so that they do not have to tell people everything in order to feel that they are being truthful. Elyse demonstrates this cultural coping mechanism throughout her interview as she notes various situations in which she withheld information to protect the missionary identity from being revealed. She refers back to her upbringing in a country where high corruption caused most of the Christians and missionaries she knew to withhold information about imports. This prevented officials from charging exorbitant bribes that were presented as taxes. Elyse's cultural framework allows her to withhold the whole truth in certain situations without experiencing moral identity dissonance.

Derek (Type 2.5) once discipled a group of new BMBs in a small house church in an area of high persecution for converts from Islam. When interrogated by police, Derek withheld information and even lied not for his own safety, but to protect vulnerable BMBs. Derek demonstrates the combination of theological and cultural coping mechanisms that he engages to resist moral identity dissonance successfully:

> I think we follow the model that Jesus modeled. Obviously, Jesus didn't lie. But Jesus, when faced with hard questions, would either ask a question back to the authorities to direct [the conversation] in a different direction, or he would tell a story. Or sometimes, he would just be silent. And so I think those are three great responses that I used. But then, as Westerners, we have a high value of telling the truth. I think it's one of the things that people have [to know] when they come [to the field]. If they're going to be persecuted, they need to have a good theology of [pause]. When your interrogations happen, what is your theology of telling the truth to authorities who are working for the evil one?
>
> Because essentially, *ultimately*, they are working for the god of this world. I think our [local Arab BMB] brothers and sisters taught me that. They [asked me], "Why do we have to obey these authorities if they're working for Satan? We don't need to tell them everything. If we lie, we lie. And that's just part of it." People have got to come to a [balance of] being Christians and submitting to authorities that are put in place, [but also] Peter and John [said], "You're telling us to not share. We can't *not* share. And so we have to listen to God and not to you." And I think there is that element there of [pause]. You have to have good theology of how you're going to answer.

Derek notes the tension and conflict in Scripture regarding submission to authorities and obedience to God. He feels that these passages apply to his interrogations, and that part of subverting Satan's schemes involves lying to or misleading authorities about ministry activities when the government tries to prevent Muslims from becoming Christians. Derek's strategy in interrogations was to give as little helpful information as possible, and not disclosing the whole truth. At several points in his interrogations, he told police he had given them all the names of missionaries or BMBs when he had not. In the end, Derek decided that, along with the BMBs he knew, sometimes it may be necessary to lie in challenging situations in order to protect vulnerable people. These robust coping strategies enable Derek to resist moral identity dissonance.

Many participants feel that telling a partial truth but not the whole truth is an ethical choice, especially compared to lying directly. Even if the partial truth leads to a false conclusion, this is often acceptable to many participants, but not all. In the hierarchical control model, moral identity is one of the highest-level identities that a person has.[16] Certain situations

16. Burke and Stets, *Identity Theory*, 145.

may put people in a position to act in conflict with higher-order identities, creating a discrepancy that must be resolved.[17] One option for relieving the discrepancy involves continuing in the behavior and shifting the identity to align with the chosen behavior. Groups aid resistance to moral identity dissonance and can help the individual continue in the practice by providing a context in which the practice meets the community's expectations.[18] Many participants refer to the missionary community in their interviews as passing on the acceptable practices for concealing the missionary identity, often through stories of their experiences.

The other option for resolving the discrepancy in moral identity is a radical reorientation to verify the moral identity.[19] Blake notes that over time, his behaviors of concealing and leading others to a false conclusion were forming him into a chameleon. Ultimately, his family left the GCC for other reasons, but his experience with moral identity dissonance was one factor preventing them from returning to the Arabian Peninsula. He now works as a missionary to Muslims in a non-RAN, where his evangelistic work is legal. His missionary identity is still prominent, but the moral identity is the higher-level identity that has realigned the standards of behavior so that both identities can be verified. Other participants also coped with moral identity dissonance with radical reorientations, such as changing jobs to reduce deception, or leaving the field entirely.

Dissonance #3: Vocational Identity Dissonance

Another category of dissonance arising from interviews is vocational identity dissonance. In this type of dissonance, the participants experience conflict between their vocational roles and their core sense of self. Participants in both categories of job takers and business owners experience some vocational identity dissonance, but business owners report more frequently that they feel a lower sense of alignment with their vocation. Some business owners—especially Type 2s—first entered the field with few vocational qualifications, such as business training or expertise in a particular area or consulting work. Their organizations often encouraged these missionaries to start a business to gain a visa, and sometimes provided BAM training or mentorship. Some Type 2 business owners flourished in their tentmaking

17. Burke and Stets, *Identity Theory*, 225.

18. Burke and Stets, *Identity Theory*, 145.

19. Burke and Stets, *Identity Theory*, 226.

endeavors and had opportunities to integrate work and ministry. Others, whose personal identities and values clashed with the requirements for entrepreneurial ventures, floundered and experienced tentmaking as inordinately stressful. These participants tend to see work in opposition to ministry, as a necessary burden to bear for the sake of the gospel.

Blake is one such Type 2 business owner who felt that work competed with his own sense of personal identity. Blake felt a strong sense of calling to be a missionary in the hardest places from a young age, and he had been preparing to proclaim the gospel among the unreached since he was fifteen. His vocational plan was that he would do whatever he had to in order to accomplish this task. He held a certificate in teaching English, but had never taught English beyond what was required for his certification in TESOL (teaching English to speakers of other languages). He had originally planned to go to Yemen, but war broke out just before he left for the field, thwarting those plans. As a result, he was underprepared for maintaining a visa in the GCC, where English-teaching jobs often require a master's degree and several years of experience. After completing language school in the GCC, he took over the ownership of a functioning business in another city. His clients were mostly other expatriates in his city. He described his business venture as "the most soul-sucking, like difficult . . . I think even if I had a degree in international business, the way that businesses worked, and the levels of government bureaucracy were just a little bit beyond my ability to cope. I would not wish running a business in that country on anyone." Blake felt a strong sense of dissonance between his vocational identity and his personal identity. His personal aptitudes were in highly relational skills; he identified administrative duties as among his lowest personal aptitudes. Unfortunately, he found that the skills most often needed for his particular role in his business were highly administrative.

When locals ask Henry (Type 2) why he came to the GCC, he explains that a job opportunity came up, though it was his missionary calling to UPGs that actually drew him to the gulf. He works for a company started by his missionary organization, performing administrative tasks. He values the company's work in the community and appreciates that it provides visas for his family. In addition, working for a company owned by his organization's leaders provides time flexibility for ministry, and eliminates the need to conceal his missionary identity from his employer. But he describes his job as "an emotional and physical drain" and hopes to someday shift to a vocational role more aligned with his personal aptitudes. He is in no hurry to change jobs, however. His teammates are job takers, and he is concerned that taking a job will reduce time and capacity for ministry—an experience his teammates currently struggle with.

All participants in this study performed real jobs in actual companies, even if those jobs could not supply their complete income needs. However, Richard and Sally came closer to "tent faking" than other participants, and this caused a profound sense of vocational identity dissonance. Richard and Sally (both Type 2s) arrived in the GCC under the identity of students studying Arabic. However, upon their arrival, the Arabic class they had registered for did not have enough students to move forward. They lived on tourist visas for a year, looking for residence visa opportunities, but their plans kept falling through. Their mission organization finally asked them to start their own business in order to secure a visa, doing trainings for students. Other tentmakers with this organization had used this vocational identity in the past. However, the mission organization's policy was for missionaries to put minimal hours towards the business—around two to four hours per week—to leave more time for ministry. Over time, Richard and Sally found this policy profoundly detrimental to their identity in the country. They perceived that locals did not trust them because of their inability to answer questions about their work in a legitimate and convincing way.

Sally felt that their organization's approach to evangelism and policies toward vocational work prevented them from developing trust with locals:

> We read it takes, on average, seven years for a [Muslim] to come to know [God]. And so we started realizing, especially here, it's going to take *relationships*, it's going to take time, it's going to take getting close to people. But we see that some other personalities, they don't really have that in their mind. They have this motto, "[God] is at work. We want to go to the places and to the people where he's already at work, and partner with him there!" And so what that looks like practically for them is running from person to person to person, just skimming the surface, finding out, "Are they open? Are they ready today?" If not, moving on. And so it's not a big deal if you don't have a solid business identity, because you're not going deep with too many people anyway. Several staff in our region have tried this strategy for many years, and it hasn't produced the results most people expected or hoped for.
>
> I think we've really asked the question "Why?" Because we also bought into that [idea] when we first moved here. But even if [God] was at work in their life, they wouldn't trust you and tell you after knowing you for twenty minutes. So I think we started

> realizing it's going to take deep relationships with people, and that requires vulnerability and sharing life.

Sally found that their missionary identity was constantly at risk of discovery because they did not have a clear and truthful vocational identity in the community. Though she identifies herself as an open person who values vulnerability and authenticity, she closed herself off from locals to prevent her missionary identity from being discovered. She avoided deepening relationships with the people she was trying to reach, because she felt they could see through the façade she was constructing.

Richard also felt a deep sense of dissonance between his personal identity and his vocational identity in his minimalist business practices. Richard identifies himself as a hard worker with high integrity, as well as a driven and competent problem-solver. He left a very successful vocational role in the US to be a missionary. However, on the field, his organization actively discouraged him from developing the consulting business. This created problems when a local man invited Richard for coffee. He asked many questions about the business Richard supposedly ran. It quickly became clear that the Arab knew much about business, and Richard knew very little. Compounding the stress, the local man was a police officer. Richard grew increasingly concerned that his flimsy vocational identity would cause his missionary identity to be discovered. A similar situation happened again with an Arab business owner, who questioned Richard extensively about the business model to try to help Richard. Richard found these conversations enormously stressful, causing him to avoid developing close relationships with locals. He perceived that locals were interpreting him as an incompetent businessman at best, and a shameful charlatan at worst. When Richard and Sally brought up their identity concerns to their organizational leaders, they were told that they were letting fear, rather than faith, guide their decisions. Their organizational leaders told them to pray for boldness.

Richard describes this dissonant experience as one of having a "split identity"—of being one person in some circles, and another person entirely in others. This dissonance is characterized by an experience of deep inauthenticity:

> It's not enjoyable; that is not who I am. It's a complete lack of authenticity. And that's really hard, long-term here, to not be authentic. We read one source that said that's one of the most stressful things anyone can do, is be something that you are not. And it's

> definitely true, because every second you have to filter what you're saying and what you're doing to try to be this thing. Because it doesn't naturally flow from who you are.

For Richard, vocational identity dissonance led to an experience of being deeply incongruent with his core self.

William's (Type 2) vocational identity dissonance is especially interesting among participants, because he was the only participant who obtained a visa by pastoring an expatriate church. The other pastors at the church knew his primary purpose for being in the GCC was to reach Arab Muslims for Christ, but he says only about a third of the congregation knew his missionary identity. His role in the expatriate church involved discipling new believers, often African or Indian expatriates, but his primary calling was with gulf Arabs:

> My role was, anyone that would come to faith, typically Africans, a few Indians, I walked with them for six to eight weeks and got them on the runway toward discipleship. And, then the rest of the day was trying to meet [local Arab Muslims] because I made it really clear with [the senior pastor] that I was there to do gulf Arab work. And so graciously, they said, "That's wonderful." So the church was great.

In his vocation, William made a distinction between his clerical role and his missionary role, which he generally did not experience as dissonant roles. However, his vocational identity dissonance arose while discipling new believers from a background of poverty and injustice. William felt embarrassed about his vocation and middle class lifestyle, and that people paid for him to read the Bible with others in a foreign country. In contrast, those he discipled got their visas through backbreaking, underpaid manual labor:

> So these guys that I would meet with, Africans that were brought in for construction work. A few of them, their passports were taken. They'd gone to the mosque and they'd be pushed to the back. They weren't able to worship with the Arabs. And they were so burned [out] and confused. And you'd go on their Facebook page, and they'd have suits on. It was really clear, they're telling everyone back home [that] they were [working] in an office. They were working, but it was awful.
>
> Anyway, they would come to faith and come to the church, [saying], "Islam is not the answer." It was really cool. But getting to know them, they asked [me], "What do you do?" And these guys are scraping their backs just to build pavement or roads. I've really

> struggled with this. "Oh, people are just paying me to live here." I can't even remember how I articulated a lot of that. But it was very much like, "I work for the church. I'm here to encourage people, disciple people, and the Scriptures really matter to us." And I was just talking my way through it. I really wrestled with that. Not even on a visa level, just like, "What the heck am I doing, talking to these people?" And they probably wouldn't have been judgmental or condemning. But I felt a bit of shame.

As a pastor, William presented a clerical identity to the public. However, he still largely concealed his missionary purposes towards gulf Arabs, as well as his sources of funding.[20] This concealment resulted in embarrassment while conversing with his congregants whom he perceived might have judged him for living a comparably extravagant lifestyle for easier work. These congregants did not see the sacrifices and labor of missionary service that William had to conceal. It appeared to them that he did very little work and yet received a visa that they broke their bodies to get, for a much more substantial financial return. This created dissonance between his vocational identity and his core self, resulting in feelings of shame. When their team broke down, William and his family left the GCC for a few years, but they plan to return soon. However, William is not pursuing a clerical identity at an expatriate church again; he plans to start a business instead. He feels this vocational identity will be much more aligned with the lifestyle his family will live among gulf Arabs in order to reach them.

Coping Strategies for Vocational Identity Dissonance

Coping mechanisms for vocational identity dissonance are often less defined for participants. Several participants currently have jobs they do not enjoy. The primary coping strategy is to remember their primary purpose: reaching UPGs with the gospel. This motivation provides some measure of resistance to vocational identity dissonance but several participants note that it might not endure forever. The vocational identity dissonance was rarely so disparaging that it required an immediate and significant change. However, several participants note that they hope for a change in the future to align their vocational roles with their personal aptitudes.

20. The pastors of expatriate churches in the GCC are often funded by churches and supporters in their passport countries, with either very little or no supplemental income from the expatriate church itself.

Richard and Sally experienced the most significant vocational identity dissonance of all participants, to the degree that they could not verify their core identities. Sally grew concerned about the type of person her lack of legitimate vocation was leading to, which brought a sense of despair:

> I've felt hopeless. Because I feel like I'm changing, my personality is changing. And sometimes I don't like who I'm becoming. And so then I feel hopeless. I'm [not] able to do this for a long time.

As a result of this dissonance, Richard and Sally made significant changes in order to verify their identities, aligning their personal values with their vocation. They switched to a different team that valued vocational identity more than their first team leaders did. In addition, they are starting a new business venture that demonstrates a higher alignment with their personal skills, education, interests, and ministry goals. They are hopeful that this change will eventually give them greater identity consonance and a legitimate identity in the community. Their goal is for a visa platform that creates openness and transparency, rather than concealment and fear of discovery. They believe this change will enable them to stay in the GCC long-term.

Compared to job takers, business owners may be more vulnerable to vocational identity dissonance. Several business owners have little or no training in the roles they are performing, or feel a substantial mismatch between their vocational roles and their personal identity or aptitude. Type 2 business owners sometimes express more ambivalence about making a profit, and experience more anxiety about their funding sources being discovered. Because of their unclear vocational roles and income, business owners are likelier than job takers to be accused of being missionaries. This leads to more instances of misleading or concealing behaviors to manage the missionary identity.

Dissonance #4: Missionary Identity Dissonance

For participants, the missionary identity is a prominent identity, but one that requires concealment in RANs. Missionary identity dissonance is the distress arising from the inability to verify the missionary identity. The expectations and behaviors of the missionary identity include developing relationships with locals, sharing the gospel with Muslims, discipling and teaching BMBs, and developing indigenous church leadership. While participants who are business owners experience vocational identity dissonance more frequently, job takers experience missionary identity dissonance more frequently. Two main causes emerged from interviews for missionary identity dissonance among job takers: (1) the time requirements for the job impeded other ministry activities, and (2) many job takers encountered few local Arabs in the workplace. These factors contribute to an experience of competition between the vocational and missionary role identities, preventing vocation-ministry integration.

Most participants—across Prescott's tentmaker types, job takers, and business owners—express strong opinions that vocation is important for mission, and that missionaries need robust theologies of vocation. However, many participants also simultaneously express that their vocation both helps and competes with their missionary identities in various ways. Job takers in this study report that the struggle for time and energy is one of their biggest hurdles to verifying their missionary identity. In these situations, many tentmakers end the workday so exhausted that spending time with locals—especially in Arabic—seems impossible or undesirable. This is especially challenging in the UAE, where Emiratis comprise a little over 10 percent of the total population and are often difficult to engage with.[21] In addition, many missionaries who expected to use their vocation as part of their ministry were disappointed when the two role identities did not complement each other well on the field. Some participants lament that they work with few local Arabs; instead, they work primarily with expatriates, further dividing vocation and ministry from one another. Demanding vocational environments, combined with few opportunities to engage with local UPGs at work, sometimes leads to personal crises about whether the missionary can do what they came to do. These crises led several participants to quit their jobs and find new ones, change fields, or change their visa types.

Brad (Type 2.5) works in the finance industry. He has worked in his profession in the United States, and then in two different GCC countries. His experiences of working in Arab-run companies as an expatriate have been difficult, and ultimately prompted him to move his family from one GCC country to another nearly two years ago. He remarks that the company cultures in the gulf frequently exhibit unreasonable deadlines, understaffing, unhealthy relational dynamics, and long hours. While he had more Arab co-workers in his job in the first GCC country, now the colleagues he works with are mostly expatriates from non-Arab backgrounds. His job currently drains his energy and time so much that he struggles to leave

21. Total Population by Country.

his house to connect with local Muslims, leaving him unable to verify his missionary identity by fulfilling his calling:

> It's hard when there's a lot of pressure in the work environment to feel like [pause]. I don't really feel like I'm doing what I want to do here. I mean, I want to be intentional in the workplace. And it feels like I'm separated from locals in the workplace right now. And so if work is terrible, and I don't feel like I'm doing what I want to do here, if I come home drained from the workplace every day, and I just don't want to leave the house [pause]. Why am I here?

Brad strongly believes that vocation and ministry can and should go together. However, work and ministry feel much less integrated now that he has fewer interaction with Arabs at work—the people group he feels called to reach and whose language he learned. He maintains hope that he will see more unity between work and ministry in the future, noting that he has only been in this job less than two years. However, his vocation currently leaves him unable to fulfill his missionary calling, the primary reason he and his family moved to the gulf.

Simon (Type 2.5) has been in the GCC for nearly three decades. He started his missionary career with a series of business-owning ventures, some on his own and some in partnership with his missionary organization. Especially in the first decade, Simon experienced both vocational and missionary identity dissonance. Simon, mentored by BAM practitioners and church planters separately, envisioned bringing both role identities together. He wrote a business plan, secured investors, and put in significant hours to make a financially sustainable business. He hoped this business would provide a legitimate identity in the GCC, allowing him to develop trusting relationships in his community.

Simon and his wife, Rosemary, faced many challenges as tentmakers. One of the most significant was conflict with others on the field who preferred to work fewer hours for business in order to make more time for ministry. Simon recalls with frustration the business and financial practices of his colleagues, who developed their businesses very little. These practices made Simon wary of tentmaking endeavors altogether:

> I deal with a lot of PTSD [Simon and Rosemary both laugh]. There were points where I backed out of anything tentmaker-ish, because there's just such dissonance in terms of values. There's so much PTSD. And we struggle with our sending organizations

> that recruit out of Christian colleges, people that have never even thought about working before coming out here.

Simon also laments the recruitment strategies of mission organizations that fail to recruit actual business professionals to run businesses, and he believes this hurts the overall missionary goals. Simon's particular balance of business and ministry were incongruent with some in the wider missionary community. Simon notes that work and ministry in the GCC looked nothing like his—or his colleagues'—pre-field expectations.

It took a long time for Simon and Rosemary to balance vocation and ministry in a way that led to congruence. They both experienced missionary identity dissonance for many years because of the toll of Simon's work. He often worked between sixty and eighty hours per week, sleeping in his office rather than at home. He calls this time "purgatory," especially because he worked so hard without taking a salary from the business, living on full support. His family, which included young children then, was under severe strain. There was little time for ministry beyond building relationships with the local women Simon had hired to work in his office, and local gender norms prevented Simon from developing these relationships much. Rosemary, who describes herself during that time as "underwater with the kids," had little contact with locals, and little capacity for ministry. While the business looked outwardly successful as a tentmaking venture and other missionaries commented that it was, Rosemary knew the company was not successfully bringing business and ministry together into an integrated whole:

> I was like, this is *not* why we came here. And I am *done*. Yeah, it was hard. It was so hard because we would meet people and they [said excitedly], "You guys are doing it!" And it's like, [shakes head no]. There were some neat things happening on my side [in ministry relationships with locals]. But Simon wished that I was in his world [to interact with the local women at his office]. But I'm like, I can't. And actually, I don't really *want* to enter his world, because his world is driving me nuts.

Simon and Rosemary's marriage and team life were full of conflict over the business, and Rosemary grew to resent the business for the fractures it caused in her family. Simon and Rosemary recognized that this business model was not conducive to the reproducing church-planting ministry they both felt called to. Rosemary recalls Simon's dissonance in both his ministry and business role identities, saying, "Simon, at this point, is feeling like a fake. He feels like a fraud in both these areas [business and ministry]." After much prayer, Simon sought additional training and employment options to create more margin in his schedule—for family and relationships with locals outside of work.[22] Today, Simon is employed in a local business, having transitioned from business owner to job taker. He can use his business aptitude and vocational education at work, achieving the excellence in vocation he deeply values without being in charge of everything. At the same time, he has a thriving ministry engaging with locals, discipling BMBs, and mentoring the next generation of missionaries. As Rosemary watched her husband emerge from his dissonant experiences, she exclaimed, "I remember you!" The real Simon had gotten lost in all the turmoil of their first decade on the field, but he was now coming into his authentic identity.

Job takers face both joys and challenges for expressing a Christian witness through their vocation. In fact, when asked whether their job helps them in ministry or competes with ministry, almost every participant answered, "Both." Though several teachers in the GCC saw teaching as a way to integrate vocation and ministry, Holly (Type 2) felt that teaching complicated ministry rather than enhanced it, causing missionary identity dissonance:

> I think the longer I worked there [at the school], the more I felt like [teaching and ministry] were increasingly at odds with each other. In some ways, it's kind of funny, because technically I was interacting more with [locals] when I was working [as a teacher], but it was certainly not ministry-focused in any way. It was very, very professional. At the beginning, developing relationships with students was very much off [limits], just for professional reasons.
>
> But it was also not a possibility developing relationships with coworkers. There were maybe one or two, but they were not very deep friendships. I think the biggest issue was just time and energy. We were all working full-time, a lot of them are also moms or also students at the same time. These are not people who have time for relationships. And of course, it was a very English-heavy

22. Simon noted in his interview that while he once desired to integrate work and ministry, he now minimizes gospel-centered conversations at work because of power dynamics between employers and employees. He found that locals almost always agreed to read the Bible with him when they worked with him. He later realized they may not have felt they had a choice. Alternatively, they may have feigned interest to get promotions or raises. Thus, Simon generally keeps his ministry relationships separate from his work relationships.

> environment, and that's why they paid me—to speak English in that environment.
>
> So I didn't feel that I developed deep relationships or what I would call "visiting relationships" within the city where I had moved to, because the work was such a huge chunk of my time. At the same time, I also felt like I regressed significantly in my language abilities, which impacts how I connect with people, both at work and outside of work. But in terms of what I felt ministry should look like, which is more personal interactions with people, [teaching] didn't really allow for that. I know other people do function well in those environments, but I didn't.

Holly found that her sense of professionalism prevented her from developing deep relationships with her students and colleagues. Her struggle for time and energy after working a full-time job in order to make space for "visiting relationships" was a tremendous struggle that culminated in her searching for other means of gaining a visa. With the inability to verify her missionary identity through her vocation, Holly significantly changed her environment, her visa, and how she was known in the community to facilitate her ministry goals more effectively. She ultimately quit her stable teaching job for more uncertain opportunities elsewhere in the GCC to increase ministry focus, a transition she was in the midst of during her interview.

Some job takers noted the tensions within the missionary community regarding the "real work" of missionary activity. Because job takers must devote a significant amount of time and energy to their vocation, they find that their organizations or other missionaries on the field sometimes question when they finally get around to the "real work" of evangelism, discipleship, and church planting. Many job takers strongly believe that their vocation allows them to be missional to those around them, and that their faithfulness in the workplace *is* ministry. Steve (Type 3), working in an international finance corporation, expresses frustration with the ideas of what a church planter should do every day, and how that differs from what he as a professional does every day:

> There are certain people that have made comments in our country that have said, "Oh, so when do you actually get to go out and *do ministry* if you work full-time?" [I reply], "Well, my job is part of my ministry, actually."

Steve feels a strong calling to his vocation and a strong congruence with that identity. This has sometimes caused other missionaries in the community to question his missionary identity and commitment. The role partners of other missionaries and sometimes supporters in the US fail to verify his missionary identity.

Naomi (Type 2.5) laments that in the mission community, she sometimes feels that full-time job takers are viewed as inferior to business-owning missionaries with more time flexibility. Naomi goes on to say that she is happy to work with fully supported missionaries; she wishes everyone would "bless each other" as they all walk in their callings from God. However, she does not think that fully supported missionaries always feel that way about her family as job takers who must balance a full-time workload in addition to ministry responsibilities. Such attitudes foster missionary identity dissonance, as those with full-time jobs feel that others in the mission community do not verify their missionary identity.

Nathan (Type 2.5) experienced a mild form of missionary identity dissonance common to job takers in the GCC when his vocation competed with his missionary identity. Nathan is a business professional for a start-up company in the GCC, and also provides training to businesses around the gulf. In general, he feels a high degree of alignment with his vocational identity, and he firmly believes in the principles of BAM that integrate business and mission. Because he works part-time for the start-up, and because he can schedule training seminars as he chooses, he has more flexibility with his vocation than many tentmakers. As a result, he can invest deeply in Muslim and BMB relationships.

However, he recalls one situation where his missionary identity competed with his vocational identity. A BMB he had been discipling was suicidal after experiencing significant family and community persecution. Nathan spent a significant amount of time with this BMB, staying up late into the night and trying to encourage and pray with him. The next day, when his boss asked Nathan how he was, he said things were good, which was not true. The next question was whether he had finished a report assigned to him. He had been up until three that morning with the BMB, and could not complete his work for the company that week. At the beginning of the interview, Nathan and his wife had both described him as hard-working, perfectionistic, and someone who finishes what he starts. Nathan, due to how his two role identities collided in this situation, was not able to receive verification for his personal identity from his boss, who could not know the concealed reasons why Nathan did not complete his work.

In most of the GCC, local populations are often highly resistant to the gospel. Missionaries may go for long periods without having spiritually fruitful conversations, discipleship opportunities, or the opportunity to facilitate church planting. In such situations, the missionary identity cannot easily be verified. Tansy describes how this low degree of apparent spiritual success can impact a missionary's identity:

> When you know your calling, then you tend to equate your identity with how you're fulfilling that calling. And in the Western world, oftentimes, reports of what's happening is how Western people identify who you are, like your success or your failures. So for example, in Africa, [missionaries showed the] Jesus film and 3000 people prayed to receive Christ. And those are documented, you know, "Look at what we did!" You don't hear that here. And because that is, or has been in the past, such a publicized method of success [pause]. I mean, we hear it everywhere, you know? Then the [missionaries] themselves want to equate that with their identity.

Tansy then contrasts apparently successful missionaries in Africa with the ten to twenty believers in the whole country when she arrived in the GCC. When a missionary goes to the field with a vision of evangelism and discipleship but then sees very little spiritual fruit, it can create profound missionary identity dissonance. Tansy describes missionary friends whose churches did not verify their missionary role identities because they had not planted a church:

> We've had [missionaries] that have been here for probably thirty years, and went back to their home country. People had stopped supporting them because they hadn't planted a church yet. Because they don't recognize the groundbreaking of prayer, or the seed sowing that has to take place. The timing of the Lord, right? It was very, very hurtful, after serving in such a hard place for so long, that one of their main churches had quit supporting them.

Tansy notes that highly visible spiritual fruit—-such as conversion of thousands of people in Africa—is not yet happening to that degree in the GCC. Yet missionaries' identities are often dependent on ministry success for verification. Tansy warns that this is dangerous not only for the missionaries themselves, but also for the BMBs they may disciple, who need to know that their identity is in Christ, not in visible success.

Coping Strategies for Missionary Identity Dissonance

Coping mechanisms for resisting missionary identity dissonance differ from other types of dissonance. The participants identify their missionary purposes as the primary reason for moving to the gulf, so having an unverified missionary identity often creates significant distress that needs resolving. When their job puts them in contact primarily with expatriates, some participants reframed their missional goals to include all people in their spheres of influence. Others, however, felt a particular calling from God to certain people groups that they could not ignore. They had also invested considerable time learning the language and culture of gulf Arabs, which they did not want to waste. These participants often grew frustrated with the language regression they experienced in the workplace, and the lack of time to invest in relationships with locals outside of work. Tentmakers in such situations often viewed work as a necessary means to an end so that they could invest more time in their "after-hours" job as missionaries, leading to higher competition between vocation and ministry rather than integration.

Sometimes the missionary and vocational role identities competed, and participants chose one identity to verify over the other. When Nathan experienced tension between his two roles of vocation and missionary, he coped by allowing the higher-order identity to control the lower-order identity. In the hierarchical control system, the missionary identity controlled the behavior, and his vocational identity lost as he prioritized his role of discipling a BMB. This caused him to be briefly perceived by his employer as lazy, since Nathan could not reveal why he had not written the report. Nathan's overall tension about this situation was mild, knowing he had chosen to do the right thing when his vocational role conflicted with his missionary role. A few participants described similar situations in which they made a choice that prioritized their missionary identity over their vocational identity, such as refusing promotions that might reduce their ministry opportunities.

When participants consistently could not verify their missionary identity due to the dynamics of their vocation, their responses often aligned with the hierarchical control system model. Many participants made drastic changes in order to verify their higher-order identity of the missionary identity. They found employment in another company or even in another country, significantly changed the business model being used, or switched the visa type from job taker to business owner or vice versa. Ten of the thirty-eight participants had previously made such drastic changes specifically for the purpose of increasing ministry opportunities. In addition to those ten, two women who had been homemakers had started businesses, and one woman was starting a new vocation soon to increase ministry opportunities.[23] Therefore, thirteen of the thirty-eight participants made significant vocational changes in order to increase ministry opportunities and reduce competition between their role identities.

In addition to drastic changes, several participants described how viewing life on the field as a marathon rather than a sprint helped them when they felt dissonance with their missionary identity. The participants who had been on the field the longest had achieved more consonance between their vocation and ministry, which will be further discussed below. Rosemary quoted the book of Hebrews as she considered how perseverance over a long period of time, even when ministry does not seem fruitful, helps her resist dissonance:

> In Hebrews it says, "Run the race that is marked for you, fix your eyes on Jesus." And it's really hard in these seasons to think about what kind of race you're trying to [run]. A short-termer who comes in for three months or six months, or even a year, is going to run a different race than a family who is going to move in and try to live their life [there]. So, what's the race for you *in this season*?
>
> And it's really hard because a short-term person or short-term team can come in and [I] could [think], "I am such a failure. They're out there every hour and met six people. I only met two people this week." [But you have] to evaluate, because when you're running a marathon, sometimes you can find a rhythm. We are huge Narnia fans. There's that line when Aslan comes behind the horses and scares Bree [in the book *The Horse and His Boy*]. Because Shasta says they're going as fast as they can. And then the writer says, "He's going as fast as he *thinks* he can." And so there definitely are these moments still to evaluate [whether you're going at the right pace].
>
> The longevity [issue] is, we can all get into a pace one way or the other. Simon and I, we'll get into a season where we're sprinting. And I think sprints are there, you hit a sprint season. You are hosting a short-[term] team, you are doing something big, but then you [realize], "Oh, actually, this is not an actual livable pace."

23. One additional participant, still a job taker, said he is working toward being self-supported through savings and opening a consulting business in order to increase time devoted to church-planting activities.

By considering her ministry as a long-term marathon, Rosemary resists dissonance against her missionary identity, particularly when short-term teams come in and are able to do more ministry than she can in a short time. Many participants coped with missionary identity dissonance through prayer and waiting, trusting God to provide opportunities or major changes if needed. Giving the situation time was a frequent coping mechanism. Several participants, such as Brad in his new job, were in a season of hopeful waiting that their missionary roles would increase soon.

In contexts of low spiritual fruit, vocation also provided some resistance against missionary identity dissonance. Participants with a strong vocational identity, whether they are business owners or job takers, have the benefit of an additional identity to fall back on, verified through successful and engaging work and social interactions at their job. A strong vocational identity proved important for managing participants' sense of personal and social identity when the missionary identity could not be verified. Those with jobs they enjoyed and where they were respected and had healthy colleague dynamics were more likely to resist existential crises when missionary activities were few.

A final coping strategy for missionary identity dissonance is a careful process for evaluating ministry success and therefore the missionary identity for verification. Tansy says the realities of working as missionaries in a spiritually resistant place mean that missionaries must evaluate their work and their identities with care:

> So now for the identity of [missionaries]. They come here wanting to disciple others. And yet, life hits and it's hard, right? The average for an MBB to come to Christ is five to seven years. And in the gulf, generally eight to ten, right? Maybe there's some change in that and for some people these days, a little sooner, but it's a lengthy time, right? So it's very important for a [missionary to understand] that their identity needs to come from Christ, how Christ sees them, first and foremost. Because as they get to work with an MBB, that MBB needs to know who they are in Christ. So our identity comes from Christ.
>
> But we do need to evaluate our work. Are we really living in the purpose that we've come here to do? And if you're going to identify as a [missionary], then are you being intentional with your time? We teach [missionaries] to figure out how they're going to evaluate that. How many conversations were you able to curve to give glory to God? That might have been inserting the word, it might have been expressing something that God has done for you lately,

> it might have been praying for that person. But if you're going to count something, let's count how many times we've done that. How many times have you entered into a new relationship with a local, in an effort to build trust and understanding to earn the right to share the gospel with them? They really don't care what you know, if they don't know that you care about them and that they can trust you.

Tansy remarks that even though a missionary may not be able to measure conversions or church plants as markers of ministry success, missionaries still need ways of evaluating whether they're doing their job faithfully. These evaluation criteria help the missionary verify their missionary identity in the absence of visible spiritual fruit.

Dissonance #5: Friend Identity Dissonance

Friend identity dissonance is the final category of identity dissonance that participants describe. The need to conceal the missionary identity prevents tentmakers from sharing certain aspects of their lives with their friends, whether with Muslim locals, BMBs, or other non-missionary expatriates. Participants often describe the experience as wearing a mask and never truly being their authentic selves with these friends. This category of dissonance overlaps with dual identity dissonance, but specifically focuses on inhibitions in friendships. Greater familiarity increases the likelihood of needing to conceal, sidestep, mislead, or even lie to prevent the missionary identity from being revealed. These actions prevent participants from verifying the friend identity, as their assumed expectations of the friend role include openness, authentic sharing of the self, and trust.

Brooke (Type 2) is concerned about her integrity when offering to pay for a meal out with a Muslim friend, as the concealed truth behind the funding means she is not as generous as she appears to her friend:

> I still think it can be a little misleading in friendships. If you [say], "Oh, I'll cover this meal," [but] it's a ministry meal. You're not covering it personally, but it looks like you are. I'm *appearing* to be so generous. That does not mean that's being generous. There are people behind me being generous. So there's a little bit of an integrity thing there.

Brooke feels a dichotomy between how she presents herself to her friend and her actual financial situation. While her friends think of Brooke as generous for covering meals, Brooke relies on the generosity of her supporters to cover ministry meals. This leaves Brooke unable to verify the friend identity with behaviors of honesty and gift-giving.

Amy (Type 2.5) once lied to her local Muslim friends to manage the identity of a short-term missionary who came to her city without a job. Amy says she hates introducing short-term missionaries with no clear vocational identity to her Arab friends, because she feels forced to lie to them and break their trust:

> These are people that I love and trust that I'm introducing [the short-term missionaries] to. And even one of my [local Arab] friends was like, "I don't get it, Amy, why is she living in that nice apartment? She said that she doesn't have a job. I don't understand. It doesn't make sense to me." And I'm like, I don't know how to [pause]. I just kind of blew it. I said, "She's young. She can live off her parents," blah blah blah, which was all a lie. I just made that up, it's not even true. But I knew that she was going to be questioning, wondering. And I don't want to lie to people. I want to be as honest as I can possibly be.

Amy is frustrated and feels forced to lie to protect short-termers' missionary identities. Lying produces moral identity dissonance, and makes Amy feel like a bad friend when she breaks the trust her local friends place in her.

In addition, because Amy juggles multiple role identities—some that must be concealed—difficulties also arise for her when she cannot let her Muslim friends know about the other parts of her life. Amy values spending time with locals in their homes, babysitting their children, and deeply sharing her life with her Muslim friends. Amy's mission organization is training her in leadership skills through a program for missionaries. She also spends significant time with other missionaries for team meetings, prayer, and ministry projects. Amy hides these missionary activities from her Arab friends, who cannot understand why Amy always seems tired. She describes the dissonance of not being authentic and open with close friends about these parts of her life:

> They see that I'm so tired a lot of the time, because *I am*. But they're like, "All you do is work a job and you go home. You're single, you don't have a family." And they [have] no idea that I'm basically working two full-time jobs, and studying Arabic, and doing all these other things, and doing leadership courses. And yeah, when I'm doing leadership courses, I do share some of the information [that I'm learning]. I kind of vaguely share, but sometimes I wish I could more specifically share some of those things, or explain to

> them why I'm so exhausted. I feel like they can't quite understand that dynamic.

Because Amy withholds some aspects of her life from her friends, they misunderstand her and cannot imagine why she experiences exhaustion, especially as a single woman with no family responsibilities. This creates dissonance between Amy's self-concept and her friend identity.

Participants involved with the expatriate community, such as with the expatriate church, struggle to verify the friend identity with expatriates who cannot know about their missionary identity. Richard and Sally (both Type 2) say they found themselves avoiding locals and expatriates in their free time because they did not want them to get too close and discover their true identities. They express that they often only want to be around other missionaries because they can let their guard down around them. In other social fields, they feel they must filter themselves, which is exhausting.

Many mission organizations require their personnel to achieve some level of formal theological education. As a result, expatriate church leaders often expect tentmakers to serve the local expatriate church by leading Bible studies or teaching, a challenge several participants described. Laura (Type 2) and her husband explained to their expatriate church leaders that their priority was in building relationships with locals, rather than attending church Bible studies and prayer meetings. Laura had avoided going to Bible studies but ended up in one for a few weeks while her children attended another program during that time. She contrasts how the expatriate church perceives her with her true identity, which she feels she must conceal from them:

> I went to a Bible study two or three years ago. And I would go in, I just wanted to hear, I didn't want to take over. But I did end up sharing, and everybody [started] asking me questions, and I'm seen then as the expert. And I know why, but then there are the questions of "Why don't you give to *us*? Why don't you serve *us*?" Not that anybody specifically says that, but there are comments. There is that tension.
>
> So I'm trying to imagine it from their point of view. I mean, it would look quite selfish. Like, what *am* I doing? Because I can't show them that I'm teaching SA [spiritual Arabic, taught to missionaries who are language students]. And I can't tell them that up until last summer, my husband and I were the leaders for our organization in the gulf. So there was admin, and there was planning conferences, and there was pastoral stuff. And the people in

> the church had no idea about all that. So it looks like we're just going home and watching Netflix every evening and not going to Bible studies.

Laura's social identity within the church is profoundly dissonant with her personal identity as a committed Christian, as she cannot fulfill the expectations of the expatriate church community. She cannot tell them how she spends her time, which she significantly invests in her role identity as a missionary and a leader in her organization. She perceives that other expatriate Christians think of her as selfish by not serving the Christian community more. She allows them to imagine her and her husband streaming movies every night instead, severely impacting her relationships with them. This perception causes dissonance between Laura's personal identity and her friend identity in the expatriate church, preventing her from being fully known.

Participants particularly experience friend identity dissonance with BMBs. As their relationships with BMBs grow deeper, missionaries often become more conflicted about revealing their missionary identity to BMBs. Nearly all participants express opposition to telling BMBs about their missionary identities for several reasons. The primary reason is that it could potentially put BMBs in a more tenuous position. If the police are trying to find out information about the missionaries, and they know they can get this information from BMBs, it might put the BMBs at greater risk for interrogation and harm. Disclosure of organizational ties can potentially place a burden on the BMBs to decide how to manage the missionaries' identities before authorities. If the BMBs do not know about the missionary identity, they will not have to decide whether to lie to protect the missionaries. Second, several participants mention the risk to the broader missionary and BMB communities, especially if a BMB returns to Islam. If one missionary's identity is revealed, the identity of those they associate with could be compromised, too.

Concealing a missionary identity among BMBs becomes difficult if multiple team members are involved with the same BMB, as happened with Christy. Fatima noticed that all her American friends were going to Cyprus, not knowing they were attending an organizational conference together. Another time, she saw they all went to another city in the country, but they had not invited her. They traveled to attend a multiagency meeting for GCC missionaries. Fatima's feelings were hurt, sensing she was being left out and that her friends were withholding information. Even though it was painful, the team held to the practice of withholding organizational ties and missionary identities from BMBs. However, it made Christy feel like a bad friend.

Sam has had significant experience discipling BMBs in the GCC, and these experiences influence his reasons for not telling BMBs of his missionary identity. One Arab, working for the government, pretended to be a new believer and became a part of their BMB house church. This man recorded conversations, putting the entire BMB community at risk in an area of high persecution for converts from Islam. Sam believes that had he disclosed his missionary identity to the BMB group, the government would have become aware of his and other missionaries' identities much sooner. The police frequently interrogated the BMBs in this church, and Sam was thankful they did not have more information that could increase their risk.

However, not disclosing his missionary identity to BMBs led to another unexpected issue. One BMB came to Sam with the newspaper, saying there was an article about undercover missionaries living in another city in the country. The BMB said, "We need to contact those people! Because you and me, we don't know what we're doing here. We need to contact those guys, because they're professionals, and they will help us to really grow this church!" Sam laughed in frustration as he recalled this story, pretending to be stabbed in the heart repeatedly. He could not tell this BMB he *was* one of the "professionals" who had been trained in church planting to help grow the local church.

Sam says this issue causes many heated discussions within the mission community, as missionaries disagree about how much information to disclose to BMBs. However, Sam cautions against missionaries disclosing their missionary identities to BMBs out of a sense of guilt or a need to be fully known. Sam recognizes this friend identity dissonance and the inner turmoil it causes:

> Once you've been working alongside people for several years, you love these people and you want to be fully honest with them and not have any secrets. So certain people have different levels of how much they want to reveal about who they are with believers, because they love them.

Sam says that while more open disclosure might make *missionaries* feel better, it places additional burdens on BMBs they don't need to carry, especially in a context where persecution is common.

Coping Strategies for Friend Identity Dissonance

Nearly all participants express some experience of friend identity dissonance as they withhold information from various friendships. This causes distinct barriers to tentmakers being fully known in friendships. From interviews, the primary coping mechanisms for friend identity dissonance are (1) avoidance of social fields, (2) theological coping strategies, (3) emphasizing what is revealed rather than what is concealed, and (4) reasoning that it was for the friend's good. This final strategy has already been discussed; the other three coping mechanisms are described below.

Using the hierarchical control model, the prominent role identity of missionary sometimes competes with the friend identity, which impacts how others perceive and befriend the participants. Several participants note the time and energy it takes to invest in relationships with Muslims, disciple BMBs, maintain Arabic skills, and fulfill vocational and organizational obligations—significant aspects of the missionary identity. When weighing the expectations of these roles with the friend identity, the missionary identity often takes prominence in order to fulfill a divine calling. This impacts tentmakers' behavioral and relational choices in friendships. In their relationships with expatriates, participants are not able to verify their personal identity as highly committed Christians. This is a strong contrast from supporting churches at home that know the tentmaker as a missionary. The discrepancy between how expatriates view the participants and how the participants view themselves prevents intimacy and authenticity in friendship. As a result, avoiding non-missionary expatriate friends is a common coping strategy among tentmakers in the GCC. Many accept the discrepancy and dissonance as part of the cost of being a missionary in a RAN.

For many participants, theological coping mechanisms are also important for resisting friend identity dissonance. Of these, the most prominent is the example of Jesus. Participants frequently note that Jesus often omitted information to people, using discretion and even purposefully obscuring some of his teachings through parables, so that some audiences would not fully understand his identity as Messiah. Paul describes how Jesus's example of omission and ambiguity helps him frame his own discretionary practices with friends:

> Looking at Jesus [pause]. The more I read the Gospels, the more I see that Jesus was amazingly comfortable with ambiguity. And [he was comfortable with] *leaving* ambiguity, where we would

> think, "No, give them the answer, give the five reasons why, and the whole apologetic answer." [But] he was more than happy with giving a pebble and leaving them scratching their heads, [wondering], "Did he just say what I thought he said? I'm not sure." And he left it that way.

Amy also uses narratives of Jesus withholding information from some social fields as a coping mechanism against friend identity dissonance. In addition, she and other participants emphasize what they reveal to friends, rather than what they conceal. Amy describes how this openness and vulnerability with her local friends means they *do* know the real her, even if they do not know about her missionary identity:

> To be honest, I would say that in comparison to maybe my fellow [missionaries], I am extremely vulnerable with locals. I would say a lot of locals pretty much know everything about my life. There are obviously some things that they do not know. But I don't know that I feel bad. I don't feel like I'm hiding something because they don't know *those* things. I am so transparent with so many other things about my life. I feel like that's really helped with discipleship and with friendships. Those people feel safe with me, because I'm telling them about current struggles. Not just five years ago, I struggled with X, Y, and Z. I'm very honest about my personal struggles. And I think that's really opened a lot of doors, and has helped me to live, not this life of "I'm this secret person, and nobody really knows what's going on" kind of thing. I don't feel that way, honestly, at all. I feel like people here *really* know me. They know a lot about who I am.

Amy considers that what she reveals to her local friends is far greater than the things she conceals, and that the vulnerability she displays with her friends means that they know the truest things about her. This helps her resist friend identity dissonance.

FACTORS OF TENTMAKER IDENTITY CONSONANCE

Identity consonance is the experience of a unified and integrated identity in which there is little or no distressing disparity between different role identities. Several participants express high levels of identity consonance and integration in their interviews, even if they previously experienced dissonance in their missionary career. These participants feel at peace with themselves and how they present their identities across various social fields. I identified consonance based on their expression of minimal tension between multiple role identities, resolution of inner conflict through defined coping mechanisms, and confidence in their social identities across many social fields. Of the thirty-eight participants, I designated eleven as experiencing identity consonance based on their interview responses. I analyzed the interviews of participants expressing identity consonance, and five factors contributing to identity consonance emerged. These are: (1) low hiddenness, (2) high vocational alignment, (3) low competition between ministry and vocation, (4) robust coping frameworks, and (5) longer time spent on the field. These are each discussed below.

Consonance Factor #1: Low Hiddenness

Participants who experience high identity consonance frequently express that they have very little to hide. Jude (Type 2) says that he does not experience the dual or secret identity that many other missionaries do. He attributes this to the fact that his vocations, which have changed over the years, have always lined up with community perceptions about him:

> They know that I really am doing the things I'm doing. I think that probably cuts down a bit on the stress. Some that kind of do a company that really doesn't do anything, or they make up a persona, [saying], "This is what I'm here for," but they're not really doing that. And people can see that they're not really doing it. I think that would be a stressor on people to try to keep that hidden, that they're not really doing the things that they say they're doing. With our organization, we don't encourage people to do that. We encourage them to really be doing the things they say they're doing.

Jude, who has decades of experience in the GCC, says his advice to new missionaries is to avoid "tent faking" by setting up shell companies that do nothing in reality. This creates more things to hide, and makes the tentmaker seem suspicious in the community. In contrast, Jude does real work publicly, interfacing with the local community and frequenting GCC government offices. Though one GCC country expelled Jude for his evangelistic activities, he believes that the tangible services his business offered the community protected him from deportation for a time. In fact, he built such trust in the community through his business that several local Muslims defended him to government authorities when Jude was accused of *tabsheer* (Arabic for evangelism, but with connotations of coercion). As discussed in chapter 5, even when he was questioned about his missionary activities by police, he openly clarified how he shared his faith without coercion. Jude also has experienced little or no hiddenness from his employers and co-workers, as his workplaces have all been established by either his missionary organization or himself. He does not have to hide his missionary identity from his work colleagues, and he has time flexibility to devote to missionary tasks. Jude receives sufficient identity verification for both his missionary and his vocational identities through the interactions he has with others in the field. Jude expresses very low hiddenness overall, contributing to an experience of higher identity consonance.

Denise (Type 2.5) worked as a full-time freelance writer and editor for years in the US for her organization and other publishers. When she moved her work to the GCC, she saw it as a continuation of how she had always lived her life in the US—as a writer whose goal in life is to bring glory to God in everything she does. Denise is open with Muslims about the fact that she believes God led her to come to the GCC, and that her life—like all Christians—should be a witness to Jesus wherever she goes. In this way, she emphasizes what she proclaims rather than what she conceals, which she says is really very little. Her relative lack of hiddenness leads her to an experience of identity consonance. Of the eleven consonant participants, five own their own businesses or work for a business started by their organization, and work only with other missionaries. One additional participant is known as a housewife in the GCC but is a field leader in her missionary organization. This employment situation allows participants to reduce hiddenness in their everyday lives, as they do not have to conceal ministry activities from employers or co-workers.

Consonance Factor #2: High Vocational Alignment

The second factor emerging among consonant tentmakers is high alignment with their vocational identities. Ten of the consonant participants are currently employed; five as business owners, five as job takers. All ten express a high level of commitment to their vocational identity in their interviews. This finding is highly significant for tentmakers in the GCC. Having received appropriate education and training in their vocation, and with many relationships and connections in their field, these participants express that they would be employed in this type of job had they not been missionaries in the GCC. They frequently indicate that their job helps them have a clear and stable identity in their country of service that makes sense to the locals. They also express that their vocational roles align well with their personal aptitudes.

Paul (Type 2.5) regularly trains others in high-level technical skills required for employment at the GCC company he works for. He feels a high degree of consonance with his vocational identity because the roles of his vocation match his natural aptitudes:

> [I'm] very conscientious, I love rules. I mean, I like *to follow* rules. I find security in [them] and that's why I love my job. That's why my job fits so much, because it's all about rule keeping and compliance.

Originally, Paul had trained in another field during university, but then discovered he did not really enjoy that work. He considered trying to get a job in that field in the GCC anyway, taking any job that would get him to the mission field sooner. However, an older missionary gave him some advice that shaped how he views vocation and ministry:

> I sought a lot of counsel, and I expected people to say, "What are you doing? No, you have to stay, take whatever job [you can find]." Because there are books that will say, take whatever will get you here, *then* take whatever will keep you here longer, and *then* maybe find something you like.
>
> But this older gentleman, he referred to a three-legged stool: family, ministry, and work [Paul holds three fingers upside down, sitting on his other hand like a stool]. His assumption was that, with God's grace, the family would be okay. But he said, "Ministry is going to be really hard. And if two of the three [legs] aren't strong, you're going to go home [he removes two fingers from the stool, causing it to topple]. If you hate your job, and ministry is going poorly, even if you have a really strong family, you're not going to stay. And so there needs to be something that you can really enjoy." That's just what he observed.

Paul's three-legged stool corresponds to research affirming the benefit of multiple role identities to self-concept; if verification in one role identity fails, a person can depend upon another prominent identity for a time.[24] At this advice, Paul spent the next eight years becoming trained in his current industry before returning to the Middle East—a counterintuitive move in the midst of evangelical urgency for the salvation of UPGs, he says. He loves his job, and feels a strong consonance between his personal identity

24. Iyer et al., "More the Merrier," 710–11.

and his role in his company. When ministry relationships or opportunities wane or become discouraging, he has his other role identities of vocation and his family to lean on. This helps him achieve stability until his missionary identity can be reaffirmed and verified.

Business owners also experience consonance when their vocational roles align with their personal aptitudes and interests. Rosemary is highly passionate about education in a specialist field, and she started a business that allows her to express those interests. Denise's freelancing work is a continuation of her previous work as an editor and writer, which she loves. Leslie's work in her organization's business allows her to use her training in marketing, and she expresses high interest and alignment with her field. Whether they are business owners or job takers, participants demonstrate a high degree of identity consonance and integration when their vocational identity is aligned with their education, work experience, and personal aptitudes.

Consonance Factor #3: Low Competition Between Ministry and Vocation

Closely related to high vocational alignment is low perceived competition between ministry and vocation. Participants experiencing high identity consonance and integration describe minimal competition between their vocational and missionary role identities. Eight of the eleven consonant participants were Type 2.5s, who feel an equal calling to their missionary and vocational roles. The other three were Type 2s, who feel more called to the missionary identity. Prescott predicts that Type 2.5s may experience more tension between their multiple role identities, which he describes as "schizophrenic."[25] Eight out of seventeen Type 2.5s in this study expressed consonance. In contrast, three of the seventeen Type 2s achieved consonance. In this study, Types 2 and 3 were more likely to experience dissonance, and Type 2.5s likelier to achieve consonance. This is summarized in the table below.

25. Prescott, "Identity and Platform," 17–18.

Table 7: Identity Consonance and Prescott's Tentmaker Types			
	Type 2	**Type 2.5**	**Type 3**
Total Number of Participants	17	17	4
Participants Expressing Consonance	3	8	0
Participants Expressing Dissonance	14	9	4

Some vocations provide a natural way for Muslims in the community to know and trust participants. This allows participants more opportunities to share about their faith as they work. Denise prayed for a long time for God to lead her to a Muslim woman to share her faith with. As she wrote in a new café one day, she met the owner, a local Muslim woman. Denise has found this relationship to be a wonderful way to verify both her vocational and missionary identities simultaneously. The café owner, a successful businesswoman, commissioned Denise to help her write her memoir. As they spend time together crafting this book, Denise can share her faith as their relationship deepens.

Paul acknowledges some tensions between his vocation and his purposes as a missionary, noting that his unpredictable schedule and his employment alongside more expatriates than Arab Muslims can make evangelism and discipleship more difficult. At times, however, his job has allowed for making connections with Arabs within the industry, which have later blossomed into relationships where he has shared the gospel or discipled BMBs.

Sam, a skilled technician, was one of the few Western expatriates working in the first GCC firm that employed him. He never hid his Christian identity from his work colleagues, and spent his breaks sharing stories of Jesus with his Arab colleagues. In his interview, he shared many stories of how his vocation gave him a platform for displaying Christlike character that surprised locals, and how he had abundant opportunities for sharing his faith. At one point, he met with a group of technicians in the desert at night weekly to discuss the prophets of Christianity and Islam, and to read Scripture together. Someone eventually told the company that this was happening, and the discussion group got shut down, as it violated company policies. However, Sam says when his vocational and missionary identities conflict, he feels little dissonance—he chooses his calling and core identity of church planting. Though Sam expresses a high degree of vocational identity, and integration of his work and ministry in general, he now intentionally avoids taking certain promotions or leadership training at work. He affirms that while excellence in his vocation would honor God, his core identity is in church planting and discipleship among Arab BMBs. Gaining more responsibilities at work and higher status in the company had, in the past, conflicted with his core identity as a church planter—a conflict he was currently avoiding by taking a job he is overqualified for, and which has no upward mobility. As a result, Sam experiences high identity consonance and little tension between his missionary and vocational role identities. His missionary identity takes priority.[26]

Martin, a university professor, abides by university policies that forbid discussing religion and politics in the classroom. However, he does not experience this as a conflict between work and ministry. He invites continuing discussions with adults after class. He also appreciates that his work hours are less strenuous than those of other tentmakers in the GCC, allowing him extra time for building relationships outside work that help him fulfill his missionary calling.

Consonant participants often believe that they can fulfill their divine calling to reach Arab Muslims, and that the restrictions of their vocation do not prevent them from verifying their missionary identity. Eight of the consonant participants could share their faith at work with co-workers, or use their vocation as a platform for sharing the gospel in some way. Two consonant participants kept their evangelistic activities separate from work, but felt their vocational identity helped them build trust in the community that led to ministry after work hours, and that the way they worked demonstrated their Christian character.[27] Highly consonant tentmakers can verify their missionary identity in their social interactions, and do not experience much competition between their vocational and missionary role identities.

26. I have categorized Sam as a Type 2.5, but he was one of the most difficult to categorize. He describes his primary calling and "core identity" (his words) as a church planter. However, he also expressed throughout his interview a strong vocational calling and a general sense of integration of vocation and ministry. In the future, he hopes to be self-supported through savings and start a consultancy so that he can devote more time to church planting.

27. One consonant participant was unemployed and relied on her husband's vocation for her visa and identity in the community.

Consonance Factor #4: Robust Coping Frameworks

Participants who exhibit strong identity consonance articulated the most well-considered frameworks for their missionary identity in a RAN in their interviews. They described multiple overlapping coping mechanisms, including theological and cultural strategies. Highly consonant participants frequently cited several Bible verses or narratives that helped them frame their lives as missionaries in RANs. In addition, they resisted black-and-white thinking, noting cultural differences in expectations of behavior for discretion and openness, especially in a context of persecution. In contrast, participants expressing higher dissonance provided fewer and less descriptive coping mechanisms in their interviews.

Leslie, a Type 2.5 businesswoman, recognizes that some would frame her work as illegal. She does not disclose to locals that churches fund her, and she is careful how she gives information in order to protect her missionary identity. However, she says that she rejects the label of her work as "illegal" because she isn't coercing anyone to convert, which is how Muslims understand the work of missionaries:

> It's not illegal for me to be a Christian. And it's not illegal for me to talk about my faith, is it?[28] Maybe at one point it was. Right now, it's not illegal inviting discussion. I think if you're framing that kind of discussion a different way, it's helpful for me personally, because at the end of the day, it's not my job to convert anyone. That's not why I'm here. That's not what I'm called to. I think if we have a more humble perspective of our own calling, it also helps the conversation because my calling is to *go*. Like, go into all the world, preach the gospel, teach, baptize. *That's* the calling. The calling is not to convert people. And that's not even possible for me to do. Like, that's not something *a person* can do.
>
> So when you're looking at the laws themselves and going for [forced] conversion, I don't feel like that applies to me. Yes, I'm here. Yes, I'm a Christian. Yes, I talk about Jesus. Yes, I love him. Yes, if some people want to know about it, of course, I'm going to talk about it. [If] people want to ask me about what the Bible says and how we teach. And absolutely, if I find another Christian who wants community, absolutely. If someone is looking for baptism, yeah, I'll do that. I think the framing has helped me a little bit.

28. In Leslie's context, it is technically not illegal for Christians to talk about their faith *if* a Muslim asks them. However, other missionaries in her city said that Christians have been accused of proselytization in the past when Muslims asked about the Christian faith and then later reported the Christians for answering.

> It does kind of offend me when people are like, "Oh, you're doing something illegal," even if it's family, or things. No, I'm not! I'm not coming to destroy or to hurt or to colonize or to force my perspective. I'm really just coming as a witness. And I'm doing that with passion. I'm doing that with obedience. And I'm making sacrifices to do that. And I'm not going to try to do more than that.
>
> And I think that leaves us at a helpful place that helps us avoid some of the mistakes of past generations. If we're just witnesses, and if it *really is* about what the Holy Spirit's doing, [then] he's the one doing the illegal stuff. In Scripture, there's no law against these fruits of the Spirit, there's no law against doing good works. There's no law against [those]. That's true. That doesn't mean in a court of law, it wouldn't be seen as that. But as far as my own conscience, I feel good.

Leslie recognizes that while the government or Muslims do not see things the way she does, her own conscience is at peace with her role as an obedient witness to Jesus. She lives in a context of high persecution for converts from Islam, and missionaries have been deported in the past for baptizing BMBs, reading the Bible with them, or helping them form fellowships—all activities Leslie is willing to do if locals want her to. The current laws frame missionary activity in coercive language, and she assumes a local court would find her guilty of coercion. This articulate framing of her task, even if local authorities may disagree with the interpretation, enables Leslie to have a deep sense of consonance and integrated identity.

None of the highly consonant participants report currently experiencing moral identity dissonance. Most say they have been in very few situations where they felt they had to lie. Derek is the one exception, who lied to interrogators to protect other missionaries and BMBs, as described above. However, he spent more time explaining his theological and ethical frameworks than any other participant, which he felt confident in, expressing no current moral identity dissonance. Thus, participants who articulated stronger frameworks for their concealing practices and missionary identity resisted dissonance more successfully.

Consonance Factor #5: Longer Time Spent on the Field

A final and significant factor for consonant participants is longer time spent on the field. The figure below shows the eleven consonant participants' length of time in the GCC:

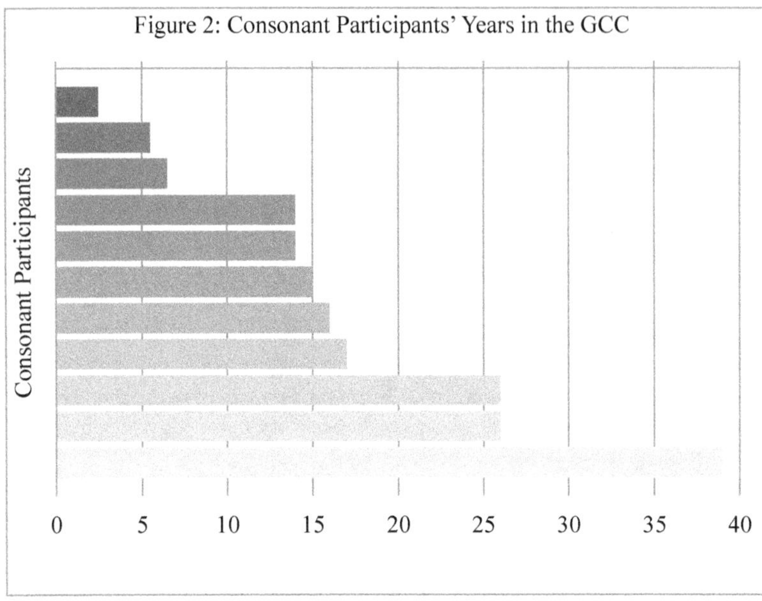

Eight of the eleven consonant participants had been on the field at least fourteen years, with an overall average of sixteen and a half years in the GCC. This does not necessarily mean that time on the field *causes* greater consonance; perhaps identity consonance enabled greater longevity on the field. Participants' stories often revealed great dissonance that they had overcome, and this took time and experience as they learned. As noted above, many tentmakers made drastic changes to achieve consonance between various aspects of their role identities. Four of the eleven consonant participants had made major changes to their vocation, visa type, or country of residence to reduce the dissonance being experienced. Their previous experiences on the field also formed significant parts of their frameworks for resisting various types of dissonance, which took time. The three consonant participants who have lived in the GCC for less than ten years were also some of the most articulate participants of the study. It may be that their robust coping frameworks helped them overcome dissonance in a shorter time. In addition, these three participants report experiencing minimal levels of hiddenness and low competition between vocation and missionary role identities. The other factors of their identity consonance may make up for what they lack in time spent in the GCC. Nearly all participants in this study describe the most dissonant time on the field as their initial years of living on the field, often during language school. Several participants expressing more dissonance had recently moved from one GCC context to another and were in a season of dissonance as they figured out their new context.

CONCLUSION

This chapter has presented the findings of interviews and participant observations, focusing on the impact of practices related to managing the missionary identity in RANs. The interviews reveal five categories of identity dissonance experienced by participants as a direct result of having a missionary identity in some social fields, which they conceal in others. Participants employ various coping and reframing strategies, which help them resist the distressing experience of dissonance. Eleven of the thirty-eight participants experience identity consonance and integration. The analysis of the interviews of these eleven participants yields five factors for identity consonance. The final chapter discusses the key findings of this study and their significance. In addition, recommendations are made for tentmaking missionaries and their organizations based on the results of this study. Finally, chapter 7 concludes with suggestions for future research regarding missionary identity in RANs.

7

Discussion, Recommendations, and Future Research

BEFORE THE DISCOVERY OF oil in the twentieth century, the Bedu people of the Arabian Gulf wandered the treacherous sands of the desert for millennia. Wilfred Thesiger, a British military officer and explorer, crossed the Arabian desert in 1945 with Bedu companions on a dangerous government expedition. His book *Arabian Sands* recounts this journey, and he describes with awe how Bedu trackers navigated his party through the sand dunes by examining camel dung and windswept tracks. By camel sign and intimate knowledge of the landscape, Thesiger's Arab companions could tell which specific tribes had traveled through that area, how long it had been since those tribes had found water, where water was located, where camels had grazed, whether camels in their party were calving, and where the tribes had gone next.[1] Additionally, their social navigation skills in the desert were just as life-saving as their physical navigation skills. Limited natural resources led to frequent raiding, and the Bedu used interactions with other tribes to gauge danger and safety as they traveled. Thesiger remarks, "The Bedu are always well informed about the politics of the desert. They know the alliances and enmities of the tribes and can guess which tribes would raid each other. No Bedu will ever miss a chance of exchanging news with anyone he meets, and he will ride far out of his way to get fresh news."[2]

1. Thesiger, *Arabian Sands*, 61–62.
2. Thesiger, *Arabian Sands*, 62.

Today, most Bedu in the Arabian Gulf have traded their tents for air-conditioned homes, and they find their way through sand dunes in SUVs with satellite navigation systems. But the "politics of the desert" remain embedded in the environment—for both the indigenous populations and the many expatriate guest workers who now dwell together. As a small subculture within this landscape, evangelical missionaries must now learn the subtle art and science of maneuvering across the ever-shifting terrain beneath them. Fueled by a divine calling to see the unreached receive the gospel of Christ, they use the signals of their companions to steer through complex social and ethical situations surrounding their identity and purpose in the country.

SUMMARY OF THE STUDY AND DISCUSSION

This study explores the practices and strategies for managing a missionary identity on the Arabian Peninsula, where many evangelistic church-planting activities are illegal. The primary aim is to understand how having a missionary identity back in the US and having a non-missionary identity overseas impacts a person's self-concept. This study uses ethnographic methods that place a high value on the context of a group with shared understandings and meanings, allowing tentmaking missionaries to narrate their identities and self-perceptions. It explores the various ways in which missionaries present and manage their identities across different social fields. With some role partners, tentmakers present and perform their missionary identities. With other role partners, participants conceal their missionary identity, often creating the dynamic of a dual identity.

Chapter 5 explores how missionaries present, conceal, and manage their identities, organized by the role partners with whom they interact: the Muslim community, the missionary community, BMBs, the expatriate community, children of tentmakers, and the world back home. The study reveals that when social fields overlap into one shared context, tentmakers often struggle to know which identity to perform, creating complexity and confusion in managing their missionary identity. Chapter 6 explores the impact of the hidden identity and the tensions experienced between the multiple role identities of participants. The impact on self-concept is described using the framework from identity theory, which includes identity dissonance and consonance. Identity dissonance describes an experience of inner tension and disharmony between the multiple aspects of the self. Dissonance results when a person cannot verify their identity in the interactions with role partners, which causes a disparity in how they view themselves and how others view them. Dissonance is a distressing experience that leads to a divided sense of self. Five categories of identity dissonance emerged from participant interviews: the dual identity dissonance, moral identity dissonance, vocational identity dissonance, missionary identity dissonance, and friend identity dissonance. These five categories are described in the table below.

Table 8: Five Categories of Tentmaker Identity Dissonance

Type of Identity Dissonance	**Description**
Dual	The experience of living a secret, double life that creates a divided sense of self
Moral	The experience of violating personal moral boundaries, resulting in behavior that is incongruent with a person's self-concept
Vocational	The experience of conflict between a person's vocational roles and their core sense of self
Missionary	The distress arising from the inability to verify the missionary identity when a person feels called to be a missionary
Friend	The experience of being inauthentic or "masked" with friends, resulting in an inability to verify the friend identity

Participants employ various coping strategies to mitigate emotional distress and resist dissonance. These coping strategies primarily include theological and cultural frameworks, as well as reframing strategies. When prominent identities remain unverified for too long and cause significant distress, some participants change their environments drastically to verify these identities.

Some participants achieved identity consonance, an experience of harmony and low tension between the multiple aspects of the self. Among thirty-eight participants, eleven were identified as experiencing identity consonance and integration. The interviews of these participants were analyzed to discover five factors associated with identity consonance, presented in figure 3 below.

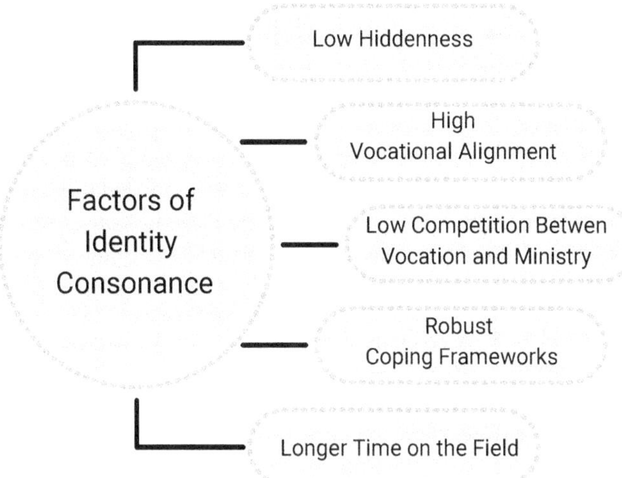

First, consonant participants experience low degrees of hiddenness in their lives overall. This includes openness about their calling and activities as ambassadors of Jesus, disclosure of church funding or investment, and presenting a transparent spiritual or clerical identity. These participants felt they hid very little of their lives from Muslim social fields. The second factor for identity consonance is high vocational alignment. When tentmakers have jobs in which they are well trained, that they enjoy, and that allow them to use their natural aptitudes and interests, they experience higher identity consonance. This factor was shared by all ten of the employed consonant participants, making it a powerful factor for identity consonance. Third, a perception of low competition between ministry and vocation is a factor for tentmaker identity consonance. When tentmakers felt they could both do their work and fulfill their divine calling to reach UPGs, there was a higher degree of identity consonance. Four of these participants had made drastic changes during their time on the field, such as changing visa types or moving to a new country, in order to decrease competition between vocation and ministry and to increase ministry opportunities. Fourth, participants expressing higher levels of identity consonance were also the most articulate of robust coping frameworks for managing their identities in a high-security context. These frameworks include theological and cultural reasonings that allow them to resist or overcome identity dissonance. Finally, participants achieving higher identity consonance have lived on the field longer, usually more than a decade. Time and experience have allowed them to adjust the management and presentation of their identities so that they experience congruence and authenticity across multiple social fields.

Integrated Identities in a Globalized World

This study is an important contribution to the growing body of literature regarding tentmaking missionaries' identities in restricted access nations (RANs). Increasingly, missiologists recognize the emotional, ethical, theological, and relational issues with maintaining a hidden missionary identity in RANs. Technology and globalization make the hidden identity more challenging to keep concealed. As noted in the literature review, some missiologists advocate for a more integrated identity centered on the vocational identity, and argue for separation from missionary organizations in order to reduce or eliminate hidden identities. This involves changing the core goals from church planting and discipleship to "blessing the nations" or interfaith dialogue—goals that can be shared inoffensively across all contexts and audiences.[3] Such an approach may be effective for many Christians seeking to glorify God among the nations through their vocation.

However, changing the core goals may not be possible for some. This study shows that many church-planting missionaries view their core selves as cross-cultural ambassadors whose primary objective is to proclaim the gospel of Christ and disciple new believers, often seeing their vocation as a means to that end. An identity centered on a professional vocation alone is difficult to integrate when tentmakers experience their authentic core self as a person called to be an evangelist and disciple maker. Participants in this study did not express a calling to bless the nations or engage in interfaith dialogue. Instead, most articulated a personal calling by God to spread the gospel among UPGs and to facilitate the formation of indigenous churches among Arabs. Their education toward those goals included training by their organization, and rigorous linguistic and cultural studies. Their missionary responsibilities include evangelism, nurturing new believers through complex discipleship issues, and developing partnerships in the missionary community.

Due to their sense of divine calling, training, commitments, and relational connections, the participants in this study express a strong missionary identity, even if they also demonstrate a strong vocational calling alongside their missionary calling. Additionally, participants with the

3. Hale, *Authentic Lives*; Love, *Glocal*; Love, "Blessing the Nations"; Lai and Love, "Integrated Identity."

highest identity consonance feel they can fulfill God's calling to serve UPGs with little or no competition from their vocation. For many participants, even those who communicate that they integrate mission and vocation, the missionary and the vocational role identities sometimes compete. This prevents the two role identities from being entirely integrated, and the conflict leads to the more prominent role controlling the outcome. This is strongly demonstrated in the drastic measures participants took to verify the missionary identity: changing jobs, starting new businesses not required for a visa,[4] changing visa types, or moving to a new country to increase ministry opportunities. Thirteen of the thirty-eight participants had made such drastic changes. Church-planting missionaries may be unlikely to change their overall goals to interfaith dialogue or blessing the nations.

Furthermore, the strong correlation between high vocational alignment and identity consonance is a key finding of this study. All ten currently employed tentmakers demonstrating identity consonance express a high degree of alignment with their vocation. The roles they fill in their jobs match their aptitudes and interests. The vocation and the roles they perform in this vocation express aspects of the participant's personal identity, allowing for an experience of greater authenticity. Participants whose vocations made them feel fraudulent to their personal identities experience high degrees of identity dissonance. Those who do what they say they are doing—and are seen doing those things—experience higher identity consonance. In addition to the ethical and theological arguments against "tent faking," this study contributes a phenomenological argument against it. "Tent faking" may be an expedient way to get into a RAN, but the impact on the missionary's integrity and self-concept is detrimental.

Social interactions allow for individuals to see themselves as others see them—reflected appraisals of who they are and how they are perceived. When these reflected appraisals match how the person perceives themselves, this leads to identity verification. In order to receive identity verification, a person must perform the roles and behaviors congruent with their identity with role partners. A businessperson must be seen doing business, dressing and acting as a businessperson, fulfilling many of the expectations society has of a businessperson. A pilot must fly aircraft, wear a pilot's uniform, interact with airline employees, and train in the skills necessary for flying. Identity verification occurs when the internal and external, the

4. Two wives of tentmakers who already had a residential visa through their husbands' jobs started businesses solely for the purpose of increasing ministry opportunities.

personal and the social, all align together. However, suppose a person identifies as a pastor as their core authentic self, yet presents a business consultant identity to others. In that case, it may present problems if the same person rarely interacts with others as a consultant. If that person has little expertise in business, spends little or no time consulting or running the consultancy, and rarely performs the consultant identity among others, it leads to a tremendous experience of fraudulence and inauthenticity. Consonant tentmakers did what they said they were doing. They were who they said they were. And others saw them doing those things and interacted with them as they performed those roles.

Ian Prescott notes that in mission organizations and among missionaries, the question on platforms is always framed as "Which is best?" He writes of this dualistic framing:

> Is it best to go as something closer to the traditional missionary—theologically trained, financially supported by churches, and spending a few years learning the language—before selecting the profession or platform that seems to best facilitate the ministry? Or is it best to go as a marketplace professional: using the qualifications one already has and seizing the professional opportunities in unreached countries; not pausing for years to go through theological or language study; staying on top of one's professional game and simply scattering to the ends of the earth with one's profession and the good news of Jesus.[5]

Prescott encourages missionaries to think beyond the framework of either-or to embrace a both-and reality: it will require *both* theologically trained and vocationally trained ambassadors to take the good news to UPGs. He concludes, "There is clearly value in having people in as diverse a range of occupations and platforms as possible so that the gospel witness can reach the greatest variety of people."[6] Of course, individual missionaries still have to decide between platforms. In my interviews with tentmaking missionaries across a broad spectrum of vocations, I often heard this same basic dichotomy from participants: "Is it better to own a business so that we can do the traditional work of missionaries with more hours in the day? Or is it better to work in a job with professional skills?" In fact, one of my unconscious biases that this study revealed to me was that I expected to

5. Prescott, "Identity and Platform," 19.
6. Prescott, "Identity and Platform," 19.

find the answer to the question of "Which is best?" What I found instead was something much more complex.

Neither owning a business nor being employed as a professional by a GCC company predicted identity consonance. Of the ten employed consonant participants, five were business owners and five were job takers. Among this set of participants, Type 2.5s, who feel an equal calling to missions and vocation, more frequently achieved identity consonance than Type 2s, who feel more called to missions above vocation. However, time is an issue here again for the Type 2s interviewed; of the 14 Type 2s who still express dissonance, nearly all had been in the GCC less than a decade. Those who had been in the GCC longer than a decade had moved to a different GCC country within the last two years. Only four participants were Type 3s, who identify their vocation as their primary calling. This may reflect the recruitment criteria of the study, requiring membership with an evangelical church-planting organization. Type 3s may be more likely to join a tentmaking network instead of a church-planting organization. None of the four Type 3s express high identity consonance. Further research that includes a broader sampling of Type 3s may elucidate these findings more clearly. Type 3s in this study describe the highest levels of missionary identity dissonance. They were less likely to achieve language fluency due to the time restrictions of their vocation in the GCC, which reduced the number of ministry relationships they had with locals. In addition, they frequently articulated frustration with others who asked them when they would get around to "the real work" of evangelism and discipleship when they devoted so much time to vocation. From this study, the answer to which platform type might be best appears to depend on a host of factors: individual aptitudes, vocational skills and interests, and overall missionary calling and goals.

Reducing hiddenness and inauthenticity is a key factor for achieving identity consonance among American tentmakers. Participants exhibiting the highest identity consonance feel they have very little to hide about themselves. The reduction of concealment decreases the experience of living a double life, even if all concealment cannot be eliminated. All participants in this study articulate some level of concealment or withholding of their full identity and purpose in the GCC as missionaries sent by organizations. They disciple BMBs in underground churches. They meet with Arab seekers who engage with gospel materials online and who risk persecution by meeting with missionaries. Most tentmakers learn Arabic to communicate the salvation offered by Jesus, a hidden agenda which governments in the GCC would likely interpret as illegal acts of proselytization. Some level of hiddenness to protect the vulnerable and allow tentmakers to continue living in the GCC seems to be necessary. However, many participants intentionally present their identities across various social fields in ways that align as closely with the truth and their personal identities as possible. Those who were able to make more of these alignments had a greater sense of identity consonance and authenticity.

Several participants find higher authenticity and integrity by presenting an integrated identity centered on a clear *spiritual* identity rather than a vocational identity, a concept promoted by Dick Brogden.[7] They frame their presence in the gulf to all audiences primarily in terms of their spiritual identity rather than their vocational identity, though they still hold a genuine vocation. They openly tell their Muslim and expatriate friends that they believe God called them to the GCC, and that they want to share the hope that they have in Jesus with anyone who will listen. Many seek to be more fully themselves and be as open as possible about what they can. Some put their theological education on LinkedIn, or more openly identify their ordination status or pastoral identity. Some even openly share that Christians and churches in the US financially support their families or their businesses, reducing the need to hide that information. This often leads to a decreased feeling of living a double life. As Leslie, an ordained pastor and businesswoman, said in her interview, "The more you can be who you really are, the better your life is."

It is clear from this study that hiddenness and concealment among missionaries create tension, stress, and for some, even identity crisis. This study confirms what many missiologists warn us—reducing hiddenness and situations in which missionaries feel they need to lie is important. Nathan said in his interview, "Missionaries and spies have more in common than most people realize." But some missionaries are achieving alignment and consonance with their core identity by reducing hiddenness, even if they must conceal some aspects of their identity from some social fields. Reducing what is hidden, even if all hiddenness cannot be eliminated, is a vital aspect of this identity consonance for many missionaries.

Keeping the hidden identity secret is increasingly difficult in the digital age. This study shows that if the two worlds of the missionary are too separate and distant, the missionary may suffer the identity dissonance of

7. Brogden, "Identity, Security, and Community."

having a double life with a hidden identity. The issue of context collapse due to globalization is a significant issue for missionary identity today. As discussed in chapter 2, context collapse occurs when multiple social fields, which may require varied communication strategies to convey meaning accurately, flatten into one combined audience.[8] Context collapse due to technology and globalization is precisely what Rick Love discusses in *Glocal*. Love argues that all Christian communication should be assumed to be public. He writes,

> The interconnectedness of a glocal world means that we cannot communicate with each audience separately. What we say in any public setting can be heard or read around the world. In the past, we could tailor our message for a particular audience, but no longer. What is spoken to one audience is too often overheard by others.[9]

Love's solution effectively adapts a lowest common denominator method of communication as a matter of integrity.[10] Love argues for a "3D" approach, simultaneously communicating every message as if he had a Christian, Muslim, and secular audience.[11] He writes,

> Glocalization means that we can no longer have a different message or be a different person for each different audience. In the core of our being, we have to have the same message and personal identity for every audience. This doesn't mean everyone will necessarily like the message, but we must eliminate deception or any perception of deception.[12]

The questions that arise from the problem of context collapse are not easily answered. Participants express the desire to maintain high degrees of integrity in their lives and words. They also want to reduce barriers to the gospel that can come from offense and misunderstanding, as may happen if Muslims discover they are missionaries. A missionary's communication to a group of Christians in a supporting church, who have shared assumptions and beliefs, can be exposed to another social field across the world thanks to technology. However, the greater sense of consonance and integrity

8. Cole-Turner, "Commodification and Transfiguration," 5.

9. Love, *Glocal*, 23.

10. Love, *Glocal*, 5–7, 23.

11. Love, *Glocal*, 7.

12. Love, *Glocal*, 41.

across all social fields that can be achieved, the less divided and deceptive the missionary may perceive themselves to be. For the concealment and hiddenness that remains, tentmakers need robust coping frameworks. This hiddenness may be necessary to protect vulnerable BMBs or Muslim seekers in a context of high religious persecution. Theological and cultural frameworks are especially vital for resisting dissonance from the realities of a hidden missionary identity.

The Sacred-Secular Divide Reconsidered

As noted in the literature review, tension between the vocational and missionary identities in the literature is most often attributed to the sacred-secular divide common to the Western worldview. This false dichotomy is framed as a two-tier system: professional missionaries bear a superior clerical identity with a "sacred" vocation to save souls, while entrepreneurs and professionals engage in inferior "secular" vocations of the laity.[13] Symptoms of this sacred-secular divide include ambivalence regarding salary or profits, and a belief that God cares more for the soul than the body.[14] The solution to resolve this false dichotomy is nearly always to cultivate a stronger "theology of work."[15] This theology of work includes an acknowledgment that all Christians should witness to the gospel in every sphere of their lives, including that of faithful and excellent vocation. Missions is the work of the whole church, not just trained missionaries.

However, the participants in this study demonstrate that the boundaries between "clerical" and "lay" missionaries are not so distinct for tentmakers in the GCC. Many participants have *both* high levels of vocational training and seminary training, several of them with multiple master's degrees that reflect both vocational and theological education. Twenty-one of the thirty-eight participants are Type 2.5 or Type 3 tentmakers, expressing a calling to a nonreligious vocation alongside their missionary calling. Many Type 2 participants view their vocations as platforms primarily for ministry, which is their first calling. However, they perform real jobs with real skills—they are teachers, accountants, or engineers. Most participants

13. Johnson, *Business as Mission*, 156, 161–62; Lai, *Tentmaking*, 40–44, 411–13; Lai and Love, "Integrated Identity," 344, 347; Onongha, "Tentmaking in Twenty-First Century," 190–91; Bailey, "Business as Mission," 370; Roemmele, "Cloak-and-Dagger Tentmakers."

14. Rundle, "Ministry, Profits."

15. Bailey, "Business as Mission"; Bosch, "Gap Between Best Practices."

in this study affirm the value of normal work and employment, and participate in those activities to varying degrees for the sake of the gospel. For the participants in this study, identity dissonance does not primarily arise from a belief that a clerical, missionary vocation is superior to nonreligious employment. The division between sacred and secular roles does not accurately capture the source of tensions and dissonance for GCC tentmakers.

Rather, struggles with identity center around the tensions of concealment in relationships, the management of the many role identities that missionaries juggle, and a feeling of duality between their identity at home and on the field, where they sometimes have two different role identities. Missionaries sometimes find that their vocational roles compete with their missionary roles, though they went to the field expecting to integrate them. When vocation and ministry compete and both role identities cannot be simultaneously verified, participants choose which identity to operate in. Participants express this reality in tension with affirmations that their vocational work is valuable and allows them a platform for witnessing to Christ. A more robust theology of work does not resolve all the tensions experienced between the missionary and vocational callings.

BAM and tentmaking advocates rightly argue for the inherent goodness and value of business as an endeavor that can glorify God. However, some go too far in trying to integrate the sacred and secular in the world for what they call a "holistic" view of life. They sometimes conflate the biblical principle of faithfully doing everything for the glory of God with a demolition of sacred elements of worship. Michael Baer demonstrates this in *Business as Mission*:

> There is no difference between doing a deal and serving communion. Life is a whole and is holistically submitted to God's authority. Wherever they are and whatever they are doing, they are serving and worshiping the Master. There is no sacred and secular, no dichotomy. There is no business and ministry. All is sacred. All is ministry.[16]

While Christians can and should submit all aspects of their lives to God as an act of worship, equating a business deal with the Lord's Supper goes too far. They are *not* the same. Conducting a sale with godly character may be a witness to God's character; all Christian salespeople should strive to live such a life. However, a fundamental difference exists between conducting life with integrity and administering the sacraments. Selling furniture to a

16. Baer, *Business as Mission*, 142.

buying customer, even doing so with godliness, is not *equivalent* to sharing the good news of Jesus with them or praying with them. Both can be valuable before God. There is business, and there is ministry, though neither is devoid of God's presence or blessing.

Many participants in this study instinctively recognize the inherent distinction between vocation and ministry, and this is where they sometimes experience tension between vocational and missionary identities. Managing engineering projects can be a witness to God's creativity and an engineer's desire to love and please God in all he does. The job may lead to relationships of trust in which the gospel can be shared and believed. However, managing that project is fundamentally different from counseling a BMB through persecution or teaching the Bible. It is not that one activity is "secular" and one activity is "sacred." They are fundamentally *not* the same activities, and choices and prioritizations must sometimes be made between the activities to reflect a core identity and calling. There is work, and there is ministry; they often overlap and intersect, but even the overlap and intersection testify to their distinction. This can create some tension between the multiple identities a person carries.

Some missiologists argue that missionary organizations fuel the ongoing sacred-secular divide by sending seminary-trained missionaries. For instance, Rick Love argues for his new integrated paradigm of missions, which eliminates missionary organizations, saying, "The glocal paradigm of ministry believes the whole church is sent into the world, not just a few missionaries."[17] However, one does not have to accept that *only* seminary-trained and organizationally sent missionaries are part of God's mission in order to value missionary training and organizations. Church-planting organizations and missionaries do not exist to promote a "sacred" and elite class of Christians set apart from a lower caste of Christians engaged in "secular" work. Rather than comprising an elite group superior to the laity, as the sacred-secular argument assumes and exaggerates, missionaries should be viewed as a group within the body of Christ with particular skills. Cross-cultural evangelism, discipleship, and church planting require many specialized skills, including linguistic skills, cross-cultural verbal and nonverbal communication, knowledge of and ability to teach Scripture, theology and ecclesiology, pastoral care, contextualization, leadership training, and more. With such a multidisciplinary array of complex skills and knowledge needed for the task, missionaries find the networking,

17. Love, *Glocal*, 119.

training, and support of church-planting organizations invaluable—not to prop up a superior sacred identity, but to fulfill their roles and divine calling as proclaimers of the gospel effectively.

Patrick Lai, arguing against the sacred-secular division, suggests that missionaries present a *secular identity* in their country of service, centered on their vocation, rather than "wear[ing] a Christian label."[18] Lai contends that such a secular identity centered on vocation gives the missionary more credibility, and makes it more likely that someone may seek the missionary out to answer spiritual questions.[19] However, this study challenges that claim. The findings of this study include several participants who present a professional ordained clergy identity publicly, alongside their vocational identity as business owners. These participants find that credentials in theology and ordination in ministry help locals to trust them in discipleship. Tentmakers' theological education provides authority and trustworthiness, making it a beneficial asset in a hierarchical context that values religious education and expertise. In fact, missionaries who had carefully concealed their theological education or church-planting training with their local contacts later found this concealment to be a detriment in their ministry. BMBs in the GCC often prefer religiously trained professionals rather than secular professionals in discipleship and church planting. Acquiescing to this desire for theological education should not be seen as a widening of the sacred-secular divide, or as somehow disempowering the laity who do not go to seminary. Rather, it is a simple acknowledgment that various gifts and skills are needed for the mission of God.

Theologian R. Paul Stevens notes the persisting clerical-lay hierarchy in Protestant churches, corresponding to the sacred-secular divide. Stevens argues instead for *a-clericalism*, defined as "one people without distinction except in function, a people that transcends clericalism."[20] In this model which abolishes notions of the laity and clergy, the entirety of the people of God are held in equal value and responsibility for mission in the world, rather than only the theologically educated. There instead exists the people of God as a kingdom of priests, among whom (and not separate from) are leaders, apostles, teachers, pastors, and evangelists tasked with equipping

18. Lai, *Tentmaking*, 40.

19. Lai, *Tentmaking*, 41–43.

20. Stevens, *Other Six Days*, 7–8, 51–53. Stevens attributes the origination of the term "a-clericalism" to John Stott. Stevens distinguishes a-clericalism from anticlericalism, which rejects church leadership or authority to allow the laity to dominate.

the whole church for the work of ministry (Eph 4:11–12). Tentmaking missionaries often embody this model of diversity of function without the hierarchy of clericalism. They intentionally live out their faith in the workplace, merging their Christian and vocational identities in various ways for the glory of God in all spheres of life.

RECOMMENDATIONS FOR MISSIONARIES AND ORGANIZATIONS

The following recommendations based on this study fall under three headings: "Pre-Field Training," "Verifying Identities on the Field," and "Updating Our Missionary Canon." Recommendations are made for individual missionaries as well as missionary organizations.

Pre-Field Training

Missionary organizations frequently recruit at Christian universities, Bible colleges, and large missions conferences oriented toward young adults. Older teenagers and young adults in their twenties are still in the process of forming their adult identity, including their vocational identity. Recruitment of this demographic often leads to students going to seminary or Bible college in order to prepare for a missionary career. Frequently, missionary organizations require theological education. Missions programs at Christian universities and Bible colleges may also focus on training students in skills needed for cross-cultural ministry, including anthropology and cross-cultural skills, linguistics, and evangelism. These are key areas for forming a missionary identity, and important skills for cross-cultural ministry.

However, the culture of evangelical urgency in missions can often short-circuit long-term planning for identity and vocation in their country of service. Many missionaries so strongly identify with a missionary calling that they assume they will simply take any job they can, or start a business, in order to secure a visa and begin working towards fulfilling the Great Commission. This take-it-as-it-comes philosophy works out for some missionaries, as demonstrated in this study. Some learned the language and the cultural landscape of their host country, received some mentoring and support from BAM specialists in their organization, and managed to build successful and even spiritually fruitful businesses. Others floundered, feeling a deep sense of dissonance and conflict between their vocation and their personal identities, skills, and calling. However, this study shows a strong correlation between identity consonance and high vocational alignment, even for Type 2s whose primary calling is to missions. Missionaries-in-training must consider personal aptitudes and interests in their vocation alongside their missionary training. Missions programs at universities must consider how to prepare future missionaries for a vocational identity that will also be necessary in RANs. Creating dual-track programs in Christian liberal arts universities such as missions and business, missions and TESOL, missions and nursing, or missions and engineering would deeply benefit missionaries-in-training. Such educational tracks may enable future missionaries to develop authentic vocational identities alongside their growing missionary identities.

Based on the findings of this study, I also recommend that missionary organizations guide pre-field appointees through a thorough assessment process of their personalities, values, spiritual gifts, vocational skills, and missionary goals. Organizations need to help their pre-field appointees consider how their long-term identities in their host countries will be consonant with who they feel they authentically are as their core selves. This inner sense of authenticity is an integral part of identity for many Americans. If this authenticity cannot be verified over a long period, missionary attrition may increase, especially in regions with high resistance to the gospel. Facilitating growth in the missionary's awareness of their personal and social identity is a crucial part of preparation for the field. A mismatch between the missionary's internal value system and daily life and practices will likely lead to growing dissonance over time, and perhaps attrition from the field. In this study, some missionaries who valued long-term residence were matched with a vocation that provided only a short-term identity that became suspicious over time or with questioning. Other missionaries who personally devalued profit making for themselves and had no trained skills for such an endeavor took charge of for-profit businesses. This led to feelings of dissonance. Vocations on the field should not be primarily chosen by what is available or quickly gains access to UPGs, but rather primarily by alignment with the missionary's sense of self and personal values, in addition to ministry goals.

This study demonstrates that the daily practices of concealment and deception differ between job-taking or business-owning paths for tentmakers. This study reveals that reducing hiddenness across social fields is crucial for resisting identity dissonance. There are no easy options or solutions; both business owners and job takers face many challenges. Business owners in the GCC more often face questions about their financial situation. If they are not trained in business or try to do as little business as possible, they face higher levels of vocational identity dissonance. However, job takers in this study more often experience missionary identity dissonance when they are unable to give adequate time and energy to their mission organization roles. Job takers were more likely to feel more competition between their vocation and ministry than business owners. However, in this study, both job takers and business owners achieved identity consonance over time. Recognizing the benefits and challenges of each path for tentmaking may be an essential part of field preparation, as well as encouraging future missionaries that time is needed to work out new identities on the field.

I must acknowledge a conscious bias for the continuing existence of missionary organizations. I am a member of an evangelical missionary organization that focuses on making disciples among UPGs. I was sent by this organization to the Middle East, I was trained in church planting and in leadership by this organization, and I appreciate the many services that such a network provides to my whole family. I also have a positive bias toward church-planting goals among UPGs. I have worked alongside faithful church planters across many organizations who have adopted a lifestyle of perseverance, humility, and learning in order to invite Muslims into the abundant and everlasting life Jesus offers. Many of my prayers have been for indigenous Christian leadership to arise in the Arabian Peninsula, to equip local Arabs to glorify and proclaim the name of Jesus, despite the persecution and hardship they may face for his sake.

However, it is clear from this research that these specific goals of evangelical church planters often require some level of concealment and hidden identity on the Arabian Peninsula. This concealment may include information about BMBs or other missionaries, information about the sending organization and events, funding and speaking engagements at churches, or training events for church planting or evangelism. If a Christian wants to eliminate all hidden identities and agendas, they must modify their core message, overall goals, and language to avoid the offense that may occur if their purposes, missionary identity, or organizational affiliations are revealed. They may decide that their goals are simply to bless others wherever they are, to be a light in the workplace and glorify God in whatever they do, and to engage in respectful interfaith dialogue as faithful believers. If only all professing Christians lived such a life! For these Christians, a tentmaking network whose goals can be openly shared across all audiences, rather than a church-planting organization, may be the best route to take.

However, if the Christian's goal and calling is to help facilitate a healthy and reproducing indigenous church in a location where conversion to Christianity is illegal or at least strongly persecuted, some level of concealment will likely be required. Organizations must be open about this reality and the added stresses that a lifestyle of concealment and secrecy can bring. Missionaries need to confront these realities before leaving their home country, and decide if their ethical and theological frameworks can handle concealment, and how much. As Thomas Hale notes, this may depend on cultural background, personality, and many other factors.[21]

For those with more transparent and extroverted personalities, Dick Brogden's approach may be desirable in order to reduce what is concealed or withheld.[22] The more of the core spiritual self that can be openly acknowledged rather than hidden, the better for the missionary and their relationships. However, Brogden acknowledges that this must be done carefully, in a way that honors and cares for the security concerns of others in the missionary and BMB communities. Brogden is fluent in the language and highly culturally adept as an experienced missionary; newcomers to the field may need to adopt a more cautious approach as they learn a complex social landscape. Cory and Casie, even though they had significant experience across several Muslim countries, said they went on a "listening tour" when they arrived in a new city as they considered how to present and manage their identities in a new context. This listening tour included listening to the experiences of various missionaries, BMBs, local Muslims, and the diverse expatriate Christian community. Their goal is to reduce what they themselves conceal, but to do so in a way that honors the very different social groups around them.

Prior to leaving for the field, Christians sent by a missionary organization need to evaluate carefully what they will conceal and what they will be open about. Things they thought needed to be concealed might be openly acknowledged, if framed carefully. For many business-owning participants in this study, their hidden funding source was a significant stressor requiring concealment and misdirection. Funding was a particular problem for

21. Hale, *Authentic Lives*, 52–53. Hale notes that he has never met an Asian who struggles with a dual or hidden identity, as "formal identities" are a cultural norm, as are discretion and withholding of information.

22. Brogden, "Identity, Security, and Community."

those who had spent time in language school. Missionaries should consider potential ways to reduce concealment or deception regarding funding, such as open acknowledgment that their churches and Christian friends have financially supported them. This will need to be accompanied by a reason, and missionaries can describe a reason that is both true and points to aspects of their Christian faith and calling. Of course, this carries risk—as do lies, deflections, and suspiciously vague answers.

If language options are available in the home country, rather than on the field, this may reduce the necessity of misleading others during language school. However, if missionaries must attend language school full-time on the field, they could use the opportunity to share why they want to learn the language and how it is funded—as closely to the truth as possible. Perhaps they could openly acknowledge that Christian friends and family give money to them each month. They might share that they want to know the language well so they can understand the people well and even that their motivation for learning the language is to fulfill a calling from God to love and bless the people of that country. The particular context may make these suggestions unwise or complex. However, the less the missionary hides initially, the less anxiety they will experience about that information getting out.

Missionaries to the GCC must also consider their online presence and how they will manage and present their identities online. Several participants remarked how Arabs in their social circles would stalk them, hack private accounts, and run their names through internet search engines prior to meeting. The frequent strategy has been to remove all evidence of any online presence. As Jaron Evans argues, missionaries should consider intentionally narrating a clear identity online to reduce suspicion and to mitigate accidental online postings about the missionary.[23] Tentmakers can articulate in their own words who they are, who Jesus is, why they came to the country, and what their relationship with God is like. They can communicate their spiritual identity, vocational identity, family identity, and more on their own terms. This may reduce feelings of hiddenness and concealment, both for the missionary and for those with whom they interact.

All missionaries in the GCC risk police interrogations regarding their relationships to other missionaries, their organization, or BMBs. Missionary organizations often require security training for their personnel for the more significant security events of interrogation, imprisonment, and deportation. However, missionaries need to be adequately prepared for the

23. Evans, "To Be (Online)."

smaller but more frequent relational issues of daily concealment, deflection, avoidance, or even deception that their circumstances might require. These daily navigations of identity often prove very stressful over time for most missionaries, even if larger security incidents never occur. If missionaries cannot adequately meet these daily challenges in a way that aligns with their moral or theological views, they may experience dissonance or even identity crisis on the field. Greater stress was often experienced when missionaries had to conceal aspects of their missionary identity from more familiar and intimate relationships. However, suddenly revealing a hidden identity from a long-term relationship is problematic as well.

For many participants, information about BMBs or other missionaries was something they withheld, concealed, or even lied about. Lies to protect other people usually resulted in less moral identity dissonance for missionaries, but not always. Those with stronger identity consonance had a clear articulation of what was worth hiding and why. Those with more scrupulous conceptions of truth telling, and personalities oriented towards openness and transparency, more frequently struggled with a deep sense of dissonance. Organizations should facilitate workshops to help missionaries and teams work out theological, ethical, and cultural frameworks for concealment and misleading practices. Role-playing and considering how to interact with Muslim friends, expatriate Christians, and children in truthful but not harmful ways should be part of this training. Missionaries can then work out their personal boundaries and comfort levels for information sharing across various audiences. This will enable them to reduce what is concealed and prepare answers to common questions that align with the truth of their core personal identity and calling. Considerations for how to manage the collective security of other missionaries and BMBs with differing boundaries should also be part of this process.

Verifying Identities on the Field

Research in identity theory reveals that having multiple, nonoverlapping role identities can strengthen a person's self-concept. If one identity fails verification, the other identities remain unaffected for a person to fall back on until the other identity receives verification again.[24] This provides some protection against identity dissonance and crisis. A healthy missionary team or organizational culture can provide some resistance against this

24. Iyer et al.,"More the Merrier," 710–11.

crisis by strengthening verification of the missionary's multiple role identities in various ways. Below are some recommendations for missionaries and organizations for verifying the missionary identity and the vocational identity on the field.

Verifying the Missionary Identity

An identity-reflecting community is vital for missionaries in high-security contexts. Missionaries often feel misunderstood by the locals they serve, the expatriates they interact with, and the churches they attend. In addition, resistance to the gospel can be very high in RANs. Therefore, evangelism, conversions, discipleship, and church formation can often be slow processes with high failure rates. Missionaries often verify the missionary identity through ministry interactions and relationships associated with missionary activity. They may share stories of Jesus with Muslim seekers, conduct Bible studies, or coach emerging leaders of a BMB church. However, these verifications of missionary identity may not be available if the missionary is still in language school and cannot yet speak the language well enough to form these relationships. Additionally, the missionary identity may fail verification if the missionary only has interactions with Muslims who have low spiritual interest in Christianity—a common experience in the Arab world.

In fields labeled as highly resistant to the gospel, the missionary identity may need verification by interactions with different role partners to increase the salience and commitment of this prominent identity. Increased interactions and personal relationships related to the missionary identity may happen within the missionary organization, on mission teams, and through interagency field partnerships. From an organizational standpoint, leaders may need to provide additional interactions that confirm and verify missionary identities for contexts with little visible spiritual fruit. This may include sending organizational representatives to visit field members, providing in-person training, and planning in-person retreats and conferences. Training should also include reorienting field missionaries to the concept of preparing soil, planting, and watering as necessary roles in seeing a harvest in the long term, reducing the reliance on conversions or baptisms alone to verify the missionary identity or define success as a missionary. Annual evaluations of missionaries in their ministry roles can provide an additional context for verifying the missionary identity and setting ministry goals. In contexts of low spiritual fruit, measuring success and faithfulness to the missionary task may include evaluations of relationships formed, prayer engagement, intentional spiritual conversations, or other missionary activities. In these social contexts, the increased number of relationships and personal interactions by which a missionary is known as "missionary" can strengthen and verify the missionary identity, reducing experiences of identity dissonance that may arise in a RAN.

Organizations need to be aware that field leaders may receive additional opportunities for verification from their organization through leadership training, mentorship, and numerous strategy meetings sometimes not available to non-leadership members. For the sake of efficiency to cost and time, organizations may pour more resources into leadership, assuming that investment will trickle down to field members. Field members who have no leadership roles may have fewer opportunities for identity verification as missionaries, if their organization is not providing training and personal interactions as they perform the role of missionary. Teams can be an important verifier of missionary identity, if they have healthy dynamics and are able to provide equipping, support, and encouragement towards the missionary task. The more interpersonal, face-to-face verifications of the missionary identity, the stronger the missionary identity may be, even without visible ministry success.

Verifying the Vocational Identity

Tentmaking has always been, and will remain, a vital aspect of the missionary endeavor. Vocations provide legitimate identities for missionaries in foreign communities, allowing them to build trust among the people they are trying to reach. As countries continue to eliminate missionary or religious visas, foreign missionaries will increasingly need to rely on building businesses or taking employment for long-term residence. The pendulum on tentmaking has certainly swung in mission organizations since 1997, when Ruth Siemens lamented that tentmakers were often not viewed as real missionaries.[25] In this study, only two participants—a married couple—expressed that their organization forbade them from making any profit or developing a legitimate business. Five additional participants said some within the missionary community sometimes questioned their commitment to the unreached when they put in significant hours for their vocational roles. One couple and one single woman said their churches or supporters sometimes misunderstood why they had profit-making businesses when they were missionaries. For all other participants, tentmaking

25. Siemens, "Vital Role of Tentmaking," 128.

was an assumed part of their mission on the Arabian Peninsula, and their organizations encouraged, supported, and sometimes facilitated tentmaking opportunities.

Tentmakers of all kinds can demonstrate their faithfulness and integrity in the workplace as they engage in colleague interactions, perform their work well, and resist corrupt practices that may be normative in a particular culture. However, guidance in preparation and through the unique challenges that tentmakers face is critical for reducing missionary attrition. A concern for business owners arose if they had a low sense of vocational success or identity, and if they were engaged in few or no evangelistic or discipleship relationships. In other words, both their missionary and vocational identities were failing verification. These participants were more likely to experience a sense of existential crisis and wonder why they were on the field. In contrast, a strong vocational identity sometimes helped carry tentmakers along until the missionary identity could be reaffirmed in a later season.

Many missionary organizations now have BAM consultants to guide and train missionaries establishing businesses or organizations in their host countries. Business owners and job takers in this study identified regular mentorship with such consultants as crucial for enduring the challenges they faced in vocation on the field. Coaches educated in the ethical and theological issues raised by security concerns in RANs can be valuable in guiding missionaries who struggle to reconcile their actions with their moral or theological frameworks. These additional interpersonal interactions can also help verify a tentmaker's vocational identity, and help them better integrate their missionary goals with their vocation. Time and experience are crucial factors for resolving experiences of dissonance, as demonstrated by this study. Coaches can guide tentmakers through prayer and discernment for identifying areas of dissonance and realigning personal aptitudes, vocational identity, and missionary goals. This may involve a drastic change, as it did for many participants of this study. Missionary organizations can form working groups, networks, and training to support tentmakers to help increase relational interactions surrounding tentmaking in order to strengthen the vocational and missionary identities together. This creates resistance against dissonance and the sense of competition missionaries may experience between their missionary and vocational role identities. Such networks within an organization may also demonstrate that the organization values the vocational work of missionaries.

Updating Our Canon of Missionary Stories

Finally, our canon of missionary stories and experiences needs to be updated and expanded to keep up with the new world we live in. As Steve noted in his interview, we no longer live in William Carey's or Hudson Taylor's world. Missionaries no longer pack their belongings in a coffin and sail to exotic lands, forever cut off from their home world. They are rarely clearing runways in the jungle with machetes or teaching in the open air of a village with a foreign missionary identity. They straddle both the home and the field worlds through digital platforms and by returning more frequently with the ease of air travel. The field world may collide with the missionary's home world unexpectedly, creating an identity crisis and legitimate fears of discovery. Missionaries face video surveillance, phone tapping, email hacking, and being unknowingly recorded on mobile phones. They often work two full-time jobs, one of them unknown and hidden to others. They may have imagined spending their whole lives in one country, only to be denied a visa after a decade of living there. For many missionaries, their expectations of themselves and what their daily lives would look like overseas are shattered, sometimes in devastating ways. Their expectations are often formed in the imagination by the stories of missionaries from ages past who navigated a world we no longer live in.

Missiology needs more stories of modern missionaries navigating the tensions presented in this study, to give us an updated and realistic view of contemporary missions. There are many tentmaking and BAM how-to manuals for advice, but few *stories* by which we gain access to the development and management of the identities of tentmakers. We need more biographies and autobiographies of tentmakers that show the realities, frustrations, joys, challenges, successes, and failures. We need stories of missionaries grappling with the issues of security among the missionary community, how they worked with one another across differing views of security, how they loved and protected one another. We need stories of missionaries in their corporate workplaces, giving a realistic picture of what it means to be a missionary in today's globalized world. We need stories of the moral decision-making that modern missionaries face in tight situations to protect vulnerable local believers. Such stories are integral for developing our missionary identities, as we see ourselves in the wider narrative of God's mission to the unreached.

SUGGESTIONS FOR FUTURE RESEARCH

As the subject of identity is complex, this study was intentionally limited in its scope of the missionaries studied, only including Americans working for evangelical church-planting mission agencies. Further studies are needed on the experiences of identity and security from the perspectives of Global South missionaries. The demographics of global Christianity have shifted significantly over the past century. In 1900, 82 percent of all Christians lived in the Global North (primarily North America and Europe), and only 18 percent lived in the Global South (Central and South America, Africa, Asia, and Oceania). In 2020, studies reported that 67 percent of all Christians live in the Global South, and only 33 percent live in the Global North.[26] As a result of this trend, the missions-sending paradigm in the twenty-first century has also shifted from "the West to the rest" to a polycentric "from everywhere to everywhere."[27] Christians from the Global South now comprise a significant portion of the missionary workforce worldwide. While the United States still leads the world numerically in missionaries sent, the following four top senders are Brazil, South Korea, the Philippines, and Nigeria, respectively.[28] Some mission organizations are beginning to reflect this shift, and are engaging in internationalizing processes to mobilize, train, and send Global South missionaries.[29] Multicultural mission teams are becoming more common—with their attendant challenges, such as cross-cultural communication and conflict resolution.

Missiological research should reflect the shifting tides of mission praxis by considering the same issue from multiple angles of interpretation. Contextual and cultural complexities affect how people interpret their identity, moral decisions, and security issues. Global North missionaries likely experience and interpret visa acquisition, persecution, interrogation, imprisonment, or deportation in different ways from missionaries from the Global South. Understanding one issue from multiple cultural perspectives may yield a more holistic picture of the realities missionaries face. Comparative ethnographic studies will give researchers a more complete picture of the challenges missionaries face to identity and security today.

This study was also intentionally limited in its geographic and cultural scope. Additional studies identifying unique challenges in various contexts

26. Zurlo et al., "World Christianity," 10.
27. Tennent, *Invitation to World Missions*, 31–33.
28. Tennent, *Invitation to World Missions*, 13.
29. Plueddemann, "Implications of Globalizing Missions," 265.

beyond the Arabian Peninsula would be valuable. How do missionaries navigate identity and security in contexts of extreme surveillance and secular Communism in places such as China? How does this differ from contexts with low numbers of expatriates, or in developing nations? What about Islamic contexts where extremist cells and anti-Western rhetoric are common? Each context may yield a different set of missionary practices and behaviors for managing, concealing, or presenting identity.

This study also revealed interesting practices of parents concealing their missionary identities from their children. Many children of tentmakers grew up in homes that valued mission and evangelism, hearing stories of missionaries and praying for unreached people groups or the persecuted church. Even so, parents often concealed from their children their own missionary identities for many years so that children would not unintentionally cause a security breach for individuals and teams. Concealment proved tricky to navigate during HMA, as missionaries tried to assert their missionary identity and activity to supporters while keeping missionary vocabulary out of their children's mouths. Over time, these children either developed a dawning awareness of their parents' missionary identity, or they suddenly discovered it. Much has been written in recent years regarding the complexities that third culture kids (TCKs) face as their identities develop across cultures.[30] A qualitative study on the perspectives of adult TCKs who grew up in RANs, focusing on their perceptions of their identity and security management throughout their childhood, would be an interesting area of study. This would elucidate the impact of hidden missionary identity on missionary children.

CONCLUSION

According to the missionaries I interviewed, God is moving powerfully among Arabs in the GCC. The little church of the Arabian Peninsula is growing. What was stony and resistant soil in previous generations is now beginning to bear fruit. Underground churches are starting to form as local believers take considerable risks to meet together, worship, and study Scripture. In one little house church, one Arab strums the *oud* (a local stringed instrument), and another beats the *tabla* (a small drum), chanting their newly written Bedu-style worship song in Arabic. The billowing smoke and fragrance of *bukhoor* (incense) rises to God with their prayers. Nearly

30. Pollock et al., *Third Culture Kids*; Ernvik, *Third Culture Kids*; Wells, *Healthy Third Culture Kids*.

all their stories of coming to faith involve dreams of a man in dressed in white who spoke their name and gave them peace. Nearly all their stories of coming to faith also include a Western, Arabic-speaking friend who helped them understand who this man is and how to follow him. What they may not know is that this friend is a tentmaking missionary.

The world that missionaries navigate continues to grow more complex in an increasingly globalized and digitized age. This complexity is reflected in the variegated ways missionaries present and manage their identities. But more than making themselves known and understood, may the tentmakers of the Arabian Peninsula press on in making Jesus known and understood.

Appendix A: Recruitment Email

My name is A. G. Smith, and I am a PhD candidate at Columbia International University. My dissertation focuses on the experiences of identity among Christian tentmaking cross-cultural workers who maintain and manage multiple identities due to their vocation and calling in restricted access nations. The goal of my research is to help identify the unique challenges that workers like you face, so that sending organizations and fellowships can support and train them more effectively. This research arises from my and my husband's experiences living on the Arabian Peninsula as business owners, while also functioning as team leaders for our organization.

I would like to invite you to participate in my study through a confidential interview. The interview is expected to take about sixty minutes over Zoom. I recognize that there may be security concerns, and I am very sensitive to those. The call will be recorded for research purposes, but you may choose to have your camera off and to not use your real name in the interview. I recommend using a VPN (virtual private network) during the interview process, and the questions have been tailored to eliminate troublesome vocabulary. I will also be doing interviews throughout the summer of 2023 if you're out of your country of service during that time and find that would be better timing. Additionally, I will visit the gulf in September 2023 to conduct in-person interviews if this is preferred. If you or your organization have further security protocols, please let me know and I will accommodate them. Your name will never be attached to your personal information provided in the interview, and you will be assigned a pseudonym to protect confidentiality.

You may withdraw from the study at any time and for any reason. Your name and any personal information will be kept confidential and will never be published. You also have the option at the end of the interview to request a copy of the dissertation before it is published.

Appendix A: Recruitment Email

To participate in this study, you must:

1. Have an American passport
2. Be twenty-one or older
3. Have lived in a GCC country with a *residence visa* (not a tourist or student visa) for your vocation for at least two years
4. Be a member of an evangelical CP organization

If you're willing to participate, please email me at either [email] or my encrypted email at [email] or at the phone number below. If you have any questions, I'd be very happy to answer them.

Appendix B:
Semi-Structured Interview Questions

Below is the list of potential questions used for semi-structured interviews. The questions chosen for each interview, and the order in which they were asked, were heavily dependent on the flow and direction of conversation to allow space for different information to emerge. Some terms, such as "missionary," were changed during interviews online for those who preferred more security-conscious terminology. I made sure they understood my meaning as they answered, and then rephrased if the original meaning still was not clear. The code words I used are included in brackets.

INTRODUCTORY QUESTIONS

1. Year of birth
2. Gender
3. Country of residence
4. How long have you lived there?
5. What job gives you a residence visa?
6. Have you lived in other restricted access nations?
7. Where and how long did you live there?

SELF-PERCEPTION AND PERSONAL NARRATIVE

8. Can you take a couple minutes and tell me about who you are, what kind of person you are, how you or those closest to you would describe you.
9. Can you tell me the story of how you got here, serving in this country in this way?

VOCATIONAL IDENTITY

10. Tell me about your job that gives you a visa.
11. Tell me about your work environment—co-workers, employers, location, etc.
12. How did you find this job? Do you have a background in this vocation? What kinds of training or education do you have for this vocation?
13. If you weren't working as a missionary [global worker], would you want to do the job that you do?
14. Tell me about the relationship between your employment/vocation and your work in ministry [other purposes for being there]. Do they go together or compete with one another? Both?
15. What are other frustrations, challenges, or joys with that?

SECURITY ISSUES

16. Can you tell me about your approach to security?
17. How would you approach sharing the gospel [good news] with locals, knowing that it could get you in trouble?
18. Do you feel that you have to hide parts of yourself or your activities from certain people for the sake of security?
    - Churches [fellowships] back home
    - People back home
    - Muslim neighbors/friends
    - Local employers/employees/work colleagues
    - Expats who aren't missionaries [global workers]
    - Fellow missionaries [global workers]
    - Believers from a Muslim background [BMBs]
    - Your children—what do you teach them about security protocols?
    - Anyone else
19. [If they did conceal] What kinds of things do you conceal or withhold from others?
20. [If they did conceal] What is it like having to conceal parts of yourself in these ways or to navigate multiple identities?

21. Do people know you are a Christian? How do they know you are Christian?
22. Do you attend any public worship services? What is that like for you?
23. Are there people or situations you avoid in order to manage your identity and security? Who and why?
24. [If they do conceal] In what ways does this concealment impact your relationships with those people or how they see you?
25. Are there ways you've had to intentionally mislead someone, tell half-truths, or misrepresent a situation in order to protect yourself, others, or ministry projects? Tell me about it and what thoughts and feelings arose.
26. Have you ever felt compelled to lie about who you are or what you do to protect yourself, others, or ministry [special] projects? (Police interrogations? Employer's questions?) Tell me about it and what thoughts and feelings arose.
27. What is it like going back to the US and sharing about your life in the gulf? Are there things you conceal from people or churches [fellowships]?
28. Do you have special practices or rules for the churches [fellowships] you share at?
29. What helps you navigate these issues of concealment or deception related to being a missionary [global worker] in a restricted access nation? Scripture passages or anything else?

SELF-PERCEPTION AND MISSIONARY IDENTITY

30. [Based on answers to above] Do you struggle, or have you ever struggled, with not knowing who you are? Tell me about the experience if you have.
    - Have the feelings resolved, or is there an ongoing struggle?
31. Are there practices or things you've said in the past that, on reflection, you would do or say differently if given a chance to do it again?
32. Have you ever been asked if you were a missionary [global worker]? By who? What happened?
33. What other identities did people assume for you?

34. Do you think any government officials are aware of your missionary [global worker] activity?
35. Are there locals who are aware of your missionary [global worker] identity?
36. Have you ever struggled with mental health—such as extreme stress, anxiety, depression, or another personal crisis—related to managing your identity in a context of high security? What was that like?
    - Is it resolved? Ongoing? What helps?

DIGITAL SECURITY

37. Do you have any special practices for your digital security and identity? Tell me about those.
    - Email, texts
    - Phones, apps
    - Social media, photos and captions
    - Web presence, church [fellowship] websites, online content
    - Newsletters
    - VPNs
38. Have you had any challenges with internet and digital security? How did you cope with those challenges?
39. How is it managing distant relationships with people back home?
40. Do you have any concerns about your "home world" and "ministry world" [field world] colliding? Tell me about those.

IF THEY LEFT THE FIELD

41. What led you to leave the field?
42. Did identity struggles play any role in your leaving?
43. How has it been adjusting back to life in America/non-RAN? Any identity struggles?

CONCLUSION

44. My research explores challenges to identity that cross-cultural workers like you may face in contexts of high security. Is there anything that came to mind that you think is relevant but I didn't ask about?

Glossary of Arabic Terms

Abaya—A black overcoat that Muslim women wear for modesty

Bedu—Bedouin or nomadic tribes

Bukhoor—Smoky incense, usually made from heavily scented wood chips and frankincense, and used to fragrance a home or clothing. Bukhoor is also used in many Islamic religious rituals and is associated with purity and hospitality.

Eid al-Fitr—A Muslim holiday celebrating the end of the fasting month of Ramadan

Hefla—Party

Hosh—The private walled-in yard around a home

Imam—A man who leads prayers in a mosque, often seen as an authority in Islamic theology and spirituality

Injeel—The Gospels of Jesus, sometimes used to mean the New Testament

Methl—A proverb, a saying

Mobusher—Missionary. Arabs from an Islamic background often understand *mobusher* as someone sent by the government who uses coercive methods to produce conversion, including bribery, threats, or disrespecting another religion.

Oud—An Arabic stringed instrument with a short neck and a body shaped like a pear

Sheikh—A tribal leader or highly respected man

Shela—A headscarf worn by Muslim women to cover their hair for modesty

Souq—Traditional marketplace, usually consisting of stalls lined up where shoppers must negotiate prices for goods

Tabla—A small drum beaten with the hands, usually in a set of two

Tabsheer—Evangelism. *Tabsheer* has connotations of coercion in order to produce conversion, including bribery, threats, or disrespecting another religion.

Ya sheikh—A term of respect to address an elder or honored one, even if he is not a tribal leader

Bibliography

Adeney, Bernard T. *Strange Virtues: Ethics in a Multicultural World*. Downers Grove, IL: InterVarsity, 1995.

Agar, M. H. *The Professional Stranger: An Informal Introduction to Ethnography*. 2nd ed. San Diego: Academic, 1996.

Albright, Brian, et al. *Scholars Needed: The Current State of Business as Mission Research*. Business as Mission Global Think Tank, May 2014. https://www.bamglobal.org/wp-content/uploads/2015/12/BMTT-IG-BAM-Scholarship-and-Research-Final-Report-May-2014.pdf.

Al-Kindi, Abdullah K. "Press Freedom and Corruption in the GCC: Are There Better Future Horizons? An Analytical-Critical Study." In *Off and Online Journalism and Corruption—International Comparative Analysis*, edited by Basyouni Ibrahim Hamada and Saodah Wok. N.p.: IntechOpen, 2019. http://www.doi.org/10.5772/intechopen.86603.

Allen, Roland. *Missionary Methods: St Paul's or Ours?* London: World Dominion, 1930.

Amnesty International. "Bahrain, Kuwait and Norway Contact Tracing Apps Among Most Dangerous for Privacy." Amnesty International, June 16, 2020. https://www.amnesty.org/en/latest/ news/2020/06/bahrain-kuwait-norway-contact-tracing-apps-danger-for-privacy/.

Asencio, Emily K. "Self-Esteem, Reflected Appraisals, and Self-Views: Examining Criminal and Worker Identities." *Social Psychology Quarterly* 76 (2013) 291–313.

Augustine, St. *The Teacher. The Free Choice of the Will. Grace and Free Will*. Translated by Robert P. Russell. FC 59. Washington, DC: Catholic University of America Press, 2004.

Baer, Michael. *Business as Mission: The Power of Business in the Kingdom of God*. Seattle: YWAM, 2006.

Bailey, Stephen. "Is Business as Mission Honest?" *Evangelical Missions Quarterly* 43 (2007) 368–72.

Barnett, Mike. "Creative Access Platforms: What Are They and Do We Need Them?" *Evangelical Missions Quarterly* 41 (2005) 88–96.

Bebbington, D. W. *Evangelicalism in Modern Britain: A History From the 1730s to the 1980s*. London: Routledge, 1993.

Bosch, David A. "The Gap Between Best Practices and Actual Practices: A BAM Field Study." *Christian Business Academy Review* 32 (2017) 32–44.

Bourdieu, Pierre. *Outline of a Theory of Practice*. Translated by Richard Nice. Cambridge Studies in Social Anthropology 16. Cambridge: Cambridge University Press, 1977.

Brogden, Dick. "Identity, Security, and Community." *Journal of Biblical Missiology*, July 6, 2020. https://biblicalmissiology.org/blog/2020/07/06/identity-security-and-community/.

Brubaker, Rogers, and Frederick Cooper. "Beyond 'Identity.'" *Theory and Society* 29 (2000) 1–47.

Burke, Peter J., and Jan E. Stets. *Identity Theory.* 2nd ed. New York: Oxford University Press, 2023.

Burke, Peter J., et al., eds. *Advances in Identity Theory Theory and Research.* New York: Kluwer Academic/Plenum, 2003.

Byrne, Barbara M. "Validating the Measurement and Structure of Self-Concept: Snapshots of Past, Present, and Future Research." *American Psychologist* 57 (2002) 897–909.

Cole-Turner, Ron. "Commodification and Transfiguration: Socially Mediated Identity in Technology and Theology." *HvTSt* 75 (2019) 1–11.

Co-Operation Council for the Arab States of the Gulf. "Charter of the Cooperation Council for the Arab States of the Gulf . . ." United Nations Treaty Collection, May 25, 1981. No. 21244. https://treaties.un.org/doc/Publication/UNTS/Volume%20 1288/volume-1288-I-21244-English.pdf.

Crabtree, Meghan A., and David R. Pillow. "Consequences of Enactment and Concealment for Felt Authenticity: Understanding the Effects of Stigma Through Self-Distancing and Motive Fulfillment." *European Journal of Social Psychology* 50 (2020) 1227–47.

Creswell, John W., and Cheryl N. Poth. *Qualitative Inquiry and Research Design: Choosing Among Five Approaches.* 4th ed. Glasgow: SAGE, 2018.

Crocetti, Elisabetta, et al. "Personal and Social Facets of Job Identity: A Person-Centered Approach." *Journal of Business and Psychology* 29 (2014) 281–300.

Doster, Leigh. "Teen Identity, Social Comparison and Voyeurism in Social Media: An Investigation of UK Millennial Consumption Behaviours in Facebook." PhD diss., Royal Holloway University of London, 2018. https://pure.royalholloway.ac.uk/en/publications/teen-identity-social-comparison-and-voyeurism-in-social-media-an-/.

Duffy, Matt J. "Arab Media Regulations: Identifying Restraints on Freedom of the Press in the Laws of Six Arabian Peninsula Countries." *Berkeley Journal of Middle Eastern and Islamic Law* 6 (2014) 1–31.

Dunaetz, David. "When Technology Does More Harm Than Good: Technostress in Missionary Contexts." SSRN, Mar. 28, 2022. From *Journal of the Evangelical Missiological Society* 2 (2022) 112–28. https://papers.ssrn.com/sol3/papers.cfm?abstract_id=4047459.

Dunkel, Curtis, and Colin Harbke. "A Review of Measures of Erikson's Stages of Psychosocial Development: Evidence for a General Factor." *Journal of Adult Development* 24 (2017) 58–76.

Erikson, Erik H. *Identity: Youth and Crisis.* New York: Norton, 1968.

Ernvik, Ulrika. *Third Culture Kids: A Gift to Care For.* Mariestad, Sweden: Familjegladje, 2019.

Evans, Jaron. "To Be or Not to Be (Online)." *Seedbed* 32 (2021) 11–20.

Fetterman, David M. *Ethnography: Step-by-Step.* 4th ed. Applied Social Research Methods 17. Thousand Oaks, CA: Sage, 2020.

Foyle, Marjory F. *Honourably Wounded: Stress Among Christian Workers.* Grand Rapids: Monarch, 1987.

Garrison, David. *Church Planting Movements: How God Is Redeeming a Lost World.* Midlothian, VA: WIGTake, 2004.

———. *A Wind in the House of Islam.* Monument, CO: WIGTake, 2014.

Geertz, Clifford. *The Interpretation of Cultures: Selected Essays.* New York: Basic, 2017.

Gibson, Dan. *Avoiding the Tentmaker Trap.* N.p.: WEC International, 2002.

Global Media Insight. https://www.globalmediainsight.com.

Goffman, Erving. *The Presentation of Self in Everyday Life.* Doubleday: New York, 1959.

Government of Bahrain. "Facts & Figures." Government of Bahrain, last updated Oct. 23, 2025. https://www.bahrain.bh/wps/portal/en/BNP/HomeNationalPortal/ContentDetailsPage/!ut/p/z1/rVLLbsIwEPyVXDhG3gRjx8eoiEclRBsIEF-QydOFOCEY2v59zaEHQJBW6t52vbM73hnEoQpxJU4yF1pWSuxMHnGydsY9GHnPAK997MLbggXkaeLAZNhFy8sGFoYDIN5wgDHxAtqjiF88zxkB4ro-dmfDLkzhGu_MQzALxn4wHfQdwM4l_t5-uBM-_A7_gGALfoE44nUsExThHqVZwsAmlDAbpwzbXsaozRIcgxs7SeaJc3esdKoLFG1UvRZNB8SmOmpLF6m1lSpPqvKntBFFI6TqQJPuhE4TS1e1jA8dyESsD5ZQiZXJ_Nikh-tv3PLkj6-oPBNrEaJtxtWEWytEhiS9S3JsxDjJ9AOFqmpK473ZHo87AvTSJpfxs3zf77lvZKiUTj81Wv2nDnUZmii97pe9DbyPeVbs8m-TO1kx/dz/d5/LolDUmlTVoEhL3dPaoFKRnRnLzROV3FpQSEhL2Vu/.

Greenberg, Joshua, and Sean P. Hier. *Surveillance: Power, Problems, and Politics.* Vancouver: University of British Columbia Press, 2009.

Growing Participator Approach. https://www.growingparticipation.com.

Hale, Thomas, III. *Authentic Lives: Overcoming the Problem of Hidden Identity in Outreach to Restrictive Nations.* Pasadena, CA: William Carey, 2016.

Hamilton, Don. *Tentmakers Speak: Practical Advice from Over 400 Missionary Tentmakers.* Ventura, CA: Regal, 1987.

Harris, Zachary. "Theological Critique of Security." *Evangelical Missions Quarterly* 40 (2004) 328–35.

Hofstede, Geert. *Culture's Consequences: Comparing Values, Behaviors, Institutions, and Organizations Across Nations.* 2nd ed. Thousand Oaks, CA: Sage, 2001.

Hogg, Michael A., and Kipling D. Williams. "From I to We: Social Identity and the Collective Self." *Group Dynamics: Theory, Research, and Practice* 4 (2000) 81–97.

Iyer, A., et al. "The More (and the More Compatible) the Merrier: Multiple Group Memberships and Identity Compatibility as Predictors of Adjustment After Life Transitions." *British Journal of Social Psychology* 48 (2009) 707–33.

Jia, Fanli, and Tobias Krettenauer. "Recognizing Moral Identity as a Cultural Construct." *Frontiers in Psychology* 8 (2017) art. 412. https://www.doi.org/10.3389/fpsyg.2017.00412.

Johnson, C. Neal. *Business as Mission: A Comprehensive Guide to Theory and Practice.* Downers Grove, IL: IVP Academic, 2009.

Kirk, Andrew. *What Is Mission? Theological Explorations.* Minneapolis: Fortress, 2000.

Kruger, Kurt T. *Tentmaking: A Misunderstood Missiological Method.* Eugene, OR: Wipf & Stock, 2020.

Lai, Patrick. *Tentmaking: The Life and Work as Business as Mission.* Downers Grove, IL: InterVarsity, 2005.

Lai, Patrick, and Rick Love. "An Integrated Identity in a Globalized World." In *From Seed to Fruit: Global Trends, Fruitful Practices, and Emerging Issues Among Muslims,* edited by J. Dudley Woodberry, 337–53. Pasadena: William Carey, 2008.

Lewis, Jonathan, ed. *Working Your Way to the Nations: A Guide to Effective Tentmaking.* 2nd ed. Downers Grove, IL: InterVarsity, 1996.

Little, Don. *Effective Discipling in Muslim Communities: Scripture, History, and Seasoned Practices.* Downers Grove, IL: InterVarsity, 2015.

Locke, John. *An Essay Concerning Human Understanding: Second Treatise of Government.* Eighteenth Century Collections Online. Hertfordshire, UK: Wordsworth, 2015.

Love, Rick. "Blessing the Nations in the 21st Century: A 3D Approach to Apostolic Ministry." *International Journal of Frontier Missiology* 25 (2008) 31–37.

———. *Glocal: Following Jesus in the 21st Century.* Eugene, OR: Cascade, 2017.

Lynch, Marc. "Digital Activism and Authoritarian Adaptation in the Middle East." *Project on Middle East Political Science Studies* 43 (2021) 4–7.

MacIntyre, Alasdair. *After Virtue.* 3rd ed. Notre Dame, IN: University of Notre Dame Press, 2007.

Majumdar, Samirah, and Virginia Villa. "Globally, Social Hostilities Related to Religion Decline in 2019, While Government Restrictions Remain at Highest Levels." Pew Research, Sept. 30, 2021. https://www.pewresearch.org/religion/2021/09/30/globally-social-hostilities-related-to-religion-decline-in-2019-while-government-restrictions-remain-at-highest-levels/.

Marcussen, Kristen, et al. "Mental Illness as a Stigmatized Identity." *Society and Mental Health* 9 (2019) 211–27.

Markus, Hazel Rose, and Shinobu Kitayama. "Culture and Self: Implications for Cognition, Emotion, and Motivation." *Psychological Review* 98 (1991) 224–53.

Mausz, Justin, et al. "Role Identity, Dissonance, and Distress Among Paramedics." *International Journal of Environmental Research and Public Health* 19 (2022) art. 2115. https://www.doi.org/10.3390/ijerph19042115.

McCall, George J., and J. L. Simmons. *Identities and Interactions: An Examination of Human Associations in Everyday Life.* New York: Free, 1978.

Mlotshwa, Langelihle, et al. "Exploring the Perceptions and Experiences of Community Health Workers Using Role Identity Theory." *Global Health Action* 8 (2015) art. 28045. https://www.doi.org/10.3402/gha.v8.28045.

Morris, Robert D. "Shrewd Yet Innocent: Thoughts on Tentmaker Integrity." *International Journal of Frontier Missions* 15 (1998) 5–8.

Myers, Bryant. *Walking with the Poor: Principles and Practices of Transformational Development.* Maryknoll, NY: Orbis, 1999.

National Centre for Statistics & Information: Sultanate of Oman. https://data.gov.om.

Nehrbass, Kenneth. "Managing Missionary Identity in the Digital Age: How Missionaries Utilize Digital Media Among Multiple Social Groups." *Missiology* 46 (2018) 183–95.

Novak, Michael. *Business as a Calling: Work and the Examined Life.* New York: Free, 1996.

Office of International Religious Freedom. *2021 Report on International Religious Freedom.* United States Department of State, June 2, 2022. https://www.state.gov/reports/2021-report-on-international-religious-freedom/.

Ononga, Kelvin Okey. "Tentmaking in the Twenty-First Century: Theological and Missiological Implications for Contemporary Adventist Missions." *Andrews University Seminary Studies* 53 (2015) 183–96.

Ott, Craig, and Harold A. Netland, eds. *Globalizing Theology: Belief and Practice in an Era of World Christianity.* Grand Rapids: Baker Academic, 2006.

Parks, S. Kent, et al. "Hidden and Forgotten People Including Those Who Are Disabled." Lausanne Movement, 2004. Lausanne Occasional Paper 35. https://lausanne.org/content/hidden-forgotten-people-including-disabled-lop-35a#2.

Paton, David M. *Roland Allen: The Ministry of the Spirit.* Cambridge: Lutterworth, 2006.

Pew Forum on Religion and Public Life. *Global Restrictions on Religion.* Pew Research, Dec. 17, 2009. https://www.pewresearch.org/religion/2009/12/17/global-restrictions-on-religion/.

Philpott, Daniel. *Religious Freedom in Islam: The Fate of a Universal Human Right in the Muslim World Today.* New York: Oxford University Press, 2019.

Plueddemann, James E. "Theological Implications of Globalizing Missions." In *Globalizing Theology: Belief and Practice in an Era of World Christianity*, edited by Craig Ott and Harold A. Netland, 250–66. Grand Rapids: Baker Academic, 2006.

Plummer, Jo, ed. *BAM and Mission Agencies: Why and How Agencies Engage in Business as Mission.* BAM Global, May 2024. https://bamglobal.org/report-mission-agencies/.

———. "What Is Business as Mission? A Short Introduction." Business as Mission, Jan. 25, 2024. https://businessasmission.com/what-is-business-as-mission-a-short-introduction/.

Plummer, Jo, and Mats Tunehag, eds. *Business as Mission and Church Planting: Fruitful Practices for Establishing Faith Communities.* BAM Global, Jan. 2014. https://www.bamglobal.org/wp-content/uploads/2015/12/ BMTT-IG-BAM-and-CP-Final-Report-January-2014.pdf.

Pocock, Michael, et al. *The Changing Face of World Missions: Engaging Contemporary Issues and Trends.* Encountering Mission Series. Grand Rapids: Baker Academic, 2005.

Polkinghorne, Donald E. "Narrative and Self-Concept." *Journal of Narrative and Life History* 1 (1991) 135–53.

Pollock, David D., et al. *Third Culture Kids: Growing Up Among Worlds.* 3rd ed. Boston: Brealey, 2017.

Porfeli, Erik J., et al. "A Multi-Dimensional Measure of Vocational Identity Status." *Journal of Adolescence* 34 (2011) 853–71.

Poston, Larry. "'Shrewd as a Snake, Innocent as a Dove': The Ethics of Missionary Dissimulation and Subterfuge." *Evangelical Missions Quarterly* 49 (2013) 412–19.

Prescott, Ian. "Issues of Identity and Platform in Bringing the Good News." *Evangelical Missions Quarterly* 57 (2021) 16–19.

Quinn, Diane M., and Valerie A. Earnshaw. "Concealable Stigmatized Identities and Psychological Well-Being." *Social & Personality Psychology Compass* 7 (2013) 40–51.

Quinn, D. M., and S. R. Chaudoir. "Living with a Concealable Stigmatized Identity: The Impact of Anticipated Stigma, Centrality, Salience, and Cultural Stigma on Psychological Distress and Health." *Journal of Personality and Social Psychology* 97 (2009) 634–51.

Reese, Robert. "John Gatu and the Moratorium on Missionaries." *Missiology* 42 (2014) 245–56.

Reporters Without Borders Index. https://rsf.org/en/index.

Riessman, Catherine Kohler. *Narrative Methods for the Human Sciences.* Thousand Oaks, CA: Sage, 2008.

Roemmele, Michael. "Cloak-and-Dagger Tentmakers Need Not Apply." *Evangelical Missions Quarterly* 29 (1993) 164–69.

Rundle, Steve, and Min-Dong Paul Lee. "The Motivations, Backgrounds, and Practices of Business as Mission Practitioners: Insights from an International Survey." *Missiology* 50 (2022) 420–41.

Rundle, Steven, and Tom A. Steffen. *Great Commission Companies: The Emerging Role of Business in Missions.* 2nd ed. Downers Grove, IL: IVP, 2011.

Rundle, Steven L. "Ministry, Profits, and the Schizophrenic Tentmaker." *Evangelical Missions Quarterly* 36 (2000) 292–300.

Russell, Mark L."The Use of Business in Missions in Chiang Mai, Thailand." PhD diss., Asbury Theological Seminary, 2008.

Rutt, Steven Richard. *Roland Allen: A Missionary Life.* Cambridge: Lutterworth, 2018.

Saint Arnault, Denise, and Laura Sinko. "Comparative Ethnographic Narrative Analysis Method: Comparing Culture in Narratives." *Global Qualitative Nursing Research* (2021) 1–8.

Santer, Nicholas, et al. "Narratives of the Self in Polymedia Contexts: Authenticity and Branding in Generation Z." *Qualitative Psychology* 10 (2023) 79–106.

Shaheed, Ahmed. "Binary Threat: How Governments' Cyber Laws and Practice Undermine Human Rights in the MENA Region." *Project on Middle East Political Science Studies* 43 (2021) 8–16.

Shipman, Mike. *Any-3: Anyone, Anywhere, Anytime.* Monument, CO: WIGTake, 2013.

Siebert, Jared. "Tending to the Tentmakers." In *Tentmakers: Multivocational Ministry in Western Society*, edited by James W. Watson and Narry F. Santos, 94–106. Eugene, OR: Wipf and Stock, 2022.

Siemens, Ruth. "The Vital Role of Tentmaking in Paul's Mission Strategy." *International Journal of Frontier Missions* 14 (1997) 121–29.

Smith, Steve, and Ying Kai. *T4T: A Discipleship Re-Revolution.* Monument, CO: WIGTake, 2011.

Somers, Margaret R. "The Narrative Constitution of Identity: A Relational and Network Approach." *Theory and Society* 23 (1994) 605–49.

Stefan, Robert J. *Business in Islam: Contextualizing Business and Mission in Muslim-Majority Nations.* APTS Press Monograph 5. Eugene, OR: Wipf and Stock, 2020.

Stets, Jan. "Examining Emotions in Identity Theory." *Social Psychology Quarterly* 68 (2005) 39–74.

Stets, Jan E., et al. "Exchange, Identity Verification, and Social Bonds." *Social Psychology Quarterly* 81 (2018) 207–27.

Stevens, R. Paul. *The Other Six Days: Vocation, Work, and Ministry in Biblical Perspective.* Grand Rapids: Eerdmans, 1999.

Stott, John. *The Lausanne Covenant: Complete Text with Study Guide.* N.p.: Lausanne Movement, 2009. https://lausanne.org/wp-content/uploads/2021/10/Lausanne-Covenant---Pages.pdf.

Stryker, Sheldon. "From Mead to a Structural Symbolic Interactionism and Beyond." *Annual Review of Sociology* 34 (2008) 14–31.

———. "Identity Competition: Key to Differential Social Movement Participation?" In *Self, Identity, and Social Movements*, edited by Sheldon Stryker et al., 21–40. Social Movements, Protest, and Contention 13. Minneapolis: University of Minnesota Press, 2000.

———. "Identity Salience and Role Performance: The Relevance of Symbolic Interaction Theory for Family Research." *Journal of Marriage and the Family* 30 (1968) 558–64.

Stryker, Sheldon, et al., eds. *Self, Identity, and Social Movements.* Minneapolis: University of Minnesota Press, 2000.

Taylor, Charles. *A Secular Age.* Cambridge, MA: Belknap, 2007.

———. *Sources of the Self: The Making of Modern Identity.* Cambridge: Cambridge University Press, 1989.

Taylor, Gary. "Don't Call Me a Tentmaker." *International Journal of Frontier Missions* 15 (1998) 23–26.

Tebbe, James A. "For Tentmakers: A Matter of Integrity." *Evangelical Missions Quarterly* 25 (1989) 48–51.

Tennent, Timothy C. *Invitation to World Missions: A Trinitarian Missiology for the Twenty-First Century.* Invitation to Theological Studies 3. Grand Rapids: Kregel, 2010.

Thesiger, Wilfred. *Arabian Sands.* Dubai: Motivate, 1994.

Third Lausanne Congress. *The Cape Town Commitment: A Confession of Faith and a Call to Action.* N.p.: Lausanne, [2010]. https://lausanne.org/wp-content/uploads/2021/10/The-Cape-Town-Commitment---Pages-20-09-2021.pdf.

Thoits, P. A. "Mechanisms Linking Social Ties and Support to Physical and Mental Health." *Journal of Health and Social Behavior* 52 (2011) 145–61.

———. "Personal Agency in the Accumulation of Multiple Role-Identities." In *Advances in Identity Theory and Research*, edited by P. J. Burke et al., 179–94. New York: Kluwer Academic/Plenum, 2003.

———. "Role-Identity Salience, Purpose and Meaning in Life, and Well-Being Among Volunteers." *Social Psychology Quarterly* 75 (2012) 360–84.

Thorne, Sally. "Verbatim Quotations in Qualitative Research Reports: On the Use and Abuse of Verbatim Quotations in Qualitative Research Reports." *Nurse Author & Editor* 30 (2020) 4–6.

Total Population by Country. https://worldpopulationreview.com/countries/.

Triandis, Harry C. *Individualism and Collectivism.* New Directions in Social Psychology Series. Boulder, CO: Westview, 1995.

Trueman, Carl R. *The Rise and Triumph of the Modern Self: Cultural Amnesia, Expressive Individualism, and the Road to Sexual Revolution.* Wheaton, IL: Crossway, 2020.

Tunehag, Mats, et al. "Business as Mission." Lausanne Movement, 2004. Lausanne Occasional Paper 59. https://lausanne.org/occasional-paper/business-mission-lop-59.

Valandra, V. "Reflexivity and Professional Use of Self in Research: A Doctoral Student's Journey." *Journal of Ethnographic & Qualitative Research* 6 (2012) 204–20.

Van Biema, David. "Religion: Missionaries Under Cover." *Time* (June 30, 2003) 36–44. https://content.time.com/time/subscriber/article/0,33009,1005107,00.html.

Watson, David, and Paul Watson. *Contagious Disciple Making: Leading Others on a Journey of Discovery.* Nashville: Nelson, 2014.

Watson, James W., and Narry F. Santos, eds. *Tentmakers: Multivocational Ministry in Western Society.* Eugene, OR: Wipf & Stock, 2022.

Wells, Lauren. *Raising Up a Generation of Healthy Third Culture Kids: A Practical Guide to Preventative Care.* Canby, OR: Self-published, 2020.

Willis, Rebecca. "The Use of Composite Narratives to Present Interview Findings." *Qualitative Research* 19 (2019) 471–80.

Wilson, J. Christy, Jr. *Today's Tentmakers: Self Support: An Alternative Model for Worldwide Witness.* Wheaton, IL: Tyndale, 1979.

Winter, Ralph D. "The Highest Priority: Cross-Cultural Evangelism." In *Let the Earth Hear His Voice: International Congress on World Evangelization Lausanne, Switzerland*, edited by J. D. Douglas, 213–41. Minneapolis: World Wide, 1975.

Wolcott, Harry F. *Ethnography: A Way of Seeing*. 2nd ed. Lanham, MD: AltaMira, 2008.

Woodberry, J. Dudley, ed. *From Seed to Fruit: Global Trends, Fruitful Practices, and Emerging Issues Among Muslims*. Pasadena, CA: William Carey, 2008.

World Economic Outlook. https://data.imf.org/en/datasets/IMF.RES:WEO.

World Watch List. https://www.opendoorsus.org/en-US/persecution/countries/.

Worldwide. "Dick Brogden." Worldwide, n.d. https://www.worldwidemission.org/dick-brogden.

Yamamori, Tetsunao. *God's New Envoys: A Bold Strategy for Penetrating "Closed Countries."* Portland, OR: Multnomah, 1987.

Yeoman, Barry. "The Stealth Crusade." *Mother Jones*, May/June 2002. https:/www.motherjones.com/politics/2002/05/stealth-crusade/.

Yin, Robert K. *Qualitative Research from Start to Finish*. New York: Guilford, 2012.

Zaman, Sahira, and Anis ul-Haq. "Impact of Role Identity Salience Between Inter-Role Conflict, Domestic and Professional Outcomes." *Journal of Behavioral Sciences* 33 (2023) 48–68.

Ziadah, Rafeef. "Surveillance, Race, and Social Sorting in the United Arab Emirates." *Politics* 44 (2021) 605–20. https://www.doi.org/10.1177/02633957211009719.

Zurlo, Gina A., et al. "World Christianity and Mission 2020: Ongoing Shift to the Global South." *International Bulletin of Mission Research* 44 (2020) 8–19.

www.ingramcontent.com/pod-product-compliance
Lightning Source LLC
LaVergne TN
LVHW050614100826
845148LV00011B/1591